The Dormition and Assumption
of the Virgin Mary

APOCRYPHES

COLLECTION DE POCHE DE L'AELAC

Direction

ANNE-CATHERINE BAUDOIN
ALAIN DESREUMAUX
ZBIGNIEW IZYDORCZYK
ENRICO NORELLI
JEAN-MICHEL ROESSLI

Volume 17

Maquette de couverture :
Vincent GOURAUD

Composition et montage :
Alain HURTIG

© 2023, Brepols Publishers n.v., Turnhout, Belgium
All rights reserved. No part of this publication may be reproduced,
stored in a retrieval system, or transmitted, in any form
or by any means, electronic, mechanical, photocopying, recording,
or otherwise without the prior permission of the publisher.
D/2023/0095/116
ISBN 978-2-503-60616-3
e-ISBN 978-2-503-60617-0
DOI 10.1484/M.APOCR-EB.5.133716
ISSN 1263-946X
e-ISSN 2565-9219
Printed in the E.U. on acid-free paper

The Dormition
and Assumption
of the Virgin Mary

Translated with an Introduction
by Stephen J. SHOEMAKER

BREPOLS

For my beloved niece,
Siobhan Marion Shoemaker

APOCRYPHES

AELAC'S PAPERBACK SERIES

To be published

Les Actes éthiopiens d'Étienne,
par Damien LABADIE

La Maríu Saga. Une vie de la Vierge en vieil islandais,
par Christelle FAIRISE

*The Vision of Adomnán and The Two Sorrows
of the Kingdom of Heaven*,
by John CAREY

APOCRYPHES
AELAC'S PAPERBACK SERIES

A FRAGMENT OF PAPYRUS found in the tomb of a Coptic monk in Egypt, a fable telling the story of the manger, a Romanesque fresco on a Poitevin wall, a serialized Latin novel detailing the adventures of the apostles ... all bear witness to the variety and wide diffusion of Christian writings known as Apocrypha.

In turn sought after and rejected, exploited and reviled, translated and forgotten, apocryphal works remain mysteriously and powerfully evocative. A mere mention of the word "Apocrypha" frequently summons intimations of an unexpected revelation, of a secret finally unveiled, of a long-forgotten truth. However, those who plunge into apocryphal literature in hope of discovering knowledge they have long sought after may discover only disappointment. Some Apocrypha, indeed, claim to initiate the reader into truths about Jesus: one, the *Gospel according to Thomas,* reports an esoteric teaching He entrusted to his disciple Thomas; another, the *Gospel of Nicodemus*, faithfully relates the story of Jesus's visit to hell as narrated by two men He had brought back to life. Many others, however, have no such pretensions: the *Letter Fallen from Heaven* appears only to justify the payment of tithes and the observation of Sunday. Similarly, stories about an apostle turning the wife of a high Roman official away from her conjugal duties (as in the *Acts of Philip*, for example) merely reflect some contemporary sexual mores, here a call to chastity in marriage. For those who thirst after glimpses of eternity, documents such as these are of scant attraction. And yet, if readers approach them without expectations of profound, secret revelations about Jesus, his disciples, or His kingdom of heaven, Apocrypha can be a source of enduring profit and pleasure.

Indeed, the import of apocryphal texts lies elsewhere: they reveal how Christians at different times and in different places understood and represented the figure of Jesus, the meaning of his message, the role of the apostles, the origin of their local churches, and other similar topics. Apocrypha testify to the issues that stirred and provoked early Christians to respond with stories and reflections: what is the true nature of Christ, asks the *Ascension of Isaiah*; and how was He both royal and divine, asks the *Acts of Pilate*.

Some Apocrypha are very old and reflect traditions contemporaneous with those that ultimately appeared in the *New Testament*. To historians of Christianity and biblical scholars, such texts offer a unique perspective, still little explored, on the nascent forms of Christian traditions. They do not give access to historical truths about Jesus or His apostles any more than do the canonical gospels, but they shed light on how the first Christian communities lived and what they believed.

Imagination was in Apocrypha a vehicle for profound, creative reflection. Thus, the mid-second century *Infancy Gospel of Thomas*, a narrative of the various miracles and misdeeds of the child Jesus, does not simply construct a biography of His early years that indulges in unbridled, or sacrilegious, imagination. Rather, the text questions the very terms of the Incarnation, wondering at the fullness of divine grace made manifest in the infant Jesus. *Thomas* also attempts to explain what the *Gospel of Luke* meant by saying that "the child grew and became strong in spirit." As reflections on exegetical, dogmatic, and moral issues of the utmost importance to the early Christian communities, the Apocrypha in the present collection reveal their richness, not to those who seek in them what such texts cannot offer, but to those who heed Paul Valéry's sentiment that "all stories gain depth as fables."

Far from projecting a unified image of Christianity, Apocrypha introduce us to a profusion of its doctrines, mythologies, and languages. The picture of Christianity that emerges from these texts is that of an ensemble of astonishingly diverse communities. Bearing witness to this diversity, many Apocrypha have come down to us in multiple versions. Thus, the *Doctrine of Addai* has been transmitted in Greek, Syriac, Coptic, Ethiopic, Arabic, Armenian, Georgian, and Slavic forms. Each bears the marks of the socio-cultural environment that produced it, and each in its own way preserves various inflections of doctrine in the first centuries of Christianity.

That is why, when Christianity became the religion of the Empire and the authorities attempted to give it a unified image, some Fathers of the Church reviled Apocrypha as carriers of nonconformity and heresy. Today, however, as scholarship rediscovers the extraordinary profusion of Christianities in the early centuries, there is a need to place within public reach those ancient sources carrying traces of that richness and—sometimes in just a few lines—illuminating the still shadowy traces of Christianity's past.

Faced with such diversity of practice, belief, and text, the early Church had some difficult choices to make. The *Apocalypse* attributed to John came close to being excluded from the canon; the *Shepherd of Hermas* narrowly missed out on being included. In fact, one could argue that there is no intrinsic difference between the canonical and the apocryphal.

The *New Testament* came about when ecclesiastical authorities selected, from a wide range of texts, a smaller corpus to serve as a point of reference for the Christian faith. Many works not chosen continued to nourish Christian piety for centuries and inspired traditions still alive today. For instance, monastic readings for the feasts of the Apostles in the *Martyrology* draw on edifying stories going back to the apocryphal *Acts of the Apostles*; and the names of Caspar, Melchior and Balthazar, the three Magi whom the evangelical tradition refrains from naming, already appear in Coptic paintings in the Egyptian oasis of Bawit (6th-7th century).

To forget Apocrypha is tantamount to erasing the frescoes in our Romanesque churches and smashing the stained-glass windows in our Gothic cathedrals; to rendering forever incomprehensible Dante's *Inferno* and many pages in Flaubert. As ignorance of Christian history grows ever more obvious and disturbing, it is a matter of some urgency to translate and disseminate at least some of the apocryphal texts long a part of our religious and cultural memory.

This present series offers translations from the original sources edited and published in the *Series Apocryphorum* of the *Corpus Christianorum*. The translators are also scholars engaged in original research and members of the *Association pour l'étude de la littérature apocryphe chrétienne* (AELAC). Aiming to make apocryphal literature accessible to a broad spectrum of readers, individual volumes introduce each text with a historical preface, provide simple but precise notes, and include indexes. Translators hope that they will lead their readers on exciting journeys of discovery, beyond initial horizons and into the colourful, instructive, and rewarding world of Christian Apocrypha.

Table
of Contents

Acknowledgments	3
Introduction	5
Translations	
The *Book of Mary's Repose*	55
The *Six Books Apocryphon*	175
The Greek Revision of The *Book of Mary's Repose*	235
The Latin Revision of the *Book of Mary's Repose*	257
The Latin *Transitus Mariae*	269
A Unique Early *Dormition Fragment* in Georgian	285
A Liturgical Apocryphon from *Jeremiah* for the *Dormition of the Virgin*	289
The *Homily on the Dormition* Attributed to Basil of Caesarea	293
Bibliography	321
Index	
General Index	337
Ancient Writings Index	349

Acknowledgments

THE SEED FOR THIS COLLECTION of translations was planted during a conversation with Jean-Michel Roessli and Jean-Daniel Kaestli, while watching Greece play in the 2014 World Cup in a pub in Thessaloniki. As it turned out, our discussion met with more fruitful results than the Greek team that evening, ultimately yielding the present collection of translations of several early Dormition narratives, most of which appear in a modern language for the first time, at least in the versions presented in this volume. I am grateful to both Jean-Michel and Jean-Daniel for initially suggesting the publication of these translations, and also for their help and encouragement along the way. Enrico Norelli also deserves great thanks, not only for his specific comments and suggestions regarding these translations but also for his insightful and inspiring work on the early Dormition traditions which has continued to shape my thinking on this corpus of traditions. My thanks also to Christa Müller-Kessler for sharing her new editions of the Christian Palestinian Aramaic and Syriac fragments of the *Book of Mary's Repose* in advance of their publication. I also must thank my collaborator on the forthcoming edition of the early versions of the *Six Books Apocryphon*, to be published as *De uita Mariae Syriace* in the series CCSA, Andrew Hochstedler. Andrew was so kind as to look over my translation of the *Six Books Apocryphon* for this volume and suggested some improved renderings of the Syriac. The anonymous reader for the series also offered some very helpful and generative comments, for which I am grateful. Thanks also to Oxford University Press for allowing the inclusion in this volume of material previously published in *Ancient Traditions of the Virgin Mary's Dormition and Assumption* in the translations of *The Book of Mary's Repose* and *Greek Mary's Repose*. Finally, I wish to express my deep gratitude to the members of the Association pour l'étude de la littérature apocryphe chrétienne for welcoming me among them, despite my embarrassing linguistic limitations (thus *la langue barbare* in which I write). Its members are as exceptional for their kindness and collegiality as they are for the rigor and excellence of their scholarship, and I have benefitted enormously from their collective knowledge and encouragement.

Introduction

I$^{N\text{ THIS BOOK}}$ we make available, in some cases for the first time, translations of early Christian narratives about the end of the Virgin Mary's life, that is, her Dormition and Assumption. Although we know next to nothing about this event that would qualify as historical knowledge, other than that it surely must have occurred, its inevitability sparked considerable imagination in the minds of the early Christians, who remembered the end of her life in an astonishing array of detailed and diverse legends. There are some forty different narratives of Mary's Dormition and Assumption that survive from the third through seventh centuries, preserved in all of the various languages of the early Christian world. Of course, some of these narratives are versions of the same underlying tradition, transmitted in different forms. Indeed, as we will see in a moment, many of the narratives fall within one of two distinctive literary families. Yet even so, the variation among all of these early versions is, despite their similarities, often substantial, so much so that we must in fact look to them as different narratives rooted in the same broader tradition.

For these reasons, then, it is useful to have available in translation as many of these early Dormition apocrypha as possible. In the first place, many of the most important narratives are preserved in languages not known even to most scholars of

6   THE DORMITION AND ASSUMPTION OF MARY

early Christianity. No less important is the sheer diversity of their tellings of the end of Mary's life, even in the presence of many deep similarities. Accordingly, anyone who wishes to know how the early Christians remembered and celebrated the end of Mary's life cannot read just one narrative, but they will need to read several different versions. And the present book offers just such an opportunity. This collection is hardly exhaustive, however—it cannot be—and it does not present a systematic study of the early Dormition narratives or attempt to represent the range of scholarship on this corpus. For such perspectives, I would refer readers especially to my monograph on the ancient Dormition traditions, as well of some of the more recent studies mentioned in the notes to this introduction.[1]

Our goal in this instance is neither to be comprehensive nor to provide a general overview of the entire corpus and its scholarly investigation. Instead, we have selected eight texts out of the dozens of ancient accounts, chosen for their overall importance as witnesses to the ancient traditions and also with the goal of presenting new translations of texts that have not previously appeared in English or, in some cases, in any modern language. Likewise, of necessity we have had to keep commentary and explanatory notes to a minimum. If we did not, this book would instantly balloon beyond any reasonable length for publication in this series. The first two texts alone easily deserve book length commentaries in their own right, which both presently await. Our more modest aim is instead to make these texts available to individuals who may be interested in learning how the early Christians imagined the death

1. Stephen J. SHOEMAKER, *Ancient Traditions of the Virgin Mary's Dormition and Assumption*, Oxford Early Christian Studies (Oxford: Oxford University Press, 2002).

of the mother of their savior. Much of the potential interpretive work is, for better or worse, left undone. Accordingly, this book offers new translations of eight texts representing the scope and variety of the ancient Dormition traditions, including the earliest and most important versions of the two main literary traditions. As such, it provides a quick if selective overview of this complex and fascinating tangle of early traditions regarding the end of Mary's life, without too many other encumbrances, affording an illuminating and intriguing glimpse into the worldview of the early Christians and how they remembered the beginnings of their faith and the lives of its founding figures.

Nevertheless, before we get much further, we should clarify some terminology. Mary's "Dormition," that is, her "falling asleep," refers to the event of her departure from this world, using a common euphemism for death in both ancient and modern discourse. This occasion is remembered as a time when all the apostles were miraculously gathered from the ends of the earth to be present for Mary's passing, her funeral, and burial, and her son Jesus himself comes to receive her soul at the moment of its exit from the body. The term "Assumption" refers to Mary's glorious and miraculous translation to the Garden of Paradise after her death, where she presently exists in the resurrected state, exemplifying the promise that awaits all of the faithful at the end of time. The various narratives imagine Mary's transfer in body and soul to Paradise in differing ways, and indeed a few narratives actually conclude without describing Mary's Assumption, leaving her fate after death a mystery for the reader. But most narratives, and certainly all of the earliest narratives, conclude with some sort of bodily Assumption of Mary to Paradise. And these are the events recalled in the early Christian imagination by the texts in this volume.

8   THE DORMITION AND ASSUMPTION OF MARY

The primary aims of this book are twofold. Firstly, it brings together for the first time the two earliest and most important narratives of the Virgin Mary's Dormition and Assumption, namely, the *Book of Mary's Repose*, which dates to the fourth century at the latest and is quite possibly even earlier, and the *Six Books Apocryphon*, a work whose traditions belong to the fourth century. To my knowledge, translations of these two texts from the original languages have never been published together in a modern language. In fact, the only translation of the *Book of Mary's Repose* into any modern language, from Classical Ethiopic (Ge'ez), Old Georgian, and Syriac (Christian Aramaic), was done by myself and published in my monograph *The Ancient Dormition and Assumption Traditions*.[2] The second apocryphon, the *Six Books Apocryphon*, has been translated several times into English from different early Syriac versions, as well as into Spanish and Italian, but a translation of this text in English has never been published together with other early narratives of the Virgin Mary's Dormition and Assumption.[3] Moreover, the translation included in this volume has been made from a version that has never been published before, an unpublished sixth-century manuscript.

---

2. An Italian translation of this apocryphon was published in Mario Erbetta, *Gli Apocrifi del Nuovo Testamento*, 3 vols., vol. 1/2, *Vangeli: Infanzia e passione di Cristo, Assunzione di Maria* (Torino: Marietti, 1966), 421–56. Nevertheless, this translation largely reproduces in Italian the Latin translation made by Victor Arras with his edition of the text. Likewise, this translation either summarizes or omits many very difficult passages in this text.

3. Although I published an English translation of the *Six Books Apocryphon* from an Ethiopic version in Shoemaker, *Ancient Traditions*, 375–96, this version is quite different from the ancient Syriac versions preserved in fifth and sixth century manuscripts, and it is also shorter.

INTRODUCTION 9

Thus, this volume makes these two earliest Dormition and Assumption apocrypha, or Dormition apocrypha, as I will call them for short,[4] available together in English translation for the first time. I also provide an English translation of the earliest Greek Dormition text, which is an early abridgment of the *Book of Mary's Repose*, seemingly from the sixth century. In light of this narrative's antiquity and its close relations with the *Book of Mary's Repose*, it is often essential for understanding the latter's contents in places. Unfortunately, however, this apocryphon does not have a convenient title in modern scholarship, and the title given by the text is easily confused with another important early Greek Dormition narrative, the *Transitus Mariae*, or *Translation of Mary* by Ps.-John the Theologian. For lack of a better alternative, we shall call it here the *Greek Revision of the Book of Mary's Repose*, or *Greek Mary's Repose* for short.

The second purpose of this volume is to make available in English several important early Dormition narratives that have never been translated into a modern language before their publication in the present collection. To this end this book includes translations of five ancient Dormition apocrypha that have never been translated before, three of which are translated from Old Georgian, while the fourth and fifth render the earliest

---

4. In this regard I follow the Eastern Christian tradition, which refers collectively to the Virgin's Dormition and Assumption using the single term *koimēsis*, "the Dormition." This expression is intended simply as a shorthand for "Dormition and Assumption" and is in no way meant to indicate the absence of Mary's bodily Assumption or the priority of traditions lacking this feature in any given instance. This point needs to be emphasized, given the extent to which modern dogmatic concerns regarding the Virgin Mary's Assumption have often determined the scholarship on these traditions in the previous century.

Latin narratives into English. The translation of these Latin texts appears first, since they preserve very early versions of the same traditions witnessed in the *Book of Mary's Repose* and *Greek Mary's Repose*. Indeed, these early Latin apocrypha are, like *Greek Mary's Repose*, essential for understanding the *Book of Mary's Repose* and its ancient traditions. Also like *Greek Mary's Repose*, there are no widely agreed upon names for these Latin apocrypha, and again, for lack of a better alternative, we shall call the first text the *Latin Revision of the Book of Mary's Repose*, or, again, *Latin Mary's Repose* for short. The other early Latin version that we include following this one, whose contents are equally important for understanding the *Book of Mary's Repose*, we have called simply the *Latin Transitus Mariae*.

We follow these Latin texts with a fragmentary text of a Dormition apocryphon that survives only in Old Georgian translation. This fragment preserves a particularly unusual text that is transmitted in between two fragments of Old Georgian translations of the *Book of Mary's Repose* in an early Georgian homiliary that provides liturgical readings for the various feasts of the liturgical year, including, in this case, for the feast of the Dormition on 15 August. Given this fragment's immediate context between two fragments of the *Book of Mary's Repose*, one would rightly expect it to preserve another fragment of this ancient Dormition apocryphon, and indeed, it is often presented as such in the scholarly literature on this topic. Nevertheless, it does not reflect anything in the *Book of Mary's Repose*, and accordingly it would appear that this Georgian fragment witnesses partially to some now lost early Dormition narrative.

The next text also appears here in a modern language for the first time, again translated from Old Georgian. We include this text for several reasons, not the least of which is its highly

INTRODUCTION 11

unusual nature: this apocryphon was produced by rewriting and expanding an earlier, already existing apocryphon about the prophet Jeremiah. This apocryphon takes as its basis the section on Jeremiah from a larger apocryphal collection known as the *Lives of the Prophets*. By quoting selectively from this legendary story about Jeremiah and interspersing the text with passages that draw its meaning toward the Virgin Mary, its author created a new Dormition apocryphon. It is a remarkable example of an apocryphon produced not by rewriting a biblical text but instead by rewriting an older apocryphon to make its contents apply to an entirely new subject. This text is also significant for its use as a liturgical reading at one of the most important early Marian shrines, the church of the Kathisma halfway between Jerusalem and Bethlehem, and on this basis we can be sure that it was composed and put into use sometime before the middle of the seventh century.

Finally, the last text is a lengthy account of the Virgin's Dormition and Assumption that is attributed to Basil the Great; it survives in Old Georgian and has never been translated into any modern language. Nevertheless, Basil is clearly not the author of the text, and there is little question that it is a more recent composition, dating to the early seventh century it would seem. This apocryphon is a retelling of the Dormition narrative from the *Six Books Apocryphon* that adds several new elements, including a number of features from the Palm tradition, all of which indicate its production at a later stage in the history of ancient Dormition traditions. Unlike the previous texts, this particular narrative adds very little to our understanding of the earliest Dormition traditions. Its value lies instead in disclosing how these traditions continued to develop in new ways into the Early Middle Ages.

With these eight narratives, we offer multiple representatives of three of the four main literary traditions about the

THE DORMITION AND ASSUMPTION OF MARY

Dormition of the Virgin to emerge from ancient Christianity. The most important of these traditions have been designated the "Palm of the Tree of Life" narratives, or "Palm" traditions for short, so-called on account of the prominence given to a branch taken from this mythical tree in narratives of this type. Of the two main literary traditions, this one appears to be the older, and it was also the only narrative type to circulate widely in the Christian West.[5] The *Book of Mary's Repose* is the earliest narrative from this tradition, and its Greek and Latin revisions included in this volume also offer important witness to the archaic form of this apocryphon.[6] The second major literary tradition is the "Bethlehem" traditions, and true to the name, a significant amount of action in these apocrypha takes place in Bethlehem. The *Six Books Apocryphon* is the earliest exemplar of this tradition, and the *Homily on the Dormition* by Ps.-Basil, which, as noted above, is largely a revision of the *Six Books*, also stands to a certain extent in this tradition.[7] It should be emphasized that these two main literary traditions emerged in parallel, independently of one another, in ancient Christianity, and there is no indication that one of the traditions developed out of the other.[8]

5. Stephen J. SHOEMAKER, "From Mother of Mysteries to Mother of the Church: The Institutionalization of the Dormition Apocrypha," *Apocrypha* 22 (2011), 11–47, 30–1.

6. For more on the Palm tradition, see SHOEMAKER, *Ancient Traditions*, 32–46. One should see also my published collected studies on the early Dormition narratives: Stephen J. SHOEMAKER, *The Dormition and Assumption Apocrypha*, Studies on Early Christian Apocrypha 15 (Leuven: Peeters, 2018).

7. For more on the Bethlehem traditions see SHOEMAKER, *Ancient Traditions*, 46–57.

8. This is argued at length in ibid., esp. 142–204.

INTRODUCTION   13

The two remaining texts, the Georgian fragment and the reading from Jeremiah, represent a third category of traditions that I have named the "atypical" narratives, since they do not fit into one of the two main literary categories. Other than this independence, these narratives generally do not share much in common with one another, beyond their focus on the events of the Dormition of the Virgin. The category is effectively a catch-all for the many ancient narratives that do not reflect a literary type.[9] Finally, a fourth category of traditions, which is not represented in this volume, is the "Coptic" tradition, a group which, unlike the others, is not identified on the basis of literary relations, but instead on the presence of certain distinctive Egyptian liturgical practices. The Coptic narratives are defined by their identification of the date of the Virgin's Dormition, that is, the departure of her soul from her body, on 21 Tobe, or 16 January on the modern calendar, rather than the middle of August. More recent Coptic narratives also add to this a commemoration of the Assumption of her body into heaven 206 days later on 16 Mesore, 9 August on our calendar.[10] This liturgical program is distinctive to Egyptian Christianity, and the Coptic Dormition narratives are structured around this feature. From a purely literary standpoint,

---

9. On these atypical narratives, see ibid., 63–71.

10. For more on the Coptic traditions, see ibid., 57–63; and Stephen J. SHOEMAKER, "The Sahidic Coptic Homily on the Dormition of the Virgin Attributed to Evodius of Rome: An Edition of Morgan MSS 596 & 598 with Translation," *Analecta Bollandiana* 117, no. 3–4 (1999), 241–83. See also Simon C. MIMOUNI, *Dormition et Assomption de Marie : Histoire des traditions anciennes*, Théologie historique, 98 (Paris: Beauchesne, 1995), 173–210, 447–50; Simon C. MIMOUNI, "Genèse et évolution des traditions anciennes sur le sort final de Marie : Étude de la tradition littéraire copte," *Marianum* 42 (1991), 69–143.

14   THE DORMITION AND ASSUMPTION OF MARY

however, these Coptic narratives either represent early rewritings of the Palm tradition or they are atypical.

In the translations presented in the following chapters, I have used the standard abbreviations for biblical writings, as well as early Christian and Jewish writings, established in the *SBL Handbook of Style*.[11] Also, I have inserted subheadings in the translations, all of which appear in italics. These are not present, the reader should be aware, in the original texts.

The *Book of Mary's Repose*.

This ancient Dormition apocryphon is the earliest and most important text in this corpus, and it is also one of the most important Marian texts in the early Christian tradition. Indeed, the *Book of Mary's Repose* remains one of the most significant early Christian apocrypha that has yet to be fully "discovered" by modern scholarship. Although a critical edition of the text was published with a Latin translation and commentary in 1973, this apocryphon remained almost entirely ignored for another quarter century. It was my hope that my English translation and analysis of this apocryphon in my monograph on the *Ancient Dormition and Assumption Traditions* would bring this apocryphon the attention that it deserved, but unfortunately it still remains largely ignored in most conversations about early Christian apocryphal literature and likewise the remarkable diversity of ancient Christian faith and practice.

11. Patrick H. ALEXANDER, *The SBL Handbook of Style for Ancient Near Eastern, Biblical, and Early Christian Studies* (Peabody, Mass., Hendrickson Publishers, 1999), 71–89.

INTRODUCTION   15

The only exception to this general neglect would appear to be several important and insightful articles by Enrico Norelli. Norelli proposes that we should identify this text with a group mentioned in Irenaeus, which he identifies as "the elders" and associates with the apostle John.[12] It is a speculative proposal, to be sure, and we know so little about this supposed group of "elders" that they are almost a blank slate. Irenaeus does frequently associate these elders with eschatological ideas of a material kingdom of God in the earthly Paradise, as does the *Book of Mary's Repose*. And yet, much the same ideas regarding an eschatological earthly paradise appear in Ephrem's *Hymns on Paradise*, indicating that they seem to have had a broader currency.[13] Accordingly, we do not need limit their potential source to Irenaeus' elders, whoever they may have been, if they even were a real historical early Christian group of some sort. While they certainly provide a possible early—second century!—context for the *Book of Mary's Repose*, any such connection must be recognized as highly speculative and still unproven.

12. Enrico NORELLI, "La letteratura apocrifa sul Transito di Maria e il problema delle sue origini," in *Il dogma dell'assunzione de Maria: problemi attuali e tentativi de ricomprensione. Atti del XVII Simposio Internazionale Mariologico (Roma, 6–9 ottobre 2009)*, ed. Ermanno M. TONIOLO (Rome: Edizioni Marianum, 2010), 121–65; Enrico NORELLI, "Les premières traditions sur la Dormition de Marie comme catalyseurs de formes très anciennes de réflexion théologique et sotériologique. Le cas du Paradis terrestre," in *The Apocryphal Gospels within the Context of Early Christian Theology*, ed. Jens SCHRÖTER (Leuven: Peeters, 2013), 403–46; Enrico NORELLI, "La littérature ancienne sur la Dormition de Marie: La transformation de ses formes et de ses fonctions" in *De l'(id)entité textuelle au cours du Moyen Âge tardif. XIIIᵉ-XVᵉ siècle*, ed. Géraldine VEYSSEYRE, et al. (Paris: Classiques Garnier, 2017), 63–84. I thank David Brakke for our exchanges regarding these "elders" of Irenaeus.
13. See SHOEMAKER, *Ancient Traditions*, 179–203.

16   THE DORMITION AND ASSUMPTION OF MARY

With the exception of Norelli's valuable studies, I suspect that one of the main reasons for the general sidelining of this text in most scholarship on early Christianity and Christian apocrypha is its baffling theological complexity and idiosyncrasies. And yet, of course, these are the very qualities that make it essential for this text to be better integrated into the study of ancient Christianity. The *Book of Mary's Repose* reflects a mélange of early Christian ideas and practices unlike any other that I have ever seen. Accordingly, this text offers invaluable insight into the diversity of early Christianity, revealing an early community (one assumes) whose peculiar understanding of Christianity is distinctive and yet overlaps in significant ways with many broader trends. Those interested in the diversity of early Christianity would do well to pay more attention to this particular witness.

No doubt another reason for the marginalization of this apocryphon is the complexity of its transmission, which is difficult even in comparison with the frequently convoluted histories of early Christian apocryphal traditions. The *Book of Mary's Repose* survives intact only in a translation into Classical Ethiopic, a language that unfortunately remains foreign to most scholars of early Christianity. In 1973 Victor Arras published a critical edition of the text based on two manuscripts, along with a Latin translation and extensive commentary in Latin. This edition forms the basis for my translation, and in the notes I have occasionally indicated variant readings from one of the two manuscripts, identified using the letters assigned to them by Arras.[14] Moreover, as already mentioned, significant fragments of this text survive in Syriac and in Old

14. Victor Arras, *De transitu Mariae apocrypha aethiopice*, 2 vols., CSCO 342–3, 351–2 (Louvain: Secrétariat du Corpus SCO, 1973), 1:1–84 (Ethiopic) and 1–54 (Latin).

INTRODUCTION   17

Georgian, and I have translated these fragments alongside of the Ethiopic text, on the basis of editions prepared by Michel van Esbroeck, William Wright, and myself.[15]

To this we may now add several significant fragments of the *Book of Mary's Repose* in Christian Palestinian Aramaic, as well as several new Syriac fragments, recently published in a spate of articles by Christa Müller-Kessler.[16] Christian Palestinian Aramaic was a dialect of Western Aramaic (as opposed to Syriac, which is an Eastern Aramaic dialect) in use among the Christian communities of Palestine during Late Antiquity and the Middle Ages. The Christian Palestinian Aramaic fragments in

15. Michel VAN ESBROECK, "Nouveaux apocryphes de la Dormition conservés en géorgien," *Analecta Bollandiana* 90 (1972), 363–69; William WRIGHT, *Contributions to the Apocryphal Literature of the New Testament* (London: Williams and Norgate, 1865); Stephen J. SHOEMAKER, "New Syriac Dormition Fragments from Palimpsests in the Schøyen Collection and the British Library: Presentation, Edition and Translation," *Le Muséon* (2011), 259–78.

16. Christa MÜLLER-KESSLER, "Three Early Witnesses of the 'Dormition of Mary' in Christian Palestinian Aramaic from the Cairo Genizah (Taylor-Schechter Collection) and the New Finds in St. Catherine's Monastery," *Apocrypha* 29 (2018), 69–95; Christa MÜLLER-KESSLER, "An Overlooked Christian Palestinian Aramaic Witness of the 'Dormition of Mary' in Codex Climaci Rescriptus (CCR IV)," *Collectanea Christiana Orientalia* 16 (2019), 81–98; Christa MÜLLER-KESSLER, "Obsequies of My Lady Mary (I): Unpublished Early Syriac Palimpsest Fragments from the British Library (BL, Add 17.137, no. 2)," *Hugoye* 23 (2020), 31–59; and Christa MÜLLER-KESSLER, "Obsequies of My Lady Mary (II): A Fragmentary Syriac Palimpsest Manuscript from Deir al-Suryan (BL, Add 14.665, no. 2)," *Collectanea Christiana Orientalia* 19 (2022), 45–70. Unfortunately, there are a number of errors in the notes to the text in the first article, wich is nonetheless usable.

18 THE DORMITION AND ASSUMPTION OF MARY

question were all written during the fifth or sixth century, and one set of fragments was produced in the scriptorium of the ancient monastery of Mar Saba in the Judean Desert.[17] Without question, these additional fragments are extremely important for their further confirmation of this apocryphon's antiquity: we can now point to several different manuscripts that were circulating in Syriac and Christian Palestinian Aramaic during the fifth and sixth centuries that are translations of an even earlier Greek original.[18]

Furthermore, the Christian Palestinian Aramaic fragments bring confirmation of this apocryphon's likely Palestinian provenance, and in light of the connection with Mar Saba, one strongly suspects that the fragments translated into Georgian in the Klarjeti homiliary also were originally produced in this same milieu. Yet the Syriac fragments of this text were all originally produced in fifth-century Mesopotamia, and were eventually taken to the Deir al-Suryan monastery in Egypt only in the tenth century.[19] When we add to this the sparse fragments of

17. Sebastian Brock, "Ktabe Mpassqe: Dismembered and Reconstituted Syriac and Christian Palestinian Aramaic Manuscripts: Some Examples, Ancient and Modern," *Hugoye* 15 (2012), 7–20, 12–13

18. The Christian Palestinian Aramaic fragments make certain that the apocryphon was originally in Greek: as Müller-Kessler notes "CPA versions are always dependent on a Greek 'Vorlage.'" Müller-Kessler, "Overlooked," 86.

19. Müller-Kessler, "Obsequies (I)," 35; and Müller-Kessler, "Obsequies (II)," 46–7; see also Sebastian P. Brock, "Without Mushe of Nisibis, Where Would we Be? Some Reflections on the Transmission of Syriac Literature," *Journal of Eastern Christian Studies* 56 (2004), 15–24; and Sebastian P. Brock and Lucas van Rompay, *Catalogue of the Syriac Manuscripts and Fragments in the Library of Deir al-Surian, Wadi al-Natrun (Egypt)*, Orientalia Lovaniensia Analecta 227 (Leuven: Uitgeverij Peeters, 2014), XIII.

INTRODUCTION 19

this apocryphon witnessed by a very bad Coptic papyrus at Yale, it becomes quite clear that this was a very popular text that circulated widely in the late ancient Near East. Although in some instances the text preserved in this Coptic fragment is so minimal that it is difficult to compare with the Ethiopic, in those places where the parallel is clear we have included a translation of this Coptic witness from the edition by Philip Sellew.[20] The fact that it survives today only in a bunch of erased Aramaic fragments, a Coptic scrap, some Georgian liturgical readings and a complete Ethiopic version is a consequence, no doubt, of the apocryphon's dissonance with the established orthodoxies of the Imperial Church and a process of revision that involved both theological correction of the original narrative and its abbreviation for great liturgical efficiency.[21]

Yet perhaps the most significant contribution of the new Christian Palestinian Aramaic fragments is their witness to the fact that the so-called "Story of Peter and Paul" in sections 105–131 of the complete Ethiopic text was originally part of the ancient apocryphon and is *not* a medieval insertion, as I mistakenly concluded in my earlier monograph of the ancient Dormition traditions.[22] This episode appears in the apocryphon when Jesus is about to reveal the heavenly mysteries to Paul, and the Devil interrupts, demanding the right to challenge Paul before he receives this exalted secret knowledge. The story that follows relates the contendings of Paul, who is joined by Peter, with the Devil in Rome and Philippi. In my original translation of the *Book of Mary's Repose*, I omitted this part of the

20. Philip SELLEW, "An Early Coptic Witness to the *Dormitio Mariae* at Yale: P. CtYBR inv. 1788 Revisited," *Bulletin of the American Society of Papyrologists*, 37 (2000), 37–69.

21. SHOEMAKER, "Mother of Mysteries."

22. SHOEMAKER, *Ancient Traditions*, 159–60.

20 THE DORMITION AND ASSUMPTION OF MARY

text, primarily because comparison with all of the extant early Dormition narratives revealed no indication that this story was part of the ancient tradition. Indeed, there was no evidence at all for this apocryphal legend of Peter and Paul prior to the Middle Ages, when it circulated as an independent apocryphon in Arabic with the title "The Story of Peter and Paul." [23]

After carefully studying the evidence available at the time, I concluded that this story was a medieval interpolation designed to fill out the details of the contest between Paul (and Peter) and the Devil introduced by the latter's challenge. Nevertheless, a newly discovered Christian Palestinian Aramaic fragment found among the "new finds" at Mount Sinai, published by Müller-Kessler, has now removed any doubt that this episode was a part of this lengthy, ancient Marian apocryphon. Following this discovery, Müller-Kessler identified and published additional Christian Palestinian Aramaic fragments of this section of the apocryphon from another manuscript from the fifth or sixth century, adding to our knowledge of the apocryphon's circulation as a part of the *Book of Mary's Repose* in ancient Christianity. Even more recently, Müller-Kessler has now published a fragment of this section from the *Book of Mary's Repose* in Syriac. Although this Syriac version is unfortunately very garbled and difficult to read, it clearly witnesses to this early legend of Peter and Paul.

Therefore, in light of this new evidence, I have now added a translation of this section from Ethiopic, making for the first complete translation of this apocryphon into a modern language. In addition, I have added parallel English translations for all of the new Christian Palestinian Aramaic and Syriac fragments.

23. Agnes SMITH LEWIS, *Acta mythologica apostolorum*, 2 vols., Horae semiticae 3 & 4 (London: C.J. Clay, 1904), 150–64 (Arab) and 175–92 (Eng).

INTRODUCTION 21

Thus, the translation of the *Book of Mary's Repose* in this volume adds significant new material and reflects our best and most complete understanding of this early Christian apocryphon at present. At the same time, it also bears witness to an even earlier and previously unknown apocryphal acts of Peter and Paul, which our text has seemingly incorporated and which presumably should be named *The Contendings of Peter and Paul with the Devil* (as opposed to the rather anemic title "The Story of Peter and Paul" in the Arabic version). It is a new apocryphon deserving of study in its own right among the corpus of the ancient apocryphal acts of the apostles.

In order to understand the Ethiopic version of this apocryphon (and also the fragments in other languages) as fully as possible, one must also consult numerous later versions of this narrative in Greek and Latin (especially the two early Greek and Latin revisions of the *Book of Mary's Repose* included in this book) as well as in Old Irish.[24] As readers will soon discover, in preparing my translation I have frequently made reference to these other accounts, as well as Arras' commentary,

---

24. In an earlier book, I published a list of the most important parallels for each section of the *Book of Mary's Repose* to assist readers in making the essential comparisons among all of these early editions: SHOEMAKER, *Ancient Traditions*, 415–18. Translations of the Old Irish texts can be found in C. DONAHUE, *The Testament of Mary: The Gaelic Version of the Dormitio Mariae together with an Irish Latin Version* (New York: Fordham University Press, 1942); Máire HERBERT and Martin MCNAMARA, *Irish Biblical Apocrypha: Selected Texts in Translation* (Edinburgh: T&T Clark, 1989), 119–31. Another Greek text especially important for understanding the early history of this tradition is John of Thessalonica's early seventh-century *Homily on the Dormition*, an English translation of which can be found in Brian E. DALEY, *On the Dormition of Mary: Early Patristic Homilies* (Crestwood, N.Y.: St. Vladimir's Seminary Press, 1998), 47–70.

22   THE DORMITION AND ASSUMPTION OF MARY

as indicated in the notes to the translation. The difficulties of translation are compounded by the fact that the Ethiopic text is regularly obscure in its expression and/or corrupt. Likewise, there are very many passages that cannot be rendered into sensible English, and often only the gist, at best, can be understood. Several reasons can likely explain the difficulties in comprehending these sections. Perhaps most significant is the highly esoteric nature of the text itself.[25] The *Book of Mary's Repose* often relates secret knowledge and hidden mysteries of the cosmos, information that, as is characteristic of such literature, is intended for a community of initiated spiritual elite who have learned how to understand these cryptic messages. Furthermore, it seems clear that in some instances one or more of the text's Ethiopic transmitters has sought to correct what was perceived to be theological errors in these esoteric passages, thereby obfuscating the content further. Finally, it has also been argued that the *Book of Mary's Repose* is written in an extremely archaic form of Classical Ethiopic, which is perhaps the oldest form of this language that is extant.[26] The grammar and vocabulary of the text are in fact often irregular,

25. See now also Stephen J. SHOEMAKER, *Mary in Early Christian Faith and Devotion* (New Haven: Yale University Press, 2016), 100–29.

26. Tedros ABRAHÀ, "La *Dormitio Mariae* in Etiopia," in *Il dogma dell'assunzione de Maria: problemi attuali e tentativi de ricomprensione. Atti del XVII Simposio Internazionale Mariologico (Roma, 6–9 ottobre 2009)*, ed. Ermanno M. TONIOLO (Rome: Edizioni Marianum, 2010), 167–200, esp. 187. There is every indication that the *Book of Mary's Repose* was translated from Greek into Ethiopic during Late Antiquity and does not depend on an Arabic intermediary, as is the case with many translations of Greek texts into Ethiopic. There is no extant Arabic version of this text, nor are there any telltale signs of an intermediate Arabic version.

INTRODUCTION   23

and these qualities likely reflect to some degree the antiquity of the translation's language. Presumably, the translation was made from Greek directly into Ethiopic at a very early stage, most likely in the sixth century during the Axumite period.

As already noted, many of the key themes and features of this Dormition apocryphon show strong affinities with heterodox and esoteric varieties of the early Christianity. These include, among other things, the identification of Christ as a "Great Angel," a persistent emphasis on secret and often soteriological knowledge, and even reference to a common "gnostic" creation myth. Mary's son Jesus, who in this text is identified as a manifestation of "the Great Cherub of Light," entrusts her both with a secret prayer that is required to ascend past the cosmic demiurge and his minions at death and as a secret book containing the mysteries of the cosmos, which she is to share with the apostles when they arrive for her departure. The salvific role of this prayer is further clarified with a dense summary of a cosmological myth that has strong resonance with the doctrines of the early gnostic Christians.[27] Although in some earlier publications I proposed that the *Book of Mary's Repose* should be identified with ancient gnostic Christianity on the basis of these and numerous other similarities, I have since backed away from this conclusion, in part because the category of gnostic Christianity has become so fraught in contemporary scholarship on early Christianity that its usage is not always very helpful. Likewise, I have become increasingly convinced that it is best not to try to pin this text too closely to one particular kind of early Christianity or another but instead to allow its genuinely peculiar mix of ideas to

27. David BRAKKE, *The Gnostics: Myth, Ritual, and Diversity in Early Christianity* (Cambridge, Mass.: Harvard University Press, 2010), esp. 52–62.

24   THE DORMITION AND ASSUMPTION OF MARY

stand on its own.[28] Indeed, it is not simply another gnostic text. It is something altogether different, the likes of which we have not seen before.

The narrative opens as the "great angel" comes to Mary in Jerusalem and announces her impending death, entrusting her with a book containing the secret mysteries of creation. At the angel's bidding Mary ascends the Mount of Olives, where she immediately recognizes this Great Cherub of Light as the one who was incarnate in her son Jesus. A lengthy revelation discourse ensues, which includes, among other things, various references to themes familiar from gnostic mythology and a secret prayer that is necessary for the soul to escape through the realms guarded by the Demiurge and his minions. After the great angel departs, Mary returns home where the apostles are miraculously assembled to her, arriving on clouds from the ends of the earth. When the apostles have greeted one another and offered their prayers, Peter begins an all-night discourse that is suddenly interrupted by a heavenly voice rebuking him for revealing esoteric teachings to those not ready to receive them. Peter obligingly continues with a more exoteric lesson. Then, in the morning Mary says the secret prayer that her son, the Great Angel, had taught her, and she lies down on her bier. Immediately Christ appears with Michael and a host of other angels to receive his mother's soul, which he entrusts to Michael. The Lord commands the apostles to prepare Mary's body for burial, and as they go forth from the city to the tomb, under the watchful protection of the heavenly host, the Jews

---

28. See also the very helpful comments regarding my earlier position in Enrico NORELLI, *Marie des apocryphes : Enquête sur la mère de Jésus dans le christianisme antique*, Christianismes antiques (Genève: Labor et Fides, 2009), 129–42, which in large part convinced me to change my mind on this point.

INTRODUCTION 25

launch an attack with the aim of burning her body.[29] Unsurprisingly, the heavenly powers intervene to protect Mary's body and punish the Jews, and after their chastisement and conversion, the apostles lay her body in the tomb.

For three days the apostles wait at the tomb, guarding it until the Lord will come with his angels to take it away. As they wait, Paul, who was more recently converted and did not know Christ in the flesh, begins to ask the others to share their knowledge of the hidden mysteries that he had taught them. The apostles are reluctant and refuse to reveal the secrets to him unless the Lord instructs them, and instead they eventually shift the conversation to a discussion of what they had each been preaching to their new converts, focusing especially on matters of ascetic practice. The others are shocked when Paul advocates a program of ascetic moderation, but he is soon vindicated when Christ arrives and champions the teaching of Paul, promising to reveal even greater mysteries to him in heaven. In the company of the heavenly host, Christ takes his mother's body and the apostles on clouds to Paradise, where her soul is reunited with her body. Then he personally escorts her with the apostles on a tour of the places of punishment.[30] In this context the text highlights the powers of the Virgin's intercessions on behalf of sinners in what is seemingly

29. On this aspect of the early Dormition traditions, see Stephen J. SHOEMAKER, "'Let Us Go and Burn Her Body': The Image of the Jews in the Early Dormition Traditions," *Church History* 68.4 (1999), 775–823.

30. On this apocalypse of the Virgin from the *Book of Mary's Repose*, see Richard BAUCKHAM, "The Four Apocalypses of the Virgin Mary," in *The Fate of the Dead: Studies on Jewish and Christian Apocalypses*, Supplements to Novum Testamentum 93 (Leiden: Brill, 1998), 332–62; and SHOEMAKER, *Ancient Traditions*, 179–203.

26 THE DORMITION AND ASSUMPTION OF MARY

some of the earliest evidence for this central element of Marian piety: indeed, Norelli suggests that belief in Mary's unique intercessory powers was one of the primary inspirations for the development of the early Dormition traditions.[31] Christ then returns Mary and the apostles to Paradise, where they meet with the blessed dead from the old covenant. After Paul and Peter contend with the Devil, so that Paul can learn the secret mysteries, Mary and the apostles are brought into the seventh heaven, before the presence of God. The apostles then return to earth, while Mary remains in heaven, sitting with her son at the right hand of God.

Although the *Book of Mary's Repose* is known in its entirety from relatively late Ethiopic manuscripts of the fourteenth century, we know that it was current in ancient Christianity from the various Syriac and Christian Palestinian Aramaic fragments of the text that were copied in the later fifth and the sixth centuries.[32] Moreover, through comparison with other closely related texts, such as *Greek Mary's Repose* and *Latin Mary's Repose*, included in this volume and discussed below, we can confirm that virtually all of this apocryphon's content was in circulation by this time. Furthermore, comparison with these other witnesses reveals the faithfulness with which this Ethiopic translation transmits its ancient source. The Ethiopic translation of the *Book of Mary's Repose* shows itself more faithful than, for instance, the translations of *I Enoch* or the *Apocalypse of Peter*, whose Ethiopic translations are widely regarded as largely accurate transmissions of these ancient

---

31. NORELLI, *Marie des apocryphes*, 132–6.

32. WRIGHT, *Contributions to Apocryphal Literature*, ܡܘ-ܠܒ (Syr) and 42–51 (Eng). Also MÜLLER-KESSLER, "Obsequies (I),"; MÜLLER-KESSLER, "Obsequies (I)."

documents.[33] Indeed, it is quite clear that the *Book of Mary's Repose* is significantly older than the fifth-century Syriac fragments that first bear witness to it. Since the *Book of Mary's Repose* was originally composed in Greek, we know that it must be older than these late fifth century translations.[34]

Fortunately, we can be slightly more specific than this. Firstly, the doctrinal content of the *Book of Mary's Repose* is clearly indicative of its production at an earlier time in the history of Christianity. The abundance of "heterodox" elements present in this text seems to require that an early version of the "Palm of the Tree of Life" apocryphon was already in existence during the third century, if not perhaps even earlier. This date coincides roughly with the floruit of gnostic and esoteric Christianities, such as seem to be reflected in this document, as well as with the relative disappearance of Angel Christology, one of this apocryphon's hallmarks, after the beginning of the fourth century. The initial composition of a document centered on these ideas much after this point seems comparatively unlikely.[35] Indeed, many of the earliest revisions of this apocryphal tradition openly express discomfort with these elements of their source material. The sixth and early seventh-century redactors have carefully reshaped the contents of the ancient narrative to comport better with the orthodoxies of their era, when these older expressions of Christianity had become quite foreign.[36]

33. SHOEMAKER, *Ancient Traditions*, 146–59.

34. Ibid., 33–42.

35. Ibid., 42–6, 253–6, 278–9, 284–6.

36. See SHOEMAKER, "Mother of Mysteries"; Stephen J. SHOEMAKER, "The Virgin Mary's Hidden Past: From Ancient Marian Apocrypha to the Medieval *vitae Virginis*," *Marian Studies* 60 (2009), 1–30.

Furthermore, the *Book of Mary's Repose* vigorously defends the authority of the apostle Paul, whose status as an apostle seems to be in question from the moment he first appears. In this regard the *Book of Mary's Repose* seems intent on rebutting other Christian communities that had challenged the authority of Paul. This feature would seem to locate its composition sometime in the second or third century, inasmuch as opposition to Paul is largely confined to this era.[37] Strangely enough, however, it is not Paul's attitude to the Law that is at the forefront in this matter. Instead, doubts about Paul center on his failure to receive initiation into the secret mysteries by Jesus, since he did not follow Jesus when he was teaching in the flesh, and even more so on his advocacy of ascetic moderation in contrast to the extreme, encratite views espoused by the other apostles. When the apostles discuss the degree of renunciation that they enjoin on their converts, Paul is astonished at the rigor imposed by his co-apostles, explaining that he recommends instead a more modest program of restraint. Just as their disagreement appears headed for a heated debate, Christ returns and champions the ascetic moderation advanced by Paul. Inasmuch as Mary was elevated to become the paragon of virginity and ascetic renunciation during the fourth century, her association here with a moderate asceticism seemingly aimed at married householders rather than world-renouncing virgins seems telling. One imagines that this feature is indicative of the apocryphon's production before the image of Mary as the archetypal ascetic became the norm.[38]

---

37. See Gerd LUEDEMANN, *Opposition to Paul in Jewish Christianity*, trans. M. Eugene Boring (Minneapolis: Fortress Press, 1989), esp. 197.
38. Stephen J. SHOEMAKER, "Asceticism in the Early Dormition Narratives," *Studia Patristica* 44 (2010), 509–13.

INTRODUCTION   29

Other elements also suggest such an early date, including Joseph's confession that he initially thought that perhaps he had raped the Virgin Mary while drunk one night, and Mary's fear before death because she had sinned. These remarks are sharply at variance with the belief in Mary's sinlessness, for instance, while the notion that she might have sinned seems to have been limited to the second and third centuries. By the fourth century, agreement on her sinlessness had become fairly widespread.[39] Nevertheless, one of the strongest indicators that this apocryphon was composed by the fourth century, if not even earlier, is the close literary relationship it shares with the *Apocalypse of Paul*. Unfortunately, scholarship on early Christian apocalypticism and apocrypha has long overlooked this connection,[40] a symptom, no doubt, of the general neglect of the ancient Dormition traditions. It is clear, however, that one of these two texts depends on the other, and for a variety of reasons the probability is high that the *Apocalypse of Paul* has made use of the apocalyptic conclusion to the *Book of Mary's Repose*.[41] Since the *Apocalypse of Paul* is generally dated to sometime around the turn of the fifth century,[42] this literary

39. Regarding the question of Mary's sinfulness, see e.g. Tina BEATTIE, "Mary in Patristic Theology," in *Mary: The Complete Guide*, ed. Sarah Jane BOSS (London: Continuum, 2007), 75–105, 99–102.

40. Perhaps most notably in Martha HIMMELFARB, *Tours of Hell: An Apocalyptic Form in Jewish and Christian Literature* (Philadelphia: University of Pennsylvania Press, 1983).

41. BAUCKHAM, "Four Apocalypses of the Virgin," 344–6; SHOEMAKER, *Ancient Traditions*, 42–6; NORELLI, *Marie des apocryphes*, 115, 134 n. 79; and Édouard COTHENET, "Marie dans les apocryphes," in *Maria : Études sur la Sainte Vierge*, ed. Hubert DU MANOIR DE JUAYE, 7 vols., vol. 6 (Paris: Beauchesne, 1952), 71–156, 127–9.

42. Pierluigi PIOVANELLI, "Les origines de l'*Apocalypse de Paul* reconsidérées," *Apocrypha* 4 (1993), 37–59.

30   THE DORMITION AND ASSUMPTION OF MARY

dependence adds further evidence for the *Book of Mary's Repose*'s composition in the fourth century, if not even earlier.

The *Six Books Apocryphon*.

A rather different account of the Mary's departure from this world emerges from the *Six Books Apocryphon*, a work so-called because of its arrangement according to six books. This narrative is the earliest representative of the "Bethlehem" literary tradition, the other of the two main literary traditions. In common with the Palm traditions, it shares Mary's death at her home in Jerusalem; the miraculous reunion of the apostles, who are flown in on clouds; Christ's reception of his mother's soul; the attack of the Jews; the transfer of Mary's body and/or soul to Paradise; and, in the earliest narratives at least, an apocalyptic tour of the heavenly realms and the places of punishment. Beyond this rather slim core, however, it recalls a very different memory of the events at the end of Mary's life.

Like the *Book of Mary's Repose*, the earliest direct witnesses to the *Six Books Apocryphon* are in Syriac, where the text survives intact in two manuscripts from the sixth century and in three fragmentary manuscripts—one quite substantial—from the later fifth century. The two complete early manuscripts preface this Dormition apocryphon with the *Protevangelium of James* and the *Infancy Gospel of Thomas*, thereby producing, in effect, a sort of proto-"Life" of the Virgin Mary.[43] Since the

---

43. See SHOEMAKER, "The Virgin Mary's Hidden Past,"; Stephen J. SHOEMAKER, "Mary in Early Christian Apocrypha: Virgin Territory," in *Rediscovering the Apocryphal Continent: New Perspectives on Early Christian and Late Antique Apocryphal Texts and Traditions*, ed. Pierluigi PIOVANELLI, Tony BURKE, and Timothy PETTIPIECE (Tübingen: Mohr Siebeck, 2015), 175–90.

INTRODUCTION 31

text was originally written in Greek, the existence of several Syriac versions by the later fifth century indicates a much earlier composition, and it seems reasonable to suppose that the text and its traditions most likely belong to the previous century, as other evidence confirms more directly.[44] I have made the translation published in this volume on the basis of a still unpublished sixth-century Syriac manuscript at the University of Göttingen, which I have edited as part of preparing a critical edition of this text, together with Andrew Hochstedler.[45] In the notes I have often indicated a number of variants from two very closely related manuscripts housed in the British Library that preserve a very similar version of the *Six Books Apocryphon*, one also from the sixth century (Add. 14484; A in the notes), and another from the thirteenth (Add. 14732; B in the notes). An edition of these two manuscripts was published with English translation in the middle of the nineteenth century by William Wright.[46] Likewise, at the very beginning of the twentieth century Agnes Smith Lewis published an edition of a fragmentary—yet extensive—manuscript from the later fifth century with English translation.[47] Another set of early palimpsest fragments was recently published by Sebastian Brock and Grigory Kessel, a version with similarities to the

44. SHOEMAKER, *Ancient Traditions*, 46–56; SHOEMAKER, *Mary*, 130–65.

45. Göttingen manuscript MS syr. 10. See also Wilhelm BAARS and Jan HELDERMANN, "Neue Materialien zum Text und zur Interpretation des Kindheitsevangeliums des Pseudo-Thomas," *Oriens Christianus* 77–8 (1993–4), 191–226, 1–32.

46. William WRIGHT, "The Departure of My Lady Mary from This World," *The Journal of Sacred Literature and Biblical Record* 6–7 (1865), 417–448 and 108–160.

47. Agnes SMITH LEWIS, *Apocrypha Syriaca*, Studia Sinaitica 11 (London: C.J. Clay and Sons, 1902).

32 THE DORMITION AND ASSUMPTION OF MARY

Smith Lewis palimpsest.[48] The version of the *Six Books* witnessed in these palimpsests differs significantly in some instances from the version of the Göttingen and British Library manuscripts, although I have occasionally drawn some comparisons to Smith Lewis's palimpsest in the notes to my translation.

As found in these earliest manuscripts, the *Six Books Apocryphon* begins with an elaborate liturgical invocation, indicating from the start this text's use in the context of worship, after which follows the tale of several monks from Mount Sinai who were concerned that they did not know how the Virgin Mary had departed from this life. Initial inquiries in Jerusalem lead them to Ephesus, where through incubation at the shrine of St. John they miraculously received a copy of this apocryphon. The Dormition narrative itself then begins in the second book, as Mary departs Jerusalem in the face of Jewish harassment for a second house that she has in Bethlehem. At this point the scene shifts temporarily to Bethlehem, one of the hallmarks of this literary tradition. The apostles miraculously assemble in Bethlehem, and at Mary's request they each explain how they came there from the various places where they had previously been spreading the gospel, or in the case of a few, after arising from their graves. While in Bethlehem, Mary works numerous miracles, mostly of healing, both among

48. Sebastian P. BROCK and Grigory KESSEL, "The 'Departure of Mary' in Two Palimpsests at the Monastery of St. Catherine (Sinai Syr. 30 & Sinai Arabic 514)," *Khristianskiĭ Vostok* 8 (2017), 115–52. See also Adrian C. PIRTEA, "The Syriac and Sogdian Prefaces to the Six Books on the Dormition of the Virgin Mary," in *Iranianate and Syriac Christianity in Late Antiquity and the Early Islamic Period*, ed. C. BARBATI and V. BERTI (Vienna: Austrian Academy of Sciences Press, 2021), 279–331, which draws some important conclusions regarding the date of the apocryphon's invention narrative.

INTRODUCTION   33

those gathered in Bethlehem and others at great distance. Indeed, the narrative inventories Mary's numerous miracles in three different sections.

When the Jews persuade the Roman governor to drive Mary and the apostles out of Bethlehem, this holy assembly is miraculously transported together through air, over the heads of the soldiers, to Mary's Jerusalem home. When Mary again begins working miracles in Jerusalem, the Jews decide to move against her directly, only to be scorched with fire as they attempt to attack her house. In response, the governor organizes a debate between the Jews and the Christians, in which the latter unsurprisingly triumph, and the Jews are forced to reveal where they have hidden the implements of the crucifixion.[49] Numerous additional miracles ensue, until at divine command the apostles bear Mary on her bier—while still alive—to her tomb. Along the way the Jews attack her bier, unsuccessfully, and eventually the apostles reach her tomb. Before dying, Mary offers a blessing, promising her intercessions for those who regularly commemorate her after her passing. Christ arrives, and after promising to yield to his mother's petitions, he receives her soul and transfers her to Paradise in the company of the apostles. A set of lengthy liturgical instructions then follows, giving the dates for three annual commemorations of Mary and describing the ceremonies to be observed on those occasions, which include offerings of bread and the reading of the *Six Books Apocryphon*. The final two books of the apocryphon describe Mary's resurrection and her otherworldly journey, this time without the apostles.

49. On this tradition, see Stephen J. SHOEMAKER, "A Peculiar Version of the *Inventio crucis* in the Early Syriac Dormition Traditions," *Studia Patristica* 41 (2006), 75–81.

34 THE DORMITION AND ASSUMPTION OF MARY

Theologically the *Six Books Apocryphon* is quite orthodox, particularly in comparison with the *Book of Mary's Repose*. Moreover, its Marian piety is significantly more advanced, showing a remarkably developed devotion to the Virgin.[50] Numerous miracles are assigned to the power of Mary's prayers, and she is able to work miracles throughout the world. Several of these miracles involve Marian apparitions, and in some cases she is seemingly able to bilocate. While the *Book of Mary's Respose* draws a focus on Mary's intercessions only during her visit to the places of punishment, the *Six Books Apocryphon* repeatedly invokes the unique efficacy of her petitions. Nevertheless, it is not enough to seek her prayers, but these must be joined to regular liturgical commemorations and offerings in her honor, to be observed on three different occasions during the year. The rituals enjoined by the *Six Books Apocryphon* for these occasions involve offerings of bread in Mary's honor, in a fashion strikingly similar to the practices of the "Kollyridians" as described by Epiphanius of Salamis (*Pan.* 78–9). The correspondence of these rituals with Epiphanius' account is too remarkable to be mere coincidence, and it seems clear that he somehow knew traditions from this apocryphon as he was writing in the middle of the fourth century.[51]

50. On this aspect, see now SHOEMAKER, *Mary*, 130–65.
51. Stephen J. SHOEMAKER, "Epiphanius of Salamis, the Kollyridians, and the Early Dormition Narratives: The Cult of the Virgin in the Later Fourth Century," *Journal of Early Christian Studies* 16 (2008), 371–401; also SHOEMAKER, *Mary*, 145–63.

INTRODUCTION 35

The Greek Revision
of the *Book of Mary's Repose*.

This revised version of the *Book of Mary's Repose* survives only in a single manuscript, which was edited by Antoine Wenger and published with a French translation in 1955, and again published in 1989 by Frédéric Manns, also with a French translation and a reproduction of the manuscript.[52] I have made my translation by comparing these two published editions and occasionally correcting them as necessary through comparison with Mann's reproduction. As Wenger persuasively demonstrates in the extensive study that accompanies the text's publication, this precis of the ancient Palm Dormitions was almost certainly composed by the sixth century. Through painstaking analysis and comparison, Wenger establishes that this Greek narrative, perhaps in a slightly different form, was used by John of Thessalonica as the basis for his homily on the Dormition at the beginning of the seventh century.[53] Nevertheless, as it is increasingly clear that the early history of the Dormition traditions reaches back into the fourth if not even the third century, there is no reason now to exclude the possibility that this revision of the Greek *Book of Mary's Repose* was made in the fifth or even fourth century.

This apocryphon is invaluable for understanding the earliest history of the Palm Dormition tradition. It not only confirms

---

52. Antoine WENGER, *L'Assomption de la T. S. Vierge dans la tradition byzantine du VIe au Xe siècle : Études et Documents*, Archives de l'Orient chrétien, 5 (Paris: Institut français d'études byzantines, 1955), 210–41; Frédéric MANNS, *Le Récit de la Dormition de Marie (Vatican grec 1982) : Contribution à l'étude des origines de l'exégèse chrétienne*, Studium Biblicum Franciscanum, Collectio Maior, 33 (Jerusalem: Franciscan Printing Press, 1989).

53. WENGER, *L'Assomption*, 17–67.

the antiquity of many doctrinal and literary features of the *Book of Mary's Repose*, but in a number of instances it seems to have preserved the content of this ancient apocryphon more clearly than the complete Ethiopic version. Indeed, this Greek version preserved much of the esotericism of its ancient source. For instance, the Greek revision shares the angel Christology evident in the Ethiopic text, and the near-verbal agreement between the two versions confirms that this understanding of Christ was present in the earliest layer of this apocryphal tradition. Likewise, this Greek revision affirms that the book of the secret mysteries entrusted by Christ to his mother is a primitive feature. Although Arras, in his commentary, proposed that the book had been introduced through mistakes made during translation from the Greek into Ethiopic, the presence of this arcane volume in this earliest Greek text confirms its presence in the original version of this apocryphon. This Greek revision also includes the secret prayer of ascent and preserves in Greek much of the technical jargon of gnostic and other early esoteric Christian groups that appears in the oldest version of this apocryphon.

Readers will thus discover the main significance of this Greek text primarily through comparison with the *Book of Mary's Repose* and connections drawn in the notes between these two versions. Nevertheless, the apocalyptic conclusion to the *Book of Mary's Repose* is lacking from this revised account. I suspect that its absence reflects the fact that the tradition of an apocalypse of the Virgin was already becoming independent from its origins in the Dormition apocrypha, and accordingly the Greek redactor excised it, although admittedly, this is not the only possible explanation for its omission. In this regard, the following text, the *Latin Revision of the Book of Mary's Repose*, proves itself a valuable witness to the antiquity of this apocalyptic conclusion.

INTRODUCTION   37

Two Early Latin *Dormition* Narratives.

The Latin texts that I have translated for this volume are
certainly two of the earliest versions of the ancient Dormition
narratives preserved in Latin, even if they may not be the
oldest. The rightful bearer of this honor is not clear, and it
may instead belong to an apocryphal *Transitus Mariae* attributed
to Melito of Sardis, an early Christian writer of the mid-second century who is most famous for his treatise on Passover.
Nevertheless, we have skipped over this text—important
though it is—because it is comparatively well known and has
been translated into English, among other modern languages,
several times.[54] And if perhaps either or both of these texts
may be a bit more recent and heavily edited than the Ps.-Melito
Transitus, they are nonetheless of great antiquity and close in
age to the Ps.-Melito apocryphon. More importantly, however,
both texts are extremely important for understanding the earliest
history of the Palm Dormition traditions.

The first of the two Latin texts translated in this volume we
have called *Latin Revision of the Book of Mary's Repose* (*Latin
Mary's Repose* for short), since as Antoine Wenger has demon-
strated, it shows significant fidelity with *Greek Mary's Repose*,
and since the publication of the *Book of Mary's Repose*, its close
relation to this ancient apocryphon has also become clear.

---

54. The best edition of this text is Monika HAIBACH-REINISCH, *Ein
neuer "Transitus Mariae" des Pseudo-Melito* (Rome: Pontificia Academia
Mariana Internationalis, 1962). For translations, see Alexander WALKER,
ed., *Apocryphal Gospels, Acts, and Revelations*, Ante-Nicene Christian
Library 16 (Edinburgh: T&T Clark, 1873), 522–30; Montague Rhodes
JAMES, *The Apocryphal New Testament* (Oxford: Oxford University
Press, 1924), 209–16; François AMIOT and DANIEL-ROPS, *Évangiles
apocryphes*, Textes pour l'histoire sacrée (Paris: A. Fayard, 1952), 112–
34; ERBETTA, *Gli Apocrifi, vol. 1/2*, 492–510.

38   THE DORMITION AND ASSUMPTION OF MARY

The only previous translation of this text into a modern language was into Italian, and our translation was made from Wenger's edition of its only known manuscript.[55] The second text we have decided to name, faute de mieux, the *Latin Transitus Mariae*. To my knowledge, this Dormition apocryphon has not previously been translated into any language, although there are Italian translations of a closely related and much shorter version.[56] The basis for this translation is the critical edition produced by André Wilmart on the basis of nine manuscripts that were known to him at the time.[57] We have also translated, after the conclusion of the text in Wilmart's edition, a previously untranslated ending of a more recently discovered manuscript from this same textual tradition, edited by Wenger,[58] that is especially important for its account of the apocalyptic journey by Mary and the apostles following her Assumption.

Both of these Latin narratives offer important confirmation of various primitive elements from the ancient Palm tradition as transmitted by the *Book of Mary's Repose*, while at the same

55. WENGER, *L'Assomption*, 245–56; trans. ERBETTA, *Gli Apocrifi, vol. 1/2*, 472–79.

56. This version was published in also Bernard CAPELLE, "Vestiges grecs et latins d'un antique '*Transitus* de la Vierge'," *Analecta Bollandiana* 67 (1949), 21–48. See also the translations in ERBETTA, *Gli Apocrifi, vol. 1/2*, 480–2; and Luigi MORALDI, *Apocrifi del Nuovo Testamento*, 2 vols., Classici delle religioni 24. Sezione 5: Le altre confessioni cristiane (Torino: Unione tipografico-editrice torinese, 1971), 1:879–84.

57. André WILMART, *Analecta reginensia : Extraits des manuscrits latins de la reine Christine conservés au Vatican*, Studi e Testi, 59 (Città del Vaticano: Biblioteca apostolica Vaticana, 1933), 323–62. See; G. MAROCCO, "Nuovi documenti sull'Assunzione del Medio Evo latino: due transitus dai codici latini 59 e 105 di Ivrea," *Marianum* 12 (1950), 449–52.

58. WENGER, *L'Assomption*, 258–9.

time they demonstrate the process of revising these older traditions. For instance, these adaptations remove many of the heterodoxies that stood in the earliest versions of this apocryphon, so as to update the narrative in order to conform with the limits of orthodoxy as they were becoming defined at the end of antiquity. Likewise, these Latin versions reflect a persistent trend in the later history of the early Dormition tradition toward increased brevity, undoubtedly with liturgical efficiency in view.[59] Despite these editorial efforts, much of the early tradition nonetheless remains in evidence, especially in *Latin Mary's Repose*, and it bears witness to some parts of the *Book of Mary's Repose* that, for whatever reason, are absent from *Greek Mary's Repose*. In the Latin version, we find an often faithful reproduction of the language of the original, as well as important vestiges of the ancient tradition, such as Mary's prayer to the "great cherub" and Peter's all-night discourse, including the divine warning that he should not divulge the secret mysteries to those incapable of receiving them.[60]

59. In this regard, see SHOEMAKER, "Epiphanius of Salamis,"; Stephen J. SHOEMAKER, "Between Scripture and Tradition: The Marian Apocrypha of Early Christianity," in *The Reception and Interpretation of the Bible in Late Antiquity*, ed. Lorenzo DiTOMMASO and Lucian TURCESCU, Bible in Ancient Christianity 6 (Leiden: Brill, 2008), 491–510; SHOEMAKER, "The Virgin Mary's Hidden Past,"; Stephen J. SHOEMAKER, "Apocrypha and Liturgy in the Fourth Century: The Case of the '*Six Books*' Dormition Apocryphon," in *Jewish and Christian Scriptures: The Function of "Canonical" and "Non-canonical" Religious Texts*, ed. James H. CHARLESWORTH and Lee Martin McDONALD (London: T&T Clark, 2010), 153–63; SHOEMAKER, "Mother of Mysteries."

60. Those interested in pursuing these points further should compare the various texts in light of Wenger's detailed analysis in WENGER, *L'Assomption*, 68–95.

40 THE DORMITION AND ASSUMPTION OF MARY

An Early *Dormition* Fragment in Old Georgian.

As noted already above, this fragment is transmitted uniquely in a Georgian homiliary, that is, a collection of liturgical readings, largely homilies, to be read for the various annual feasts of the ecclesiastical year. The Georgian homiliary tradition depends on the early liturgical traditions of late ancient Palestine, and much of the material found in these collections derives from this milieu. There are in fact several different Georgian homiliary collections, and despite some variation in their contents, they all depend ultimately on an older Greek model from late ancient Jerusalem. Only a single homiliary, however, transmits this Georgian Dormition fragment, the Klarjeti homiliary, so-called on account of this particular manuscript's link to this region of medieval Georgia.[61] In this homiliary, as we have noted, this fragment appears sandwiched between two fragments from the *Book of Mary's Repose*. Accordingly, this second of the three collected fragments is often indicated in studies of the early Dormition traditions as if it were another fragment of the *Book of Mary's Repose*. Indeed, in his edition, Michel van Esbroeck numbers the paragraphs of these fragments with numbers consecutive to the first fragment. Although he notes that one or more pages has gone missing in between the two fragments, he presents them as if they were in fact both from the same text, and yet, they are not.[62]

---

61. For more on this tradition, see Michel VAN ESBROECK, *Les Plus Anciens Homéliaires géorgiens : Étude descriptive et historique*, Publications de l'Institut orientaliste de Louvain 10 (Louvain-la-Neuve: Université catholique de Louvain, Institut orientaliste, 1975), which remains the most important study on the topic not written in Georgian.

62. Michel VAN ESBROECK, "Apocryphes géorgiens de la Dormition," *Analecta Bollandiana* 92 (1973), 55–75.

INTRODUCTION   41

Instead, this second fragment preserves a brief passage from an otherwise unknown Dormition narrative that is quite different from any other account that I am aware of. Nevertheless, it does share some the basic elements common to most of the ancient Dormition apocrypha. The text focuses on the moment of the Virgin's Dormition, that is, the departure of her soul from the body. Like the vast majority of other early Dormition narratives, this fragment notes the presence of the apostles for this event, as well as the arrival of Christ with the angels to personally receive his mother's soul as it goes forth. Thereafter the apostles see to her burial, going from Mount Zion to a tomb in Gethsemane, although as they are placing her in the tomb, her body miraculously ascends to heaven separately from her soul, presumably to be reunited with it in Paradise. It is difficult to date this text, but one imagines that the Georgian translation probably derives from a Greek model from the sixth-century or possibly seventh-century Jerusalem. The Georgian manuscript preserving the fragment dates to the tenth century, but there is relative consensus that the contents of the Georgian homiliary collections were compiled from materials used in Jerusalem's liturgical services during the fifth, sixth, and seventh centuries.[63] And in regard to the readings transmitted for the commemorations of Mary on and around 15 August, Michel van Esbroeck has persuasively argued that these should be dated to sometime around the

63. Van ESBROECK, *Les Plus Anciens Homéliaires*, 325–349; Tamila MGALOBLISHVILI, კლარჯული მრავალთავი *(Klarjuli mravalt'avi [The Homiliary of Klarjeti])*, Zveli Kart'uli mcerlobis żeglebi 12 (Tbilisi: Mec'niereba, 1991), 469–73, 478–88; M. MAISURAŻE et al., ათონის მრავალთავი *(At'onis mravalt'avi [The Homiliary of Athos])* (Tbilisi: Georgian Academy of Sciences, K. Kekelidze Institute of Manuscripts, 1999), 284–5.

42 THE DORMITION AND ASSUMPTION OF MARY

year 500.[64] This text has not previously been translated into any modern language, and the translation in this volume was made not from van Esbroeck's edition, but instead from Tamila Mgaloblishvili's edition of the Klarjeti homiliary.[65]

A Liturgical Apocryphon from *Jeremiah* for the *Dormition of the Virgin*.

This unusual Dormition apocryphon also survives uniquely in the Klarjeti homiliary, where it appears as a reading for the 13 August feast celebrated at the church of the Kathisma, or "Seat," of the Virgin Mary. The Kathisma church was the earliest Marian shrine in the Jerusalem region, which once stood at the mid-point of the Jerusalem-Bethlehem road. The significance of the Kathisma's location derives, as is now well known, from the Nativity traditions of the *Protevangelium of James*, and this account of the birth of Jesus was unquestionably the impetus for construction of a shrine on this spot. At the center of this Kathisma church was a large rock, on which it was believed that Mary had briefly rested before giving birth nearby, although the *Protevangelium* makes no mention of a rock or Mary's rest. Nevertheless, this apocryphon preserves an early tradition that Mary gave birth to Jesus not in Bethlehem but very near the site of the Kathisma. According to the *Protevangelium*, Mary and Joseph were on their way to Bethlehem when, at the third mile of the Jerusalem-Bethlehem road, the location of the Kathisma Church, the child was ready to come forth. Thus, Mary gave birth in a nearby cave, somewhere in a remote location halfway between Jerusalem and Bethlehem.

64. Van ESBROECK, *Les Plus Anciens Homéliaires*, 342–6.
65. MGALOBLISHVILI, კლარჯული მრავალთავი, 421–3.

INTRODUCTION   43

Although the *Protevangelium* dates to the later second century, this Nativity tradition is almost certainly even older: Justin Martyr's reference to a similar tradition in the *Dialogue with Trypho* would seem to indicate its circulation in the first half of the second century.[66] Some scholars, most notably Michel van Esbroeck and Walter Ray, have proposed with good reason that this was likely the earliest Nativity tradition of the Jerusalem and Bethlehem region, where, one should note, Justin was from (Flavia Neapolis, which is modern Nablus), and I would tend to agree. In addition to the various liturgical arguments advanced for this conclusion, it is also noteworthy that the earliest history of the Kathisma Church and the liturgies associated with it clearly identify it directly with traditions of Christ's Nativity.[67] Were this tradition not primitive to the region, I find it otherwise difficult to imagine

66. Justin Martyr, *Dialogue with Trypho* 78. See George T. ZERVOS, "Dating the Protevangelium of James: The Justine Martyr Connection," *SBL Seminar Papers* 33 (1994), 415–34; George T. Zervos, "Christmas with Salome," in *A Feminist Companion to Mariology*, ed. Amy-Jill Levine (London: T&T Clark, 2005), 77–98.

67. Michel VAN ESBROECK, "Les textes littéraires sur l'Assomption avant le Xe siècle," in *Les Actes apocryphes des apôtres*, ed. François BOVON (Geneva: Labor et Fides, 1981), 265–85, 284. The early liturgical traditions associated with the Kathisma's 15 August feast are clearly celebrating Mary's role in the Nativity, anchoring the shrine's earliest history solidly in commemoration of the Nativity. See, e.g. SHOEMAKER, *Ancient Traditions*, esp. 80–1, 91, 97–8, 116–18, 124–7. The primitive connections between this shrine, its feast, and the Nativity are clearly explained in Walter D. RAY, "August 15 and the Development of the Jerusalem Calendar" (Ph.D. diss., University of Notre Dame, 2000), which also makes an argument, necessarily speculative but also convincing, that 15 August was the original date of the Nativity as observed in the Jerusalem region in connection with this location. I

44   THE DORMITION AND ASSUMPTION OF MARY

how this tradition could have survived competition with the biblical Nativity traditions in order to give rise to the Kathisma Church and also to determine the canonical representation of the Nativity in Christian art up until the present day.

Jerusalem's early liturgical traditions evidence a strong connection between the Kathisma church and the Nativity of Christ in its earliest history. Our oldest liturgical document from Jerusalem is a liturgical text known as the Jerusalem Armenian Lectionary, whose Greek original reflects the liturgical calendar and practice of Jerusalem during the mid-fifth century.[68] The lectionary provides the appointed scriptural readings for each of Jerusalem's annual feasts, including the feast of the Memory of Mary the Theotokos, celebrated on 15 August at the third mile from Bethlehem, that is, the location of the Kathisma church. The biblical passages to be read on this occasion clearly identify the Nativity and the Virgin's role therein as the focus of this feast. The appointed lection from the Old Testament is Isaiah 7:10–16, "Behold, a virgin shall conceive," as the Christians were reading it from the Septuagint. The Epistle reading is Galatians 3:29–4:7, in which Paul emphasizes redemption by God's son, "born of a woman," which is the most Paul ever has to say about Mary and the Nativity. And the Gospel text is the beginning of Luke's birth narrative, 2:1–7, which describes Mary's birthing of Christ. Each of these verses then emphasizes the birth of Christ from Mary, a theme that is

have summarized much of Ray's arguments in Stephen J. SHOEMAKER, "Christmas in the Qur'ān: The Qur'ānic Account of Jesus' Nativity and Palestinian Local Tradition," *Jerusalem Studies in Arabic and Islam* 28 (2003), 11–39, 24–28.

68. See Hugo MÉNDEZ, "Revising the Date of the Armenian Lectionary of Jerusalem," *Journal of Early Christian Studies* 29 (2021), 61–92.

INTRODUCTION   45

confirmed by other early sources relevant to the church of the
Kathisma and the feast of the Memory of Mary.[69]

A century later, by the middle of the sixth century, this
15 August feast of the Virgin Mary had come to be transformed
into a commemoration of Mary's miraculous departure from
this world and her Assumption into heaven, and its celebration
was moved to the church of her tomb in Gethsemane. Thus we
know from the Jerusalem Georgian Chantbook and the Jerusalem Georgian Lectionary, collections whose traditions reflect
this period in Jerusalem's liturgical history.[70] The Kathisma's
Memory of Mary did not completely disappear, however; it
was transferred instead to 13 August, marking the start of what
was eventually to become a five-day commemoration of Mary
in the middle of August, as also evidenced by these early Georgian liturgical collections from Jerusalem. Yet of the Georgian
homiliaries, only the Klarjeti homiliary provides a reading for

69. A. RENOUX, *Le Codex arménien Jérusalem 121*, 2 vols., PO 35.1 and
36.2 (Turnhout: Brepols, 1971), 2:354–7.

70. El. METREVELI, Cʻ. ČANKIEVI, and L. XEVSURIANI, უძველესი
იადგარი *(Uzvelesi iadgari [The Oldest Chantbook])*, Żveli kʻartʻuli
mcerlobis żeglebi 2 (Tbilisi: Mecʻniereba, 1980); Michel TARCHNISCH-
VILI, *Le Grand Lectionnaire de l'Église de Jérusalem*, 2 vols., CSCO 188–
89; 204–5, Scriptores Iberici 9–10; 13–14 (Louvain: CSCO, 1959–60).
Regarding the date of these materials, see esp. Stig FRØYSHOV, "The
Georgian Witness to the Jerusalem Liturgy: New Sources and Studies,"
in *Inquiries into Eastern Christian Worship. Selected Papers of the Second
International Congress of the Society of Oriental Liturgies, Rome, 17–21
September 2008*, ed. B. GROEN, S. HAWKES-TEEPLES, and S. ALEXOPOU-
LOS (Leuven: Peeters, 2012), 227–67, 233–8, 246–7. Regarding the
hymnal, see also Stephen J. SHOEMAKER, *The First Christian Hymnal:
The Songs of the Ancient Jerusalem Church: Parallel Georgian-English Texts*,
Middle Eastern Texts Initiative 10 (Provo, Utah: Brigham Young
University Press, 2018), xi-xv.

46   THE DORMITION AND ASSUMPTION OF MARY

this feast, in this case an expanded version of a passage from the apocryphal *Life of Jeremiah*, from the collection of the *Lives of the Prophets* that survives uniquely in the Klarjeti homiliary.

This text is, in effect, a rewritten apocryphon used here as a liturgical reading for a Marian feast at one of the oldest Marian shrines. True to form for the Kathisma church, this reading from the Prophet Jeremiah, as it is identified, evokes the events of the Nativity while also identifying Mary with the Ark of the Covenant resting on a rock, all in the context of celebrating her Dormition and Assumption, the events around which this mid-August festival cycle centered. It is particularly interesting that, as van Esbroeck notes, this lection seems to present this apocryphal tradition as if it were a canonical text, introducing it as a reading from "the things said by the prophet Jeremiah," as if, in effect these were words from the biblical prophet himself.[71] Like the previous reading from the Klarjeti homiliary for 15 August discussed above, this Georgian translation probably derives from a Greek model from the sixth-century or possibly seventh-century Jerusalem, quite possibly sometime around 500 as van Esbroeck suggests. In any case, it must have been in use before the end of the seventh century, since shortly thereafter the Kathisma church was converted into a mosque.[72]

---

71. Mgaloblishvili, კლარჯული მრავალთავი, 409; van Esbroeck, "Nouveaux apocryphes," 365.

72. Rina Avner, George Lavas, and Irini Rosidis, "Jerusalem, Mar Elias—the Kathisma Church," *Hadashot Arkheologiyot: Excavations and Surveys in Israel* 113 (2001), 89*–92*, 89*; Rina Avner, "The Recovery of the Kathisma Church and Its Influence on Octagonal Buildings," in *One Land—Many Cultures: Archaeological Studies in Honor of Stanislao Loffreda, O.F.M.*, ed. G. C. Bottini, L. D. Segni, and D. Chrupcala, Studium Biblicum Franciscanum Collectio major 41 (Jerusalem: Franciscan Printing Press, 2003), 173–88, 180.

INTRODUCTION 47

This text has also never been translated into a modern language, and although van Esbroeck published an edition of the text with some important commentary,[73] once again I have made my translation from the edition of the Klarjeti homiliary by Mgaloblishvili.[74]

The *Homily on the Dormition* Attributed to Basil of Caesarea

This lengthy homily attributed to Basil of Caesarea presents a rather distinctive account of the end of Mary's life, even if it has some interesting points of contact with both the Palm and the Bethlehem traditions. Certainly, its author must have been aware of some of the main elements of these narrative traditions: for instance, the homily includes mention of the former's miraculous palm—although initially this palm branch is identified as an olive branch—and the latter's location of certain events at Mary's Bethlehem house. Indeed, with its opening words, it identifies as a source "the discourse of John the Theologian and Evangelist," presumably indicating the Greek *Transitus Mariae* of Ps.-John the Theologian, an early precis of the *Six Books Apocryphon* that has been translated numerous times into English as well as a number of other European languages.[75]

73. Van ESBROECK, "Nouveaux apocryphes."

74. MGALOBLISHVILI, კლარჯული მრავალთავი, 409–10.

75. Edited in Constantin TISCHENDORF, *Apocalypses apocryphae Mosis, Esdrae, Pauli, Johannis, item Mariae dormito: additis evangeliorum et actuum apocryphorum supplementis. Maiximam partem nunc primum* (Leipzig: H. Mendelssohn, 1866), 95–112. Modern translations include François BOVON and Pierre GEOLTRAIN, eds., *Écrits apocryphes chrétiens*, vol. 1, Bibliothèque de la Pléiade 442 (Paris: Gallimard, 1997), 171–88;

48   THE DORMITION AND ASSUMPTION OF MARY

Accordingly, the text's editor, Michel van Esbroeck, declares this homily "one of the most complete" Dormition narratives in existence.[76] It merges key elements of the Palm and Bethlehem traditions with certain other early traditions, such as the late apostle motif, the involvement of Ps.-Dionysius the Areopagite and his associates, and the clothing relics left behind by the Virgin after the removal of her body from this world (see more on these topics just below). All of this is set within the context of a multi-day liturgical commemoration of the Virgin in mid-August, which seems to reflect the practice of the Jerusalem Church at the end of Antiquity, in the sixth and seventh centuries. Nevertheless, the contents of this apocryphon are so distinctive, particularly in this melding of traditions, that it can only be classified among the atypical Dormition narratives.

The homily's author, in any case, is certainly not Basil: the text is much too late for this even to be a possibility. Most likely this Dormition narrative was composed sometime in the late sixth or early seventh century, as indicated by its inclusion of a four-day celebration of the Virgin's Dormition around 15 August, a structure that also indicates its production in the

J. K. ELLIOTT, *The Apocryphal New Testament: A Collection of Apocryphal Christian Literature in an English Translation* (Oxford: Clarendon Press, 1993), 701–8; Christoph MARKSCHIES and Jens SCHRÖTER, eds., *Antike christliche Apokryphen in deutscher Übersetzung*, 7. Auflage der von Edgar HENNECKE begründeten und von Wilhelm Schneemelcher fortgeführten Sammlung der neutestamentlichen Apokryphen, komplett neubearb. und um viele Texte erg. ed., vol. 1, *Evangelien und Verwandtes* (2012), 302–7.

76. Michel VAN ESBROECK, "L'Assomption de la Vierge dans un *Transitus* Pseudo-Basilien," *Analecta Bollandiana* 92 (1974), 128–63, 125.

INTRODUCTION   49

Jerusalem area.[77] Although this festal period begins only on
14 August, rather than on 13 August as in the Georgian Lectionary and the Klarjeti homiliary, it is clear that these texts derive
from the same Jerusalemite milieu. Based on its content, as will
be made clear in a moment, I suspect that this Dormition narrative is a work of the seventh century. The liturgical program,
however, suggests that it should not be dated much later than
this. The text has never been translated into a modern language
before, and I have made my translation on the basis of van
Esbroeck's edition.[78]

In addition to the features derived from the Palm and especially Bethlehem traditions, this Dormition narrative includes
two additional traditions that are typical of many later Dormition narratives, mentioned above: the presence of Ps.-Diony-
sius the Areopagite and his associates for the Virgin's Dormition, and a focus on the clothing relics that Mary left behind.
These traditions enter the Dormition narratives, it would seem,
only around the turn of the seventh century. The traditions
regarding Dionysius and his coterie derive from a passage in
the third chapter of *On the Divine Names*. There Ps.-Dionysius
the Areopagite famously refers to an assembly of the apostles,
himself included, gathered together to behold "that mortal
body, that source of life, which bore God. James, the brother
of God, was there. So too was Peter, that summit, that chief of
all those who speak of God."[79] With this notice, it would seem,

77. Ibid., 126; SHOEMAKER, *Ancient Traditions*, 132–40; MIMOUNI, *Dormition et Assomption*, 315–16.

78. VAN ESBROECK, "L'Assomption de la Vierge."

79. PS-DIONYSIUS THE AREOPAGITE, *On the Divine Names* III. 2 (Beate
Regina Suchla, ed., *Corpus Dionysiacum*, 2 vols., vol. 1), *Pseudo-Dionysius Areopagite De divinis nominibus*, Patristische Texte und Studien 33

50   THE DORMITION AND ASSUMPTION OF MARY

Ps.-Dionysius provides one of the earliest patristic witnesses to the ancient traditions about the Dormition and Assumption of the Virgin Mary.[80] As for the traditions of Mary's sartorial relics, one should note that they are much earlier than this, arising in Constantinople in the late fifth century, where the relics were held. Indeed, there is a separate literary tradition, initially independent of the early Dormition apocrypha, that chronicles the invention of these relics and their transfer to Constantinople. Yet only in the seventh century do these Constantinopolitan relics begin to appear in the early Dormition narratives.[81]

Although this homily is especially remarkable as a virtual compendium of traditions about the end of Mary's life, it is not without its distinctive qualities, to be sure. For instance, in this Dormition narrative, Mary washes the feet of the disciples and their disciples as well, a feature not found in any other account to my knowledge. Also unique is the recurring appearance of an image of Christ, a linen cloth belonging to Mary that bore the visage of Christ her son. Several times in the narrative, this relic is put to liturgical use, serving as a sort of deluxe icon, it would seem. This supernatural divine photo, if

(Berlin: de Gruyter, 1990), 141; trans. Colm LUIBHÉID and Paul ROREM, *Pseudo-Dionysius: The Complete Works*, Classics of Western Spirituality (New York: Paulist Press, 1987), 70

80. On this tradition, see now Stephen J. SHOEMAKER, "Ps.-Ps.-Dionysius on the Dormition of the Virgin Mary: The Armenian Letter of Dionysius to Titus," in *"Suddenly, Christ": Studies in Jewish and Christian Traditions in Honor of Alexander Golitzin*, ed. Andrei A. ORLOV (Leiden: Brill, 2020), forthcoming.

81. For more on these relic traditions, see esp. Stephen J. SHOEMAKER, "The Cult of Fashion: The Earliest *Life of the Virgin* and Constantinople's Marian Relics," *Dumbarton Oaks Papers* 62 (2008), 53–74.

INTRODUCTION 51

you will, belongs to a broader category of sacred objects known as *acheiropoieta* icons, which are images of Christ or Mary that were miraculously produced, without human agency: "without hands," as the Greek is literally translated. One of the earliest and most famous such items is the so-called Mandylion of Edessa, a legendary piece of cloth bearing the likeness of Jesus that was believed to have accompanied his response to the letters of the first-century King Abgar of Edessa. The relic, however, is not attested until the end of the sixth century, which is the time when such *acheiropoieta* begin to appear in the tradition.[82] Another example is a cloth given to Jesus on the way to Golgotha, which he used to wipe sweat from his face, thus imprinting it with his image (later identified in the medieval tradition as the Veil of Veronica). According to the Piacenza Pilgrim, who wrote in the later sixth century, the Christians of Memphis in Egypt claimed to possess this relic.[83] The Ps.-Basil homily seems to know yet another tradition of an *acheiropoieton* image, this one given by Christ himself to his mother. This feature is yet another sign of this narrative's production most likely in the early seventh century.

82. See, e.g. Averil CAMERON, "The History of the Image of Edessa: The Telling of a Story," *Harvard Ukrainian Studies* 7 (1983), 80–94.
83. Paul GEYER, *Itinera hierosolymitana saecvli IIII-VIII*, Corpus scriptorum ecclesiasticorum Latinorum 39 (Vienna: F. Tempsky, 1898), 189.

Dormition of the Theotokos, 13th century, St. Catherine's Monastery, Sinai. ⊚ WikiCommons.

Translations

The *Book of Mary's Repose*

1) In the name of the Father and the Son and the Holy Spirit. The Book of Mary's Repose, which is revealed about her in 5 books and in 5 heavens.

The Great Angel Christ Informs Mary
of her Death and Gives her a Secret Book.

When Mary heard from the Lord that her body would die, a great angel came to her and said, "Arise Mary and take this book, which he has given to you, he who established Paradise, and give it to the apostles, so that when they open it, they will read it before you; for on the third day, your body will die. For I will send all of the apostles to you, and they will prepare your body for burial; and they will see your glory and will not depart from you until they bring you to where you were before." And she answered and said to him, "Why then have you brought only this one book, and you did not bring a book for each one? When one has been given to the others, will they not murmur? And what should I plan? What should I do? And what is your name? If they ask me, what should I tell them?"[1]

2) And he said to her,[2] "Why do you ask me my name?[3] For it is a great wonder to be heard. When I have come, I will tell you what my name is. Then tell the apostles in secret, so

1. Cf. Exod 3.13.
2. The manuscripts read "to me," but clearly "to her" is correct.
3. Cf. Gen 32.29.

56 THE DORMITION AND ASSUMPTION OF MARY

that they will tell no one. And they will know my authority and the power of my strength: not because of the book alone, but also because of my name,[4] since it will be a source of great power. And it will be a revelation to all those in Jerusalem, and to those who believe, it will be revealed. Go then to the Mount of Olives, and you will hear my name, because I will not speak it to you in the midst of Jerusalem, lest the whole city be destroyed. You, however, will hear it on the visible mountain; but now is not the time."

3) And then Mary went and climbed the Mount of Olives, shining from the light of that angel and carrying the book in her hands. And when she came to the Mount of Olives, it rejoiced with all the trees. Then the trees inclined their heads and venerated the book that was in her hands. And when she saw them, Mary was startled, saying, "It is Jesus." And she said, "My Lord, perhaps you are my Lord? For such a great miracle has come about on your account: for I see that so many trees venerate you. Behold then, I say that there is no one who is capable of such a miracle, except[5] the Lord of Glory, who has been revealed to me."

The Christ Angel Recalls the Flight into Egypt.

4) Then he said to her, "There is no one who can do this miracle except by his hand, because he is powerful.[6] †Each[7]

---

4. A: "because of me."

5. Following the emendation suggested in ARRAS, *De Transitu*, 1:75–6 (Lat).

6. Following the suggested emendations in ibid., 1:76.

7. The remainder of this section is very confusing, and its meaning is not entirely clear. Here and elsewhere in the translation, we have placed daggers in the text as a traditional marker of textual corruption.

THE BOOK OF MARY'S REPOSE   57

one of his hears what I give, which is above every place of the world.[8] I am he who is in the trees and who is in the mountain. Do not think that the trees on earth alone were astonished! And if you have tasted from it, you will die; and if they are a little careless themselves, they will die and fall to earth. For from his birth, it is known that he is created; for his inheritance[9] [is] his various tree[s]. And when he has fallen upon them, they are not able to bear him; but he patiently bears everything, sitting upon them, and he is born above him. Therefore, I am not the one who is above everything, but I am above the trees of the holy inheritance." And when I saw the book, which is called "of the inheritance," they venerated it, because I knew it.†

5) And he said, "My mother, you did not understand my power. I first revealed it to you at the spring, where I led Joseph.[10] He was crying, the child who is glorified because he is greater than everything, and Joseph was angry with

Ethiopic	Georgian
you, saying, 'Give your breast to your child.' At once you gave it to him, as you went forth to the Mount of Olives, fleeing from Herod. And when you came to some trees, you said to Joseph, 'My lord, we are hungry, and what do	**1)** ...he was saying to you, 'Give a breast to your child.' And at once you gave him your breast, as you went forth to the mountain, fleeing from Herod. And you came beneath a single tree, and you said to Joseph, 'We are hungry, and

8. Or, "I who am above every place of this world."

9. B: "his adornment."

10. A story similar to the one told in 5–9 is found in the *Gospel of Ps.-Matthew*, 20–1 (Jan GIJSEL and Rita BEYERS, eds.), *Libri de nativitate Mariae*, 2 vols., CCSA 9–10 (Turnhout: Brepols, 1997), 1:458–70.

THE DORMITION AND ASSUMPTION OF MARY

Ethiopic

we have to eat in this desert place?' Then he rebuked you, saying, 'What can I do for you? Is it not enough for you that I became a stranger to my family on your account? why didn't you guard your virginity, so that you would [not] be found in this? And not only you, but I and my children too; now I live here with you, and I do not even know what will happen to my seven children.'

6) I say this to you Mary: know who I am and what power is upon me. And then he said to you, 'There is no fruit that you could eat in the trees. This date palm is tall, and I cannot climb it. I say to you that there is no one at all who has climbed, and there is nothing that a person will find in this desert. I have been afflicted from all sides because

Georgian

we have nothing that we could eat in this desert.' 2) Then he rebuked you and said to you, 'What can I do for you here and now to feed you? Is it not enough for you that I became a stranger to my own because of you, because you did not guard your virginity, so that you would not be found in this?[11] Not only you, but I and my children too, because I am here, and I live with you, but I do not know if something will happen to my three sons.'

3) Joseph said this to you at this time. I say this to you now, Mary, so that you will know who I am and what power is with me. I am the one who announced your birth to Joachim and about John to Zechariah; and I am the one who brought the hidden mystery to you from heaven; I am the one who killed the first-born sons of

---

11. The verb is actually in the third person singular in the Georgian: "[he, she, it] would not be found in this."

THE BOOK OF MARY'S REPOSE

Ethiopic

of you, because I have left[12] my country. And I am afflicted because I did not know the child that you have; I only know that he is not from me. But I have thought in my heart, perhaps I had intercourse with you while drunk, and that I am even worse because I had determined to protect [you]. And behold, now it has been made known that I was not negligent, because there were [only] five months when I received you in [my] custody. And behold, this child is more than five months; for you embraced him with your hand. Truly, he was not from your seed, but from the Holy Spirit. And he will not leave you hungry, but he will have mercy on you; he will provide for me, and he will remember that I am a sojourner, as you are a sojourner with me.'

Georgian

Egypt during the time of the Pharaoh. **4)** And then Joseph said to you, 'There is no tree from which we could eat in the midst of so much, except only this date palm, and I cannot climb it. But I say to you that no one has climbed it, and no one will be found in this desert. I am afflicted from all sides, because I have left my country. And I am also burdened because I did not know this child that you have, because he is not mine. But when you were pregnant, I was thinking in my heart, by what cause am I found in this, because I had orders to protect you. **5)** Behold, now it is manifest that I was not at all negligent regarding you; there are five months since I was charged to protect you, and is this child not more than five months? But you love him with your spirit, and you know that he is not born from our nature, but he is from the Holy Spirit. Now, the Spirit

---

12. In the manuscripts, "They have left."

THE DORMITION AND ASSUMPTION OF MARY

Ethiopic

7) Is this not everything that Joseph said to you? And the child stopped [nursing from] your breast, this one who is greater than all things, and he said to Joseph, 'My father, why don't you climb this date palm and bring it to her, so that my mother might eat from it, as was said about it.[13] And I will feed you: not only you, but also the fruit that comes forth from it. I will not be hungry even for one day.' And the child turned and said to the date palm, 'Incline your head with your fruit, and satisfy my mother and father.' And it inclined immediately. And who made it incline? Is it not because I have power, which was because of me?[14] And you and Joseph were satisfied,

Georgian

will not abandon you in hunger, but let him have mercy on me and feed me, and he will remember that I am a so-journer with you, and you are a sojourner with me.'

6) Did not Joseph say this to you? And did the child not stop [nursing] from your breast, this one who is greater than all things, and he said to Joseph, 'Father, have you not come to this date palm from the law? Bring and let my mother eat. Believe what I told you, "I will feed you: not only you, but also the fruit that comes from it." I will not be hungry even for one day.' **7)** And the child turned and said to the date palm, 'I say to you, O date palm, incline your head with [your] fruit to the earth, and satisfy my mother and father.' And it inclined immediately. **8)** Am I not the angel who said this to you? But the child's power is that which was done by me, by

13. B: "about me."
14. B: "It was I, and what power I have, which was because of me."

THE BOOK OF MARY'S REPOSE

Ethiopic	Georgian
because the date palm's branches were placed as a wave of the ocean on the shore, because I [had] joy and happiness in my body as it appeared.[15]	which you and Joseph were satisfied, because the date palm's branches with [their] fruit were laid upon the earth, filled with sweet fruit, which I shook with joy and happiness at this sight.
8) And he said to the date palm, 'Turn to me, O date palm; for the date palm is the greatest plant in all the land of Egypt. Arise then and be very exalted, because you humbled yourself and did my will, this service. Be exalted then, and be a sign to all the trees, because all the holy ones who humble themselves will be exalted.' And immediately it straightened up and became as [it was] before. And he blessed it and said to it, 'This is worthy of the glory of his name. You will be called by Adam's holy name, to the splendid humanity.	9) And the child turned to the date palm and said, 'O date palm, greater than all the plants of Egypt, arise and be very exalted, because you humbled yourself and did this service. Be exalted and be a sign more than all the other plants, because all my holy ones who humble themselves will be more exalted.' 10) And immediately the date palm arose and became as [it was] before. And the child blessed it and said, 'You who have become worthy of glorification, which has caused you to be named above both Adam and people of his race.
9) O date palm, who expelled you from Paradise, and you emigrated to Egypt with treachery, and you were sown	11) O date palm, what happened to you that you fell from Paradise and were led to Egypt with grief, and you

15. Both manuscripts are corrupt here. I have drawn from both to reconstruct a meaning somewhat near the Georgian fragments.

Ethiopic	**Georgian**

on the dry land, so that you would be cut down with iron? How did you come to this place, O date palm, because you are the image of every place? Did this not happen regarding you? For when the devil went forth, after he had led Adam astray, behold, you were furious with him, and you expelled him from Paradise to the land of Mastinpanes [?].[16] Arise and give me [some] of these seeds, which are in Paradise and which are on the earth, from which one eats,[17] because you have migrated from a good place and have been sown on earth. But do not fear, trees, because just as my Father sent me for the salvation of humanity, so that they convert, he also instructed me concerning the fruit, so that my friends might eat from

were transplanted to a dry place, so that iron would have dominion over you, just as the other tree[s]? How did you come to this place, unless human nature was active in all this? Behold then, how it was thus for you. **12)** When the devil went forth after Adam's deception, he [the Lord?] said to him, "Behold then, the Lord has become angry with you and is sending you out from Paradise to the earth, which is full of vegetation and the food of wild game. But arise now and give to me from all the plants that are in Paradise, and I will put them on the earth, so that when you go forth from Paradise, you will find food from them." **13)** When you passed from the good place, you were transplanted to the earth. But

---

16. Perhaps this originally read, "I/he was furious. . ., I/he expelled," as in the Georgian. Regarding "Mastinpanes," Arras suggests that the form is from the Greek word *styppyon*, so that the original Greek would have read "the land of flax," although I find this explanation less than convincing. See ARRAS, *De Transitu*, 1:77 (Lat).

17. Literally, "from which it is eaten."

THE BOOK OF MARY'S REPOSE   63

Ethiopic	Georgian

Ethiopic

it, [namely,] those who receive me in my image. And you too, date palm, migrate and descend to the original place.' And then the date palm arose before us and descended into his Paradise.

10) And who carried it, Mary? Was it not I? Not only do I raise trees, but also those people who humble themselves before God. I am the one who carries them and brings them to the place of justice. And in one day, when you go forth from your body, [you will] see where your body will rest,[18] because I am the one who will come on the fourth day. And they have allowed

Georgian

do not fear, plants, because just as my Father sent me for the salvation of humanity and for their conversion, he also gave me instruction about the plants, so that my friends and beloved might eat from them, [namely,] those who receive my image and do my command, those who were recluses in the mountains and the deserts. May they have you for food. And you too, date palm, pass now to your original place.' Then the date palm arose before us and passed into Paradise.

14) And who is the one who raised it up, Mary? Was it not I? Not only [am I] to take plants there, but also those people who humble themselves before God. I raised it up and carried it to the place of the just on the day that the souls go forth from [their] bodies; and when you depart from the body, I will come myself on the fourth day; for this extra day is allowed because our Savior

18. Both MSS are corrupt here, although by combining readings from both, the above sense can be construed.

THE DORMITION AND ASSUMPTION OF MARY

Ethiopic

for the sake of the one day: for our Savoir arose on the third day, and you then [will arise] on the fourth day. And I will also come to all those who have kept the Savior's words, and I will return them to the Paradise of rest. Their bodies will remain new, without decaying, because they took care of themselves while they were living on earth. And there they will remain until the day of the resurrection. And he will come with angels upon the earth, and they will be brought, each with their own bodies."

Georgian

arose on the third day. **15)** And not only will I lead you away on the fourth day, but all those who keep the words of our Savior. I will come again to those and lead them away to the Paradise of joy. Their bodies will remain new there, and the bodies of the holy people will not have a stench, because they took care of themselves while living on earth without sin. And they will come to the place where Adam and Eve were also, until the day of resurrection. And when the Lord will come with angels, he will lead them each with their own bodies."

The Soul's Departure from the Body.

Ethiopic

11) And Mary said to him, "O my Lord, with what sign will you come to them, and what is the sign of those who will be brought? Do they offer a sweet-smelling sacrifice, and thus you come to them, or when you pass among the

Georgian

16) And Mary said to him, "O my Lord, in what manner do you come to them, or whom do you lead? Those to whom you are [coming],[19] do they offer you their sweet-smelling sacrifice, and thus you will come to them? Or rather, do

19. Literally, "(to/of) those who you are to you."

THE BOOK OF MARY'S REPOSE   65

Ethiopic

just, and they have come, do they call your name, and you come to them? For if it is so, [tell me], so that I can do [this] and you will come to me and take me up." And he said to her, "What's the matter, mother? For when I have been sent to you, I will not come to you alone, but with all the hosts of angels. And they will come and will sing before you. For I have been sent to tell you, so that you will then give [what I tell you] to the apostles in secret, because this is hidden from those who seek it from Jesus the Savior."

12) And she said, "What will we do when we rest our body, because we do not want to abandon it on earth, because it is before us? And as it suits us to dwell in this form of ours, we want our body to be with us in that place." And then the good Christ said to her,[21] "This word [that] you

Georgian

you come to the just? Or does he send [you] to the good? Or do you not come only to the elect? Or do they call on your name in prayers, and they come to you? If there is something like this, tell me, so that I can do this too, and you will come to me and lead me away on the last day." **17)** And the angel said to her, "What's the matter, mother? For when I am sent to you, I will not be alone, but all the hosts of angels will come, and they will sing before you. I have been sent to reveal to you, so that you will tell the mystery to the apostles.

18) And because they were tired of seeking this from the Savior, Jesus Christ, they said, 'What will we do when we cast off our bodies, because we do not want to abandon them[20] on earth? If we are true and worthy to dwell in that [place], because he showed us the place, we do not want

20. Literally, "it."
21. A: "them."

66   THE DORMITION AND ASSUMPTION OF MARY

Ethiopic

seek now is great. And where I am going now, you are not able to come. But I will go and ask my Father, and I will prepare a place for your body in Paradise, where your body will remain.[22]

Georgian

our body to be in this place.'" **19)** Then the good Lord said to them, 'This word that you seek now is great, and where I am going, you are not able to go now; so I will go and ask my Father, and he will prepare a place for your bodies.' **20)** Then it pleased the Father that your bodies will be transferred to Paradise, where your bodies will be placed, and on the last day, I will resurrect them, and they will inherit eternal life, where the Father reigns, and the Son has power, and the Holy Spirit reigns with them, and they are magnified from the age unto the age. Amen.

The Christ Angel gives Mary a Secret Prayer of Ascent.

Ethiopic

13) †Now,[23] know what I will do when I send to you the prayer. I received [it] from my Father, as I was coming, and

22. Cf. John 8.21, 14.2.

23. This section and the one that follows (14) are very corrupt and divergent in the two manuscripts. I have done my best to render what sense may be found in A, but I have not attempted to represent B, which has an equally corrupt, yet slightly different, version of this

THE BOOK OF MARY'S REPOSE 67

now I say to you: today is your departure from your body, when the sun appears. And give everything that I have told you to the apostles, because they too [are coming?]. After your body has been placed, I will come on the fourth day to their body. And they will not find it, and they will fear that they do not believe my power, and they will be seized by it, and they will go to another body which is not for the apostles.†

14) † They said, 'Those who will go, how will they abandon their bodies here, because they will save another, and they will not be able to ascend without the prayer, and they will go forth from their bodies, and they will sleep for four days.' And after this, I will come and awaken them. And they will not be abandoned after four days, because I, my brother, have suffered for me to receive this odor; because of this, I have been patient until the fourth day; otherwise, I would come to them on the third day. For just as a sad person cannot [say?] the prayer there, the people of his churches, who love this world and who dwell in it. Therefore tell the apostles in secret, 'Do not reveal this,' so that they will not come into this; be-

passage. Hopefully, readers can get a sense of the topic from this translation and then come to their own judgments from the Ethiopic text and Arras' Latin translation. Comparison with this section in the earliest Greek Dormition narrative, also included in this volume, helps to better understand this passage: "Now, you want to know what you will do. When I was sent to you, I received a prayer from the Father, as I was coming to you, and now I am telling it to you so that you will say it when you go forth from the body at the rising of the sun, for thus [the prayer] is offered up. And what I tell you, share with apostles, because they too are coming. No friend of the world, who loves the world, is able to speak this prayer" (§7).

68 THE DORMITION AND ASSUMPTION OF MARY

cause, moreover, those who have desired his word, they have not said it, those who have not kept this.†

The Cosmic Ruler and the Soul's Escape from the World.

15) Mary, know from where the prayer has come and what it is, as you will need to observe it with every world. And even if a person has gained the whole world, and he has been abandoned to the beast with the body of a lion and the tail of a snake, what is his profit?[24] And even if he is wise and richer than the whole world, and he has been abandoned to the monsters, will he not forfeit all of his possessions, even his body?[25] Truly it is thus, Mary; for it is not possible to pass by the beast with the body of a lion and the tail of a snake, so as to pass through every world, because of the hatred of Satan, which he has brought on everyone. But the one who understands this completely will give all his possessions in order to save his body.

16) As this verdant stone that descended from heaven and appeared at the rising of the sun [?], the prayer, Mary, transcends your mother's [Eve's] nature, which prevails in every creature, on account of which there is death. And it will raise the dead and give life to all, and they will behold the steadfastness of God.

24. In gnostic Christian texts, the Demiurge (the Archon) is often described as "lion-like" or "lion-faced," or even as a "lion-faced serpent." Most likely, then, this "beast with the body of a lion and the tail of a snake" is a reference to the Demiurge/Archon or some sort of equivalent figure. Likewise, it would appear that here the text refers to the soul's ascent through the cosmic spheres after death, when it must successfully elude this cosmic ruler and his minions.
25. B: "in order to save his body?"

THE BOOK OF MARY'S REPOSE   69

17) But[26] on that day the body of Adam was in the glory that dwelt upon him, the body that sat lying on the earth, which he made with the Father, who was with him in counsel and participation. And this is that which was from the beginning and was even before the angels and the archangels, before the creation of the powers by me, until he sat and he was moved by the Ruler [Archon], when it was apparent that he could not arise. And God knew what was in the soul; and he rested and placed rest in his heart so that it would pray to him. And when the Father said this to Adam, he arose and was in the custody of the Father and the Son and the Holy Spirit until this day. And I hid this from the wise, and it is not even written in the Scriptures, so that the scribes would not see it and the ignorant would not hear it among their children. But I allowed it to be hidden among the cherubim, and no one could see it except for the Father, the Son, and the Holy Spirit, until this day, so that it would be revealed to the wise, as it will be. And I have sent this so that you will know it, with the apostles, on that day, and they will share it with the cherubim; but it will not be known except to the one to whom the cherubim tell everything.

18) And today who are they who will say this with their heart and soul and mind completely? For before creation are those who boast before humanity, saying, 'We are God's.' His memory arouses them as they seek recovery from their illness. And those who seek a request from those [who are before creation?], God does not hear them, because the will of God

26. There are many corruptions and disagreements in both manuscripts for this section, but they are not so severe as in sections 13 and 14 above. In general, it has been possible to reconstruct a (more or less) sensible text by relying on readings of one text or the other at a given point.

70   THE DORMITION AND ASSUMPTION OF MARY

is not among them. They will not be able to call upon God on their own account as on the account of others. And when they have cried out, shouting, God does not hear them.

The Parable of the Wormy Trees.

19) Do you not recall, Mary, that thief, when he was taken captive among the apostles while he was praying and bowing his head at their feet, saying, 'Beseech your master to bless us in friendship, and they will be healed from their affliction.' And the apostles went and they besought Jesus to bless

Ethiopic	Syriac
them, as they desired. And he sent with the apostles—was it not thus? And he said, 'Are they not the shepherds of Is-rael? They seek healing for their sheep, so that they will be praised before humanity. And they are unable to heal, because they have led astray until this day. And I gave to you so that you will believe.' And the apostles said to him, 'Lord, behold, they bow down and prostrate themselves and repent. Why do you not hear them?' And he said to them, 'You want me to hear them? But they are evil, and you know them.'	. . .them, as they desired. And he sent to them through the apostles—was it not thus? And he said, 'These are the shep-herds of the house of Israel, who are beseeching on behalf of the sheep, so that they will be pardoned and glorified be-fore humanity. And they can-not sanctify themselves, because they exalt themselves like the strong. Did I not give them many signs?' And the apostles said, 'Lord, behold, they be-seech and pray and repent and kneel on their knees. Why have you not heard them?' Our Lord said to them, 'I sought to hear them too, but there is deception in them, as you know.'

THE BOOK OF MARY'S REPOSE

Ethiopic

20) Then Jesus wanted to show the apostles the reasons why he did not hear them. And he took them up to a mountain, and he made them hungry. And they came and pleaded with Jesus and said to him, 'We are hungry, and what will we eat in this desert?' And he ordered that trees sprout before them and produce fruit. Then they bore fruit before them. And he said to them, 'When you go to these trees in front of you, and as their branches are numerous, so also their foliage is beautiful to see, eat from them.' And when the apostles went before the trees, they did not find fruit on them. And they returned to Jesus and said, 'Master, you sent us to the trees before us, and we did not find fruit on them, only their budding branches and their beautiful foliage, but there is no fruit at all.' And Jesus said to them, 'Did you not see it, because the trees are tall? Then go now, because the trees have inclined themselves, and you

Syriac

And when Jesus wanted to show the apostles the reason why he did not hear them, he took them up to a mountain, and he made them hungry. And when the apostles had gone, they asked him and said to him, 'Lord, we are hungry; what then do we have to eat in this desert?' And Jesus told them to go to the trees before them. And he said to them, 'Go to these trees that are opposite us, these whose numerous branches are splendid and beautiful from a distance, and from them you will be fed.' And when the apostles went, they did not find fruit on their branches. And they returned to Jesus and said, 'Good teacher, you sent us to these trees that are opposite us, and we went and did not find fruit on them, but only branches, which are beautiful and splendid, but there is no fruit on them.' And Jesus said to them, 'You have not seen them because the trees are standing straight up. Go then at once, because the trees are

Ethiopic

will find fruit on them and eat.' And when they went, they found the trees, and they did not find fruit on them.

21) And they returned to Jesus in great sadness and then said to him, 'What is this, a mockery? For first you said to us, "You will find tall trees, full of fruit," and we did not find [any]. Why then is this like a mockery? Teach us why this is.' And Jesus said to them, 'Go then and sit beneath them, and you will see why this is. And when they were standing, you did not see, and also when they inclined, you did not see.' And then they went and sat beneath the trees. And stinking worms came forth. And the apostles got up and said, 'Master, do you want to test us?' But he turned them back to the trees,

Syriac

inclining themselves, and you will find fruit on them, and you will be fed.' And when they went, they found the trees inclining, but they did not find fruit on them.

And they returned to Jesus again in great distress and said to him, 'What is this, teacher, that we are mocked? For first you said to us, "You will find straight trees, and there is fruit on them"; and we found none. Why are we mocked? But it is fitting that you teach us what this is that happened. For we think that what you have sought to teach us is false; for the trees were taken hold of by a visible power and bent down. If this is a test, tell to us what it is.' And Jesus said to them, 'Go and sit beneath them, and you will see what it is that is on them, but you will not find them bent down again.' And when the apostles went and sat beneath the trees, immediately the trees released stinking worms. And the apostles came to Jesus again, and they said to him, 'Teacher,

THE BOOK OF MARY'S REPOSE   73

Syriac
did you want to lead us astray,
or to turn us away from this. . .

Ethiopic
so that they did not return to the trees.

22) And the Savior answered them and said to them, 'By no means would I tempt you, but I want you to know intelligently. Look then now: know how they are planted.' And when the apostles looked, they saw that the plants had become human beings, who were praying and prostrate on their knees. And they said to Jesus, 'Lord, we saw people who were dressed in white garments, praying and prostrate on their knees, and a table was before them, and bread was placed on it. And after praying, they went and wanted to eat. But they did not find the bread that was upon it, and the one who did not partake, the flames of Gehenna devoured him.'[27]

23) And then Jesus said to them, 'For you, my good and united children, I have reserved the table, which is eternal, and also the bread. Do you not know this one, who is the one that you seek? For as they stand and pray and are prostrate on their knees, while repenting, do you not see them then? They are standing, while there is no fruit to God in them for repentance. There is none, because they desire the world and all its fine things. And when they remember its fine things and they pray to God, then he speaks to them about this table. And when they are returned to the world, he turns himself away from them.'

27. Literally, "unless Gehenna devoured him."

74 THE DORMITION AND ASSUMPTION OF MARY

The Christ Angel Continues to Explain his True Nature: The Angel of Death.

24) Now then, Mary, give the sign to the apostles so that they will tell the mystery to those who believe. The one to whom it is given will hear: thus will my name and my power be known. And I want to show them, Mary, what power was given to me from God the Father when he sent me into the world to destroy sinners and to bless the just.

25) I am the third that was created, and I am not the Son; [28] there is no one greater than me. I am the one who destroyed every firstborn of Egypt because of the great evil that was in them, and because of the great cry, and because of the blood that was shed by them. Ask the people of the earth, Mary, why I destroyed all the firstborn in Egypt.[29] Ask those who say, 'There is no one who saw us, and there is no one who knows us,' as they should know. Ask then those who believe and trust in their treasures, and they will tell you why I destroyed all the firstborn of Egypt, so that they ate many lentils in the teeth of their children [?], and they will always sin, and affliction will remain on their children. And behold, these who say, 'Nevertheless, we are.' For this mystery is among us together, with the blood of those who were destroyed. This I tell you, Mary, so that you know about these things.

---

28. B: "I am the one who was created third in divinity, and I am the Son."
29. Cf. Exod 12.

THE BOOK OF MARY'S REPOSE · 75

The Miscarriage of Eleazar's Wife Rachel and the Death of Egypt's Firstborn.

26) Listen then,[30] and I will explain for you why I destroyed the firstborn of Egypt. Was it not when the Israelites were in Egypt, under Pharaoh's yoke, and they were being tormented by those who were afflicting them? One of the Israelites named Eleazar became ill, and he could not be made to work. And the overseer came and said to him, 'Why have you not come to work? Behold, your hour has come, and you are unable.' And he answered nothing. And he went to the Pharaoh and said to him, 'O King who lives eternally, there is one of the Israelites who is unable to do his work, saying, "I am ill." What order shall we give: should we pardon him, or should we not pardon him?' And hearing this, the king Pharaoh gnashed his teeth, saying, 'I will remove your breath and your life from you and your body if you give the Israelites rest now; make them pay their debt, their bricks. Instead, bring his wife, and she will make bricks in his place. If you have not brought his wife, and the others see this, they will abandon their bricks, and they will be devastated and will stop their work. But if they see his wife coming to make bricks, they will be afraid and will work, so that they will not stop my work and will not remember their God. Go now, overseer, to my work, because when evening comes, I will come and count every quantity of bricks of the overseers, and if I do not find the number of bricks accurate, there will be nothing else except bricks.'

---

30. The story that follows, 26–31, is also known in the rabbinic literature. For parallels, see Frédéric MANNS, *Le Récit de la dormition de Marie (Vatican grec 1982) : Contribution à l'étude des origines de l'exégèse chrétienne*, Studium Biblicum Franciscanum, Collectio Maior, 33 (Jerusalem: Franciscan Printing Press, 1989), 76.

76 THE DORMITION AND ASSUMPTION OF MARY

27) And when the overseers heard from the king Pharaoh, they went forth, being disturbed, to the house of Eleazar, the sick man. And they seized his wife, whose name was Rachel, and brought her to the brickworks. And they beat her while exacting punishment for her husband's brickwork, and they brought her unto death. And they said to her, 'If you have not made these bricks, beware!' And she was very near to birth, and she was sad because of her shame, because she did not go forth from her house. And she did not allow any of the men of Egypt to see her, lest she be despised when she went forth to the brickworks.

28) And when she went forth to the works, and when she had made every brick, she was suffering very much, and she sat briefly to rest. And the overseers were there, and they beat her, saying, 'Get up, make bricks. Why have you not finished for the day?' And she said to them, 'I beseech you, have mercy on me, my lords; allow me to rest briefly, for my loins are pressed down.' Then the overseers beat her, while saying, 'We cannot have mercy on you, because today the Pharaoh will come to see the Israelite brickworks. For the king ordered me that we not help you; otherwise, we will make bricks in your place. Now then, we cannot [allow] you to stop.' And the hour of Pharaoh's coming arrived, and they sat while they made her work. And she got up and took clay in her hands and began to make bricks. And from the multitude of her beatings, while she was afraid, the fruit of her womb fell.

29) And when the workers saw this, they were afraid and withdrew. Then, one of them arose, and he came and saw two infants, and he wept with great lamentation, while she said, 'My Lord, you have repaid us according to our sin, because we have been sinners from ancient times. And now Lord, look and see our affliction, and remember the commandment that you placed on our fathers Abraham, Isaac, and Jacob, saying, "Bless-

THE BOOK OF MARY'S REPOSE   77

ing, I bless you and your seed." Now, even if we have sinned, do not carry out your wrath on us forever. With whom will I dwell, except with you, O Lord, and to whom shall I cry? To you, O Lord, for my affliction is very great. And I have lost this first fruit that was in my womb, and I am powerless before the multitude of my affliction, and I do not know what I shall do. Look, O Lord, upon my infants, because they are yours.'

30) And when Rachel said these things, Abraham, Isaac, and Jacob went to the good God. They bowed down and worshipped, saying, 'Have mercy, Father, on our descendants, and forgive them: remember the statutes that you placed on us and on our seed.' And when they said this, I was sent to her, to speak these words to her, and I said to her, 'Rachel, Rachel, God has heard your grief. For just as you saw the death of your firstborn, you will see the death of the firstborn of Egypt. And just as they caused your infants to fall, I will make their infants fall similarly. Thus I will make you see the Egyptians when their firstborn are made to fall from their mothers' wombs. And now, Rachel, arise and do your work; for God has sent me to exact a blood vengeance for you.' Because of this, I destroyed all the firstborn of the Pharaoh and the firstborn of the magicians; I destroyed them in the gates, in the middle of the night, by the power that was given [to me] by God.

31) †And[31] then Satan attacked, and he said to me, 'Do you want me to help the Egyptians?' And then, at that moment, he blew his horn,[32] which was being made manifest, while speaking with his horn. For you have put on what power has been given to you, and you will receive vengeance against those who have

31. Another very corrupt section. I have done my best to translate the passage, although, admittedly, it does not make a great of sense.
32. Literally, "voice," but "horn" seems more likely. See ARRAS, *De Transitu*, 1:84 (Lat).

78   THE DORMITION AND ASSUMPTION OF MARY

sinned and whose evil is known [for] what it is. And he turned to me, and I saw him as he was warring with me. And while he was saying this with his horn, he departed from their firstborn. And seizing him, I bound [him], and I found him entering houses, teaching the sign and giving the wisdom that he has.[33] And he said, 'I am not a firstborn, but in order that you save the people, so that he will not examine. There is no one like God; he made this sign of the firstborn, so that he would not forget and would not lose one who was not one of the firstborn. And the sign [is] in the right hand, just as the firstborn was not as they were saved.' And there were those who cried out, saying, 'Tell us; there is no firstborn among us.' And they did not believe in this sign, and they extended their hands and greatly rebuked the darkness; while wanting to go forth, they did not see a sign of their murder. And Michael blew his horn, and they were bound greatly, and then I bound.†

Joseph's Bones and the Exodus.

32) Now then,[34] O Mary, you will see my power, because I am the one who made this sign upon the earth. I am the one who went into Sodom beforehand and saved Lot and destroyed his wife. I am also the one who caused Joseph's bones to be found, which Pharaoh had hidden. For at the time when Joseph died, another king arose in Egypt. And he did not know Joseph, and he began to afflict the Israelites, and they wanted to flee from Pharaoh. And since Pharaoh knew that they would flee from him, he summoned the magicians and said to them, 'I know that you are wise; now tell me, what

33. Literally, "and being the wisdom that he has."
34. The story that follows (32–5) is also known in the rabbinic literature. See Manns, *Le Récit*, 76–7.

THE BOOK OF MARY'S REPOSE

shall I do with these people? For I heard that they were murmuring and saying, "Let us flee from him."' And the magicians said to Pharaoh, 'If these people want to flee, do as we tell you. Take the bones of Joseph

Ethiopic	Syriac
and place them in a hidden place, within your power, so that they will not find them. They will not flee and abandon them. For we have heard that [Joseph], when he was dying, made them swear that they would take his bones with them. And because of this, they cannot flee unless they take them, and they will remain under your power in Egypt.'	...and have them placed in a hidden place, under the hand of your power, so that they will not find them. And when you have done this, they will not be able to flee. For we heard that Joseph, when he was dying, made the children of his people swear that when they were going up, his bones should go up with them. And when you have done this, they will not be able to flee, unless they take them with them, and they will remain under your power in Egypt.'
33) And then Pharaoh, the king of Egypt, arose and in his anger he made a pit[35] in the middle of the river of Egypt. And he took the bones of Joseph and placed them in a stone box. And he covered	And after these things, Pharaoh, the king of Egypt, arose and ordered that there be a pit in the middle of the river. And he took the bones of Joseph and placed them in [a stone box.][36] And he plastered

35. Literally, "dirt."
36. The Syriac MS is damaged here, and with the help of the Ethiopic version it is possible to complete the lacuna as above.

80 THE DORMITION AND ASSUMPTION OF MARY

Ethiopic	Syriac
it vigorously with pitch, and he wrote his name on a scroll, saying, 'These are the bones of Joseph.' And he attached it to the box and had it buried in the middle of the pit. And again he brought about affliction, and he placed affliction upon the Israelites. And after this, the good God had mercy on them and heard their lamentation, and he wanted them to go forth from the land of Egypt. And he sent Moses, so that the God of Abraham, Isaac, and Jacob, the God of the living and the dead, would speak to them, because all the righteous live in him.[39] And he came and spoke to the Israelites, saying, 'Let us go; I will lead you.' And they said to him, 'Let us go then to the bones of our brother of old, who was with us, and who	it with pitch [...],[37] and he wrote [Joseph's][38] name on a scroll, [saying, 'These] are the bones of Joseph.' [And he placed] the scroll in the box and ordered that it be placed middle of the river. And when Pharaoh went in, he laid hard work on the Israelites, and said to them that they should go forth. And the Israelites answered and said to Moses, 'Let us go forth to the bones of Joseph, our brother of old, because he made our fathers swear that his bones would go up with the Israelites.'

37. Here is another lacuna. Unfortunately, the Ethiopic MSS disagree here, and do not suggest an obvious reconstruction.

38. Or his own (Pharaoh's) name, as the Ethiopic implies. The name is missing in the Syriac fragment, and the name Joseph was supplied by the text's editor.

39. Cf Mark 12.26.

THE BOOK OF MARY'S REPOSE   81

Ethiopic	Syriac

made our fathers swear that they would remove his bones with the Israelites.'

34) And they went with Moses to the bones of Joseph, and they did not find them. For they did not know that Pharaoh had hidden them. And when they did not find them, they rent their garments, they and Moses, and they wept before God, saying, 'Lord God of our fathers, why have you abandoned us, your people? Now then, return and save us; and send to us your good angel who will reveal to us; and strengthen your mercy. And we will not become like the land of Kerseson,[40] from which it happened that we had not tasted water, and after many days a river covered it. Now then, we have passed from it, as is your mercy, O Lord; for all our sin is not pure before you. Because of this, you have hidden the bones of Joseph our brother, so that we would know our

But Moses went, and they did not find them. For the Israelites did not know that Pharaoh had taken them away from them. And when they did not find them, they rent their garments and wept bitterly. They groaned and cried out to God, and Moses with them, 'Lord God of our Fathers, why have you forsaken your people? For you turned to us; and then after you turned, you turned your mercy away from us; and we have become like a barren land that has not seen water.' And after a long time, the river was uncovered. And when it was uncovered and had passed away, the Israelites cried to the Lord and said, 'You have remembered the sin and error of your people, O Lord; therefore you have hidden the bones of our brother Joseph, so that we will remain in this bondage

40. Perhaps a reference to the Wadi Kishon of 1 Chron 18.40–5.

82 THE DORMITION AND ASSUMPTION OF MARY

Ethiopic	Syriac
wickedness. Now then, return and have mercy on us.'	forever. Now turn to us, O Lord, and deliver your people from Pharaoh's oppression.'
35) And when they were saying these things, while the people wept with Moses, I then came, I, the angel, and I spoke to Moses, saying, 'Moses, Moses, God has heard your grief. Arise and go and strike the waters with your staff, which is in your hand, and the hidden treasure will appear.' O Mary, when Moses struck the river, it appeared on the mountain and came to dry water [sic]. And he found the written scroll, saying, 'These are the bones of Joseph.' And he took and brought them to the land, before he brought forth the Israelites. Behold then, I have shown you, O Mary, my power;	And when these things had been said by Moses and by all the people, I came and spoke, I, Michael the angel. And I said to Moses, 'Moses, Moses, God has heard your groan. Arise and go to the river, and strike the waters with your staff, and the hidden treasure will be uncovered before you.' What did you think, Mary? As soon as Moses struck the river, did not the box in which the bones of Joseph were placed appear and come to dry land? And Moses opened it and found the roll on which it was written, 'These are the bones of Joseph.' And he took them and brought them to their land [that was given] to their fathers. And after a long time, I have revealed myself. . .

Ethiopic

so that you will not fear, I have spoken to you, who is before me. Hear then my name: 'Adonai'el.'" And he also ordered that she give [the name] to the apostles, and he said to her,

THE BOOK OF MARY'S REPOSE   83

Ethiopic

"They will come to you just as I told you, and they will go with you.

Coptic

1) …All the apostles will gather to you just as I said, and my angels will watch over you…

Ethiopic

Take then this book." And the angel became light and ascended into heaven.

Mary Returns Home and Prays.

36) And Mary returned home. And then the house trembled on account of the glory of the book that was in her hand. And

Ethiopic

she secretly entered the inner chamber, and she placed the book, wrapping it in fine cloth. And she put on blessed garments, saying, "I bless you the firstborn,[41] who created the living, and I bless this sign that appeared from heaven on the earth, while you created us and dwelt in me.

Coptic

…Mary entered her bedroom and blessed God, saying, 'I bless you, the Son, the offspring of the Aeons, the one for whom I was a dwelling place. I bless you, the life that came forth from the Father, …

Ethiopic

I bless your birth, which illuminates and is not visible, which goes forth from you as your hand goes forth; and to you alone they come. I bless you, because you[42] counted me in what is your body. And you chose my sanctity with your word, so that you will choose me for this your coming blessing, and for the

41. A: "I bless the blessed one."
42. MSS: "he."

84   THE DORMITION AND ASSUMPTION OF MARY

sweet-smelling sacrifice, so that I will receive that which is a statute in every age.

37) I bless you so that you will give me my garments, [about] which you told me, saying, 'By this you will be distinguished from your relatives.' And you have caused me to enter the seventh heaven, so that I will be found worthy of this your mystery. I bless you so that I will be found worthy of your first blessing with all those who believe in you, so that you will return them to your kingdom. For you are hidden among your hidden; you [43] see those who are not seen. And you are the son of the hidden one; you are the one whom I first conceived, and [then I conceived?] [44] all those who believe in you.

Ethiopic	Georgian
Hear the prayer of your mother Mary, who cries out to you. Hear my voice and send your goodness to me, and no power will come upon me on that day, when [my soul] goes forth from my body; but fulfill for me what was said by you when I said, 'What shall I do about the power that will pass upon my soul?' And you told me, saying, 'Do not weep, O Mary my mother: neither angels nor archangels, nor	**1)** ...Hear the prayer and supplication of your mother Mary, who cries out to you, my son and God and creator. **2)** Hear my voice and send your goodness to me, so that no power comes before me at the time when I will go forth from the body; but fulfill what was said to me, O master, when I was weeping before you, and I was saying, 'What shall I do so that I will pass by the powers that will come upon my soul?'

43. MSS: "I."

44. The insertion is suggested by a similarly peculiar phrase in the earliest Greek narrative, also translated in this volume: "I have painfully given birth first to you and then to all of those who hope in you" (§11).

THE BOOK OF MARY'S REPOSE

85

Ethiopic

cherubim nor seraphim, nor any other power will come upon you, but I will come myself to your soul.' And now the pain of birth [45] has drawn near. I bless you and your three servants that were sent by you to minister in the three ways. I bless the eternal light in which you dwell. I bless every plantation of your hand, which remains forever. Holy, holy, holy, you who dwell [in the heights], hear my prayer for ever, Amen."

Georgian

3) Because you promised me and said to me, 'Do not be sad and do not grieve, O Mary, my mother, because neither of the angels, nor the cherubim, nor the seraphim, nor any other power will come upon you, but I will come myself and lead you away.' Now then the pain of birth has approached, which is the going forth of the soul." 4) And she began to pray and said, "Hear the voice of my prayer,[46] and on the path that evil spirits guard and control, in peace, save my soul."

*Mary Addresses Friends and Family
Regarding the Soul's Departure from the Body.*

Ethiopic

38) And when she had said this, Mary went forth and said to a maidservant of her house, "Go and call my relatives and those who know me, saying,

Georgian

5) And when Mary had said this, she went forth and said to a maidservant of her house, "Go and call my relatives and those that I know, and say to

45. "Pain of birth": both manuscripts actually read "way of his descent" here, but based on comparison with other narratives, it is likely that this restoration represents the original text.
46. Ps 27.2 (LXX).

Ethiopic

'Mary calls you.'" And when the maidservant went, she called them. And when they came to Mary's house, she said to them, "My fathers and my brothers, help me; for tomorrow I will go forth from my body and go to eternal rest. Arise then and perform a great act of kindness with me: for I ask you neither for gold nor silver, because all of these things are vain and corrupt. But I ask one thing of you, that you perform an act of kindness here, on this night. Let each of you take a lamp, and do not let them go out for three days, and I will tell you all of my charity before I depart from this place." And they all did as she told them. And the news was given to all of Mary's relatives and to those who knew her.

39) Mary turned and she saw all those who were standing there, and she raised her face, saying in a sweet voice, "My fathers and my brothers, let us help ourselves, and when

Georgian

them, 'Mary calls you.'" The maidservant went and called everyone, as she had ordered her. And when they entered, Mary said to them, "My fathers and my brothers, help yourselves; for tomorrow I am going forth from my body, and I will depart for my resting place, to eternal life, to infinite light. Now, arise and perform a great act of kindness with me: I ask from you neither gold nor silver, because all this is vain and corruptible. But I ask only this act of kindness from you, that you remain with me for these two nights. Each of you, take a lamp, and do not let them go out for two days, and I will speak to you from my heart, until my separation from this place. **8)** And thus they all did as she told them. And the report went forth to all of Mary's acquaintances and her friends.

And Mary looked and saw those surrounding her, and she raised her face and said in a sweet voice, "My fathers and my brothers, my mothers and my sisters, let us help ourselves.

THE BOOK OF MARY'S REPOSE

Ethiopic

we have lit our lamps, let us be vigilant, because I do not know the hour when the voice will come. I do not know, my brothers, when I will go, and I do not know the arrows that are in his hand. And also, my brothers, I have been informed when I will go forth. And moreover, it does not happen to everyone for a little while. But the one who lies in wait for everyone, the one who makes war, he does not have power against the just. And as for those who do not believe, he works his will on them. And it is not possible for the just, because there is nothing that he has with them; but when he is confused, he withdraws from them.

40) For two angels come to a person, one of righteousness and one of wickedness, and they come with death.[48] And when [death] acts on the

Georgian

Light the lamps and be vigilant, because you do not know the hour when the thief will come."[47] **9)** Because I know, brothers, the time when I will go forth, but I do not know the arrow that is in his hand. **10)** But I have been taught, my brothers, the time when I will go forth. And I do not fear, because death is universal to all, but I fear only the enemy, the one who wars against everyone. **11)** For he is powerless against the just and faithful, but he has power over the unfaithful, and he works his will on them. But he does not conquer the just, because he has no cause against them, and confused, he withdraws from them.

12) For two angels come to a person, one of righteousness and one of wickedness, and they come with death. And when death troubles the

47. Matt 24.43.

48. Cf. *Apoc. Paul.* 11–18 (Montague Rhodes JAMES, ed.), *Apocrypha Anecdota,* Texts and Studies, II. 3 (Cambridge: The University Press, 1893), 14–21.

THE DORMITION AND ASSUMPTION OF MARY

Ethiopic

soul that is going forth, the two angels come and admonish his body. And if it has good and righteous deeds, the angel of righteousness rejoices because of this, because there is no [sin] that was found upon it. And he calls his other angels, and they come to the soul. And they sing before it until [they reach] the place of all the righteous. Then the wicked angel weeps, because he did not find his part in it. And if there are evil deeds that are found in it, that one rejoices. And he takes seven angels with him, and they take that soul and lead it away. The angel of righteousness weeps greatly. And now, O my fathers and brothers, let there be no evil found in you." And when Mary had said this, the women said to her, "O our sister, who became the mother of the whole world, even if we are all afraid, what has happened to you [that] you are afraid, the mother of our Lord? The woe to us! Where should we flee when this comes to us?

Georgian

soul, the two angels come and examine the bodies of the people from the world. And if it has done the work of righteousness, the angel of righteousness rejoices, because that one has no matter with it. And he calls many others, and they come to the soul and sing before it until they arrive in the place of all the righteous. 13) Then the wicked angel, who is Satan, weeps, because he has no part with it. If someone is an evildoer, and he has done an evil deed, the evil one rejoices over him. And he brings seven more evil spirits, and he leads the spirit away, and they tear him apart. And the angel of righteousness weeps. So now, O brothers and fathers, help yourselves, and let nothing evil be found among you." 14) When Mary had said this, the women said to her, "O our sister, who became the mother of the whole world, even if we are all rightly afraid, what do you fear? You are the mother of the Lord! Woe to us! Where shall we flee, if you,

THE BOOK OF MARY'S REPOSE 89

Ethiopic	Georgian
[You are] the hope of us all [in?] patience. And if we sinners are humble, what shall we do and where shall we flee? And if the shepherd fears the wolf, where will the sheep flee?" And then all those who were standing there wept, and Mary said to them, "Be silent, my brothers, and do not cry, but glorify the one who is among you at this moment. I beg you, do not be cast down, because this is the joy of the virgin of God. But sing instead of weeping, so that it will be to every nation of the earth and to all the heavens of God, and there will be a blessing rather than weeping.	incorruptible and virgin, say this? O our expectation and intercessor and our encouragement who has committed no sin, what shall we, the unworthy, do, and where shall we flee? If the shepherd fears the wolf, where will the sheep flee?" **15)** And all those standing around her began to weep, and Mary said to them, "Be silent, my brothers; do not cry, my sisters, but glorify the one who is among you in Jerusalem. I beg you, do not cry in this way for the virgin, but cry out instead of weeping, so that it may be spread to every nation of the earth and every person of God, and there will be questioning rather than weeping.

Mary Confesses Her Lack of Faith and Sin.

Ethiopic	Georgian
41) And because of this I fear: because I did not believe in my God for even one day.	**16)** But I, brothers and sisters, I fear only from necessity, because I was unbelieving of my God for one day...

Ethiopic

Behold, I will tell you about my sin. When we were fleeing, Joseph, two of his children, and I, a terror was upon me, and I

90 THE DORMITION AND ASSUMPTION OF MARY

heard the voice of the infants behind me, saying, 'You do not weep and you do not lament: you see and you do not see; you hear and you do not hear.' And when it had said this, I turned around to see who was speaking with me. And then he had returned, and I did not know where he went. And I said to Joseph, 'Let us go from this place, because I saw an infant who is not from this world.' And then when I looked, he appeared to me, and I found that he was my son. And he said to me, 'Mary, my mother, every[49] sin is imputed to you, because you have tasted the bitter as the sweet.' I did not believe, my brothers, that I had found so much glory, until I gave him birth, since I did not at all know the menstruation of women, because of him. Now, however, I understand. And all of this took place and everything was said to me and made known to me then on the road, as was his power. And every soul hopes, both [those] of the righteous and the wicked." When she had said this, she called her family and said to them, "Arise and pray." And when they prayed, they sat and began to speak among themselves about the greatness of Christ [and] the sign that he made.

John Arrives at Mary's House.

42) And when it was dawn, the apostle John came and knocked on Mary's door. And he opened it and entered. And when Mary saw him, she was disturbed in spirit; she wept and was unable to restrain her tears, nor could she keep silent from her distress for a moment. And she cried out in a loud voice, saying, "Father John, remember what our master said to you regarding me on the day that he went forth from us, and I said to him, 'Where are you going, and with whom will you leave me, and where will I live?' And he said to me, while you

49. B: "this."

THE BOOK OF MARY'S REPOSE

91

stood and listened, 'John will take care of you.'[50] Now then, John, do not forget what he commanded you regarding me, and remember that he loved you more than them. Remember when you were reclining on his breast;[51] remember them too. And he spoke, and there is no one else who saw, except you and me, because you are the chosen virgin. †(And[52] John began to be sad, because he had removed himself). And I said to him, 'If to us, tell me, John; do not abandon me,'"†

43) And when Mary had said this, she wept in a quiet voice. But John could not bear it: his spirit was troubled, and he did not understand what she was saying, because she did not say that she would go forth from her body. Then he cried out in a loud voice, saying, "Mary, our sister, who became the mother of the Twelve, I deliberately provided for you. For I left behind the one who served you, so that he would bring you food. You do not want me to transgress the command of our Lord, which he commanded us, saying, 'Travel across the whole world, until sin is destroyed.'[53] Now then, tell me the distress of your soul." And she said to him, "My father John, perform

50. Cf. John 19.26–7.

51. Cf. John 13.23.

52. The text has become corrupt at this point, and although the close relationship between the *Book of Mary's Repose* and the early Greek versions in this section may not be immediately apparent from the translation, comparison in the original clearly indicates that the two Ethiopic manuscripts clearly transmit here a garbled version of what is expressed more clearly in the earliest Greek version. "…and he did not want me to grieve, because I am his dwelling place. Then I said to him, 'Tell me what you said to John.' And he told you the very things that you imparted to me. Now then, father John, do not abandon me" (§15).

53. Cf. Matt 28.19.

92 THE DORMITION AND ASSUMPTION OF MARY

an act of kindness with me. Keep my body safe and place me in a tomb. And guard me with your brothers, the apostles. For I heard the high priests saying, 'When we find her body, we will throw it into a fire, because the deceiver came forth from her.'" And when John heard this, that she said, "I will go forth from my body," he fell in his face on his back [?] and wept, saying, "Lord, who are we that you have shown us this tribulation, because we have not yet forgotten the previous ones so that we can encounter another tribulation. Why do I not go forth from my body, so that you might watch over me?"

Mary Shares the Secret Prayer
and Book of Mysteries with John.

Ethiopic

44) And when she heard John speaking like this and weeping, Mary begged John greatly, saying, "My father John, be patient with me in your weeping for a moment, so that I may tell you everything that the angel imparted to me." And then John arose and wiped away his tears. And Mary said to him, "Come with me"; and she said to him, "Tell the crowd to sing," so that John could read. And while they were singing, John entered the inner chamber, and she said to him, "[Behold,] the prayer that was given to me by the angel,

Coptic

...Queen of women...I am not discouraged. But the Virgin said to John, "Be patient, my brother, and I will tell you the things that I have seen."

She took him into her inner chamber to show him the book

THE BOOK OF MARY'S REPOSE   93

Ethiopic	Coptic
so that you will give it to the apostles." And she brought forth a small case that contained the book and said to him,	of the mysteries that [Jesus] had given her...

Ethiopic

"My father John, take this book in which is the mystery. For when he was five years old, our master revealed all of creation to us, and he also put you,[54] the twelve in it." And she showed him her funeral [garments] and every preparation for her funeral, saying, "My father John, I have shown you everything; but know that I have nothing in this great house except my funeral garments and two tunics. Since there are two poor people here, when I go forth from my body, give them to each one."

45) And after this, she brought him to the book[55] that had been given to her by the angel, so that the apostles would take it. And she said to him, "My father John, take this book, so that you may carry it before my coffin, for this is why it was given to me." And then John answered and said, "My sister Mary, I cannot take it

Ethiopic	Christian Palestinian Aramaic
unless the apostles have come, because they are not here. Otherwise, when they come, there will be murmuring and	...without... ...when they [come]; there will be murmuring and...

54. MSS: "us."

55. The second "book" mentioned here was most likely in the original Greek a reference to the Palm that the angel gave to Mary. The translator has presumably confused the word for palm here, *brabeion*, with the Greek word for book, *biblion*, on account of their proximity.

THE DORMITION AND ASSUMPTION OF MARY

Ethiopic

distress among us. For there is one who is greater than I among them; he has been appointed as our superior. And when they have come, it will be good."

Christian Palestinian Aramaic

For there is one who is greater than I, who stands over us. But when they come together, his will will be done.

The Miraculous Arrival of the Other Apostles.

Ethiopic

46) And after this they both entered; and when they came out of the inner chamber, there was a great tumult, so that everyone in the house was disturbed. And after the tumult, the apostles descended on a cloud to Mary's door: twelve[56] of them, each seated on a cloud. First Peter and his colleague Paul—he also came on a cloud, because he was numbered among the apostles; for he had the faith of Christ with them. And the other apostles arrived on a cloud. And the others began to look at each

Christian Palestinian Aramaic

And after these things, they came out from... At once when they came out...

With the sound of the thunder, all the apostles descended on clouds to where Mary's door was. And they were eleven, each of them was... First Peter and second Paul...

...the faith of Christ. And after them the other apostles also went toward them on clouds to where Mary's...

56. A: "ten"; the early Greek traditions report eleven. A brief passage preserved on one the Coptic fragments presumably offers a terse parallel here: "...And immediately, behold, all the apostles came to her..."

THE BOOK OF MARY'S REPOSE 95

Ethiopic	Christian Palestinian Aramaic
other, and they were amazed that they had arrived together. And Peter said, "My brothers, let us pray to God, who has gathered us with our brothers who are contending with us in the joy of the spirit. Truly,	...suddenly you came together. And Peter said, "My brothers, let us pray to God, who has gathered us together, especially because Paul is with us, the joy of our soul. For truly...

Ethiopic

my brothers, the word of the prophet has been fulfilled which says, 'Behold, it is good and pleasant when brothers are together.'" [57] And Paul said to Peter, "You have found the true testimony. For I am joyous, having returned to the faith of brothers." And Peter said, "Let us say a prayer." And all of the apostles raised one voice together, saying, "Yes, let us pray so that we will know why God has gathered us together."

47) Then, while they were each praising their brothers according to his honor, Peter said to Paul, "Arise and pray before us, because our spirit rejoices today in the faith of Christ." And Paul said to him, "Pardon me: behold, I am a neophyte, and I am not worthy to follow the dust of your feet. How shall I precede you in praying? For you are a pillar of light, and all our brothers who are present are better than I. Now then, you, our father, pray for us, so that the joy of Christ will be with us." Then the apostles rejoiced at his humility, and they also said [to Peter], "You pray before us." They confessed, saying, "We are present because of you; each of us has been sent, as he commanded, each one according to his own ordinance. And we ought to observe the glory of prayer that

57. Ps 132.1 (LXX).

96 THE DORMITION AND ASSUMPTION OF MARY

our master taught us and say it in our hearts. Where is Peter, the bishop, our father, so that he may speak this glory of prayer: O that he will listen and will pray here."

Peter's Prayer.

48) And then Peter prayed, saying, "God, our Father and our Lord Jesus Christ, has glorified me insofar as my ministry has been glorified; for I am the least, brothers, and I do this as it has been chosen. And in this way we too are one congregation that is among us all: each one glorifies the place of the others, and not a human being. For this is a command that we have received from our master, that we will love one another.[58] Bless me then, because this is what is pleasing to you."

49) And he stretched out his hands and said, "I give thanks to you, ruler of the whole world, who is seated upon the chariot of the cherubim[59] and dwells in the heights and who looks[60] upon the lowly, who dwells in light[61] and gives rest to the world, in a hidden mystery that you revealed by the cross. We do this too when we raise our hands in the image of your cross, so that by its form we will receive rest and everyone will receive rest, and you will give [rest] to those who must suffer. You loosen hard labor; you are the one who has revealed the hidden treasure;[62] you have established your Messiah among us. And who of the gods is as merciful as you? Your power is not distant from us. Who is as merciful as you, just as your Father? And he saves

58. John 15.12.

59. Cf. 4 Kgdms 19.15.

60. Literally, "knows'; nevertheless, the early Greek versions support this translation, as does the Psalm being cited: 112.5–6 (LXX).

61. Cf. 1 Tim 6.16.

62. Cf. Matt 11.28; Isa 45.3.

THE BOOK OF MARY'S REPOSE   97

those who believe in him from evil; your will has conquered
desire; your faith turns away error; there is nothing more beautiful than your beauty; your humility has cast down the proud.
You are the living one and you vanquished death; you are rested
and you have eradicated the darkness, the glory of the unique
one who is with the Father, the glory of mercy that was sent
from the spirit of the Father of truth. Maruyal, Maruyal, Mare-
natha, Beyatar, from now unto the age of the age, Amen."

Mary and John Greet the Apostles.

50) And when they said "Amen," they embraced each
other. And when they had embraced together, then, when
Andrew and Peter were together, John came into their midst
and said, "Bless me, all of you." Then they all embraced him,
each one in his order. After they had embraced, Peter said,
"Andrew and John, beloved of the Lord, how did you come
together here? How many days have you been here?" And
John said to him, "Listen then to what happened to me.
When we[63] were in the city of Nerdo/Nador,[64] while I was
teaching the twenty-eight who believed in our Savior, who
had taken hold of me, I was raised up before them, at the
ninth hour. And the cloud descended to the place where we[65]

63. MSS: "you (pl.)."
64. The meaning here is unclear, and in other early versions John
instead says "when I was in the city of Sardis..." (e.g. *Greek Mary's
Repose* 26 and *Latin Mary's Repose* 14), while in the Latin *Transitus
Mariae* in this volume, John says "while I was teaching in the city of
Agathen..." (14). ARRAS, *De Transitu*, 1:91 (Lat), offers a complex and
not entirely convincing interpretation of this phrase as meaning "in a
foreign land."
65. Again MSS: "you (pl.)."

98 THE DORMITION AND ASSUMPTION OF MARY

were gathered and it snatched me up before all those who were with me. And it brought me here. And I knocked on the door, and a girl opened it for me. And I found people with Mary, our sister, and she said to me, 'I will go forth from my body.' And I did not remain among those people who were standing with her, and my grief weighed down on me. Now then, my brothers, when you go forth tomorrow, do not weep, and there will be no disturbance: for if you weep, there will be a great disturbance. For this is what our master taught me when I was reclining on his breast at the supper: if the people who have come into her company see us weeping, they will revile us in their hearts and say, 'They also fear death.'

Ethiopic	Christian Palestinian Aramaic
But let us soothe Mary with a saying of love."	So let us encourage ourselves with the sayings of the beloved."

Mary Prays to the Great Cherub of Light and Prepares for Death.

Ethiopic	Christian Palestinian Aramaic
51) And then the apostles began to enter Mary's house, and they said with one voice, "Mary, our sister and also the mother of those who are saved, grace be with you."[66] And Mary said, "How have you entered in here, and who here has told you that I will go forth from	Then the apostles entered Mary's house together and said to her, "Mary, our sister, mother of all those who live, grace be with you." And Mary said to them, "How have you come here, or who told you that I will go forth from my body? And [how] have you come here

66. Cf. Luke 1.28.

THE BOOK OF MARY'S REPOSE

Ethiopic

my body? And how have you come together? For behold, I see that you are sad." And they told, each one, the land where they were dwelling, and how a cloud came and snatched them up and brought them here. And then they all praised her, from Peter to Paul, saying, "May God, who is able to save everyone, bless you."

52) And then Mary rejoiced in spirit and said,[68] "I bless the one who has power over every blessing. I bless the Great Cherub of Light, who dwelt in my womb. I bless every work of your hands, which obey every command. I bless the love [with which] you loved me. I bless the word of life that you have sent forth from your body, which has truly been given to us.

Christian Palestinian Aramaic

together, for I see you gathered together." And they said, "None of us is one in it from that land from which they were brought forth. And he came with them on clouds."[67]

...Then they received her, from Peter to Mar Paul, again saying, "May God who saves all, bless you."

And then Mary rejoiced in spirit and said, "I bless you who are the master of every blessing. I bless the dwelling places of your glory. I bless you, the Great Cherub of Light, who came to be in my womb. I bless all the works of your hands, which are perfected to you with complete submission. I bless the love with which you loved us. I bless the words of life that have come forth from your mouth and were given to us.

67. Something appears to be wrong with the text in the Christian Palestinian Aramaic version here.

68. Cf. Luke 1.47.

100   THE DORMITION AND ASSUMPTION OF MARY

Ethiopic	Coptic
I will send all the apostles to you when you go forth from your body'; and behold, they have gathered, and I am in their midst, as a vine that bears fruit in its time, just as when we were with you, just as [you were] a vineyard in the midst of your angels, subduing your enemies with all their works. I bless you with every blessing;	. . .my angels and my apostles will gather on the day of your departure from the body." Behold, they have gathered to me, and I am in their midst, as a vine surrounded by its fruit. I bless you [with?] every blessing and all sweetness. For there are no words in. . . today. . .

Ethiopic

what you told me is happening. For you told me, 'You will see me with my apostles when you go forth from your body.'"

53) And when she had said this, Mary called Peter and all of the apostles. And she brought them into her inner chamber and showed them her funeral [garments], in which they were to bury her. And after this, they went forth and sat in the midst of everyone who had lit a lamp [and] did not allow it to be extinguished, just as Mary had commanded them.

Peter Offers an All-Night Discourse.

54) And when the sun had set on the second day, as the third day was beginning, when she was to go forth from her body, Peter said to all the apostles, "My brothers, let the one who has learned discourse[69] speak all night until the sun

---

69. Literally, "discourse of a child." This is probably a corruption of the Greek *logon paideias*, present in the earliest Greek narratives, including the Greek precis of this text translated in this volume: "learned discourse" (*Greek Mary's Repose* 30).

THE BOOK OF MARY'S REPOSE

rises." And the apostles said, "Who is wiser than you? For we are all small before you."

55) Then Peter began to speak to them, "All my brothers, you who are in this place, at this hour, for this lover of humanity, our mother Mary, you who have lit lamps that are visible from earth, this you have done well. And I also desire that each receive the lamp of humanity: this is the lamp of the one who put on humanity, which is the three-wicked lamp that is our soul, our body, and our spirit, which three shine from the true fire. I now boast and am not ashamed, because you will enter into marriage, and moreover, you will enter and rest with the bridegroom. Thus the light of our sister Mary's lamp fills the world and will not be extinguished until the end of days, so that those who have decided to be saved will receive assurance from her. And if they receive the image of light, they will receive her rest and her blessing.

56) My brothers do not think that this is death. It is not death but eternal life, because the death of the righteous will be blessed before God.[70] For this is their glory, and the second death cannot subdue them. And believe [what] has been revealed to me and the apostles with me. And when you know the first death, behold, I will tell you about the second death. But I will tell you about the second death, that there is no one who will hear. But God the Father, whose spirit is now in our midst, is also concerned for his ministry. Moreover, it is fitting that we hear what is not heard by those who are not worthy and do not want to hear."

70. Ps 115.6 (LXX).

102 THE DORMITION AND ASSUMPTION OF MARY

*A Heavenly Voice Rebukes Peter
for Revealing Secret Knowledge.*

57) Then Peter raised his hands and said, "From where is the first death?" And while he was speaking, a great light shone in the house in the midst of them all, so that it made the light of their lamps seem dark. And a voice came, which said, "Peter, there is no one to whom you can tell this, because you are not alone. Speak this discourse in a sign that they can bear. For a doctor heals the sick person according to his illness, and a nurse raises an infant to a child."

58) Peter raised his voice and said, "I bless the blessed one; I bless you who saved our souls, so that you would have mercy on us. You have led us well, so that we do not suffer in the evil abyss. I bless the horn of our knowledge,[71] whose faith we have known." And he turned and said to them, "My brothers, we are not able to say what we wanted without the practice of every good thing. He directs us in every good thing, so that we will take care of our duty among ourselves."

59) And when he had said these things, twenty-one virgins arose one by one and fell at Peter's feet, saying, "We beg you, our father, bring us into the greatness of Christ and those who are known to him." And then Peter made them rise, saying, "Listen to me, our joy, and the glory of our honor: do not think that the speaking voice was revealed on your account. It is not so; rather [it is for] those who are standing outside, who are not worthy of the mystery. You are worthy, and [so is] everyone [who] has preserved the image of their infancy. For your glory is not of this world.

---

71. Literally, "horn of our tongue." As Arras explains (*De Transitu*, 1:93 [Lat]), probably the result of confusion between *gnōsis* and *glōssa*.

THE BOOK OF MARY'S REPOSE 103

Peter Instead Teaches a Parable about Virginity.

60) Listen then and learn what our master says to you: 'The kingdom of heaven is like a virgin.'[72] He did not say, 'it is like time,' because time passes. Nor is it like rich people, because wealth passes; but a virgin remains. But know that [a virgin] is glorious; therefore [a virgin] is artfully like the kingdom of heaven. And therefore there is nothing that you should worry about, because when he sends [death] to you, you will not say, †'Make us [know?] where we will ascend and where we will descend; our affliction, children, and great riches, and whose fields will sprout; whose luxury is great,'†[73] because there is nothing in this that you worry about. You have no concerns except for your virginity. And when [death] is sent to you, then you will be found ready, since you have nothing. And what you have is light, your virginity. Be patient then, and I will reveal to you what has been revealed to me. And be certain that you know that there is nothing that is lighter than the name of virginity, and there is nothing that is heavier than a person of the world, so that you will rejoice.

61) There was a certain rich man in a city who had great wealth. And the servants of his house were charged with a crime: when they did not obey his order, their master became angry, and he sent them away to a distant land for a long time. And then later he called those who had committed the crime and had gone away. One had built a house for himself and planted a vineyard and also [built] a bakery. And he had pro-

72. Cf. Matt 25.1.

73. The closely related *Homily on the Dormition* by John of Thessalonica is helpful for understanding the gist of this very garbled passage: "Woe to us—where shall we flee, and leave our poor children or our great wealth or our planted fields or our large possessions?" (§10: JUGIE, *Homélies mariales byzantines (II)*, 391; trans. DALEY, *On the Dormition*, 59).

104 THE DORMITION AND ASSUMPTION OF MARY

duced much additional wealth. Now the other servant, [what] he produced, he converted into gold, which is enduring. And he summoned a goldsmith and had him make a crown of gold for him, saying to the goldsmith, 'I am a servant, and I have a master and [he has] a son, and the crown that I have made [is for them].' And when the goldsmith heard, he worked his craft.

62) And after this, their time was finished, and their master sent someone. And he said to him, 'If you do not bring them in seven days, you and not I, it will be on you.' Then the one who was sent went forth with haste, and he went to that land, in order to find them, whether it be day or night. And when he apprehended them, he said to them, 'Your master sent me to you.' And he said to the one who had acquired a house, a vineyard, and additional wealth, 'Let us go, servant.' And he said, 'Let us go; but be patient with me, until I sell all the wealth that I have acquired here.' And then he said to the one that he was sent to meet, 'I cannot wait for you and be patient with you, because I have received seven days time, and it is passing. I cannot wait for you.' Then that servant wept, saying, 'Woe is me, for I will abandon all this. Woe is me, for I have been found unprepared.' The overseer said to him, 'O wicked servant, your greed has been revealed. And when your master wanted [you] and sent to you, why did you plant a vineyard for yourself in this land, and you were found unprepared, when I came to you?' Then the servant wept and said, 'Woe is me! I thought [that] I would remain in this exile forever. And if I had known that my master wanted me, I would not have produced so much wealth in this land.' Then the messenger brought him forth, bringing nothing with him.

63) While he was leading him, the other servant heard that he had been sent for him. And he arose and placed the crown on his head. And he went to the road along which the mess-

enger was traveling, looking for him. And when the messenger came, he said to him, 'Your master has sent me to you.' And he said, 'Let us go, because I have nothing here, and what I have is light. Let us go with joy. What I have is as nothing, because I have nothing at all here except this crown of gold. I had it made for this reason, hoping every day and praying that mercy would come upon me, and that my master would send and receive me from this land. For there are some who hate me and would take this crown from me. Now he has heard my prayer. Let us arise and go.'

64) Both servants went forth with the steward. When their master saw them, he said to the one who had acquired farms, 'Where is the produce of such a long time in exile?' The servant answered and said, 'My master, you sent to me a soldier, who would have no mercy on me. I begged him to be patient with me, so that I could sell what I had and not be ashamed and acquire in my hands the things that you deserve.' Then his master said to him, 'O wicked servant, now you remember to sell, when I have sent for you. Why did you not consider it in exile? You were not thinking of me there because of your wealth.' And he became angry and ordered that his hands and feet be bound, and that he be sent to another land. And then he called the one who was crowned with the crown and said, 'O good and faithful servant, you have longed for freedom, on account of which you made the crown, because it is the crown of the free. And you did not dare to wear it unless it was granted to you by your master. For a servant cannot be set free except by his master. As you desired freedom, you will find it with me.' Then he freed him, and he was placed in charge of many."

65) And Peter said this to the brothers who were with Mary, and he turned to them and said, "Listen, my brothers, to the things that will come upon you. For the virgin belongs

106   THE DORMITION AND ASSUMPTION OF MARY

to the true bridegroom, to the God of all creation. You then, the human race, are those with whom God became angry in the beginning, and he placed them in the world as in a prison and as spoils in the world for those to whom he abandoned us because of this. But the last days have come, and they will be transferred to the place where our ancient fathers Abraham, Isaac, and Jacob are. And there each one will be in the Fullness. And he will send the severe angel of death to us. And when he comes upon the souls of sinners, he afflicts them with pain for their many sins and makes them work very hard. Then he pleads with God, saying, 'Have patience with me for a brief moment, until I redeem my sins, which have been sown in my body.' But death will not allow it. How [could he]? And everyone who is full of sin, having no righteousness, will be brought to the valley of damnation. If he has works of righteousness, he will rejoice, saying, 'There is nothing that owns me, because I have nothing here except my virginity.' And he will plead, saying, 'Do not abandon me on this earth, because there are those who hate me on this earth, and they would take from me the name of my virginity.' Then his soul will go forth from his body, and he will be brought to the bridegroom with psalms, until [they reach] the place of the Father. And when the Father sees the soul, he will rejoice and place it with the other souls. Now then, my brothers, know that we will not remain in this world."

Christ Returns to Receive Mary's Soul.

66) And when Peter had said this all night, while the crowd was steadfast, the sun rose. And Mary arose and went outside, and she prayed, saying her prayer. And after her prayer, she went in and lay down. And she fulfilled the course of her life. And Peter sat at her head, John at her feet, and the rest of

THE BOOK OF MARY'S REPOSE 107

the apostles encircled her bier. And at that hour of the day, there was a tumult and a sweet, pleasant smell, like the odor of Paradise. And all those who were standing near Mary began to sleep, except only the virgins: he kept them from sleeping so that they would be witnesses of Mary's funeral and of her glory.[74]

67) And our Lord Jesus Christ came on a cloud with an innumerable multitude of angels.[75] And Jesus entered the inner chamber, where Mary was; Michael and the angels stood outside the inner chamber, singing. And when he entered the place

Ethiopic	Syriac
and found the apostles with Mary, he embraced them. And after this, Mary embraced [him] and opened her mouth, and she blessed, saying, "I bless you, the one who spoke with me and did not deceive me, and furthermore who told me, saying, 'I will not allow the angels [to come] upon your soul,' and he came to me himself. And it has happened to me, O Lord, according to your word. Who am I, a lowly one, that I have been found worthy	...and found the apostles with Mary, he greeted them and Mary. Mary opened her mouth and said, "I bless you, my Lord, my master, I bless you who did what was promised to me, so that I did not measure you. You promised, and why did you allow your angels upon my soul, but you came to me yourself?" The Lord did not answer. "Have I done for you everything of which I was worthy? For am I not a lowly one, who was

74. Regarding the question of who was put to sleep and who remained awake for the Virgin's Dormition according to the early tradition, see Stephen J. SHOEMAKER, "Gender at the Virgin's Funeral: Men and Women as Witnesses to the Dormition." *Studia Patristica* 34 (2001), 552–8.

75. Cf. Matt 24.30–1; 26.64.

108 THE DORMITION AND ASSUMPTION OF MARY

Ethiopic	Syriac
of such glory."[76] And when she said this, she fulfilled the course of her life, not turning her face from the Lord. And then the Lord took her soul and placed it in Michael's hands, and they wrapped it in a fine garment, so splendid that one could not keep silent.	found worthy of such glory?" And when Mary had said these things, her spirit went forth from her body, and with gratitude she turned her face toward our Lord. Then our Lord took her soul and placed it in Michael's hands. And he wrapped it in a precious garment, whose splendor was indescribable.
68) And the apostles saw Mary's spirit as it was given into Michael's hands: a perfect form, but its body was both male and female, and nevertheless one, being similar to every body and seven times white.	The apostles saw Mary's soul as it was given into the angel Michael's hands, which was perfect and went forth with goodness to eternal glory. It was clothed in the appearance of both male and female, with no defilement at all, but the image and splendor of the whole body cast off.
69) And Peter rejoiced and asked our Lord, saying, "Who among us [has] a soul as white as Mary's?" And he said to him, "O Peter, all of the elect who were sent here [had] such souls, because they went forth from a holy place. But, when	Peter rejoiced, saying to our Lord, "Who of us will have a soul as brilliant as Mary's?" Jesus said to Peter, "All these souls are coming and are elect. Therefore, their souls are shining because they are from the holy places, but...

76. Cf. Luke 1.38, 48.

THE BOOK OF MARY'S REPOSE 109

Ethiopic	Syriac
they go forth from their bodies, they are not found [thus], and they are not white, because in one way they were sent, and in another they are found.[77] Because they have loved [evil] deeds, their soul has become dark from many sins. And if someone guards himself as in the first days, when he comes forth from the body, he will be found white."	from their bodies, they were not found weeping, because. . . . . .found. . . . . .the body. . .of which we will take care. . .its sleep. . .like the mortal one, which you will watch over. I said much concerning them. I gave you the one possessed by the devil from my evil as signs, and it will be like from the body, of which the soul of splendor is found like their light."

Mary's Funeral Procession.

Ethiopic	Syriac
70) And the Savior said to Peter,[78] "Bring forth Mary's body, departing quickly, and go out from the left of the city, and you will find a new	Again Jesus said to Peter, "Watch over her body in gratitude, and take care not to let it fall outside of the city. Place Mary's body in a new tomb

77. Literally, "others were sent, and others were found."

78. One of the Yale Coptic fragments perhaps parallels this section, with a slightly different text: ". . .her body. Behold, I appoint you to bear witness to the things that have taken place in my mother's departure from the body, so that you will understand that hers was a birth in the manner of all others. But now, O Peter, hasten to prepare her for burial. . ."

110 THE DORMITION AND ASSUMPTION OF MARY

Ethiopic	Syriac
tomb.[79] Place her body there and guard it as I commanded you." And when he said this, her body cried out from splendor, saying, "Remember me, O Lord, king of glory, because I am your image. Remember me, because I guarded the great treasure that was given to me." And then Jesus said to her body, "I will not abandon you, pearl of my new treasure: by no means will I abandon you, the closed sanctuary of God! By no means will I abandon the one who is truly the guarantee! By no means will I abandon the one who led five guards! [?] By no means will I abandon the treasure [that was] sealed until I sought it!"	...as I commanded you." And when he said these things to Peter, Mary's body...and said, "Remember me, O God, king of...remember...
	...above...because...you...
	...great...
	...chosen...
	which is near...said the words that you brought...
	of the gratitude to you. Place one of the four toward you, and watch over...for death... which I perfected...of the mountain...
	[Several lines are completely illegible.]
	...he said, "These worthy ones will bring Mary's body to the mountain."
71) When he had said this, there was a loud noise. And Peter, the other apostles, and the three virgins prepared Mary's body for burial and placed it on a bier. And after this, those who were sleeping	...Peter...
	Mary's body and placed it on a bier.
	And after...those who were

79. Cf. Matt 27.60.

THE BOOK OF MARY'S REPOSE   111

Ethiopic	Syriac

awoke. And Peter brought the book[80] and said to John, "You are a virgin, and you must sing before the bier, so take [it]." John said to him, "You, our father and bishop, must take up the book before her, until we come to the place [of burial]." And Peter said to him, "so that none of us will grieve, let us tie [it to] Mary's bier." And then the apostles got up and carried Mary's bier. And Peter sang, saying, "When

sleeping awoke. And Peter brought them the staff,[81] and the angel... And Peter said to John, "You are a virgin,...before the bier while you carry it." He said...you...
...was asked of him, what...

When they heard Peter saying...

[Several lines are completely illegible.]
...and they carried...

80. In other early narratives, this passage concerns the Palm. This is likely another instance of mistaking *brabeion* for *biblion.*111

81. In contrast to most of the other early Palm narratives, which refer here to the tradition's eponymous palm branch, "*brabeion*" in Greek, the Syriac version uses a word (*šabtā*) that usually means "staff, scepter; rod, scourge." Nevertheless, *brabeion* can also mean either "prize" or even "rod" in addition to "palm." Thus it would seem that there were different interpretations of this Greek word as the tradition passed into multiple languages. In the West, the Latin and Irish traditions, for instance, clearly identify this object as a palm. In the East, however, its identification is more complex. In the other early Syriac and Arabic narratives, from the Bethlehem tradition, this object is also identified as a "staff," using a different Syriac word (*ḥuṭrā*), in the following story of the Jewish attack on Mary's body: in this volume, see *The Six Books* 3.27. It would seem, then, that there were two ancient traditions of interpretation, one that the *brabeion* was simply a "palm," and another, represented in Syriac, that the *brabeion* was a staff either made from palms or having palms attached.

112 THE DORMITION AND ASSUMPTION OF MARY

Ethiopic	Syriac
Israel went out of Egypt, alleluia." [82]	[Several lines are completely illegible.]

The Jewish Attack on Mary's Body.

Ethiopic	Syriac
72) And the Lord and his angels were going alongside of the bier, singing and not being seen. And they heard the sound of many people. And many people came out from Jerusalem. And the high priests heard the sound of the tumult and the voice of those who were singing and not seen; they heard the voice of many, and many people went out. And those who heard the voice were disturbed, saying among themselves, "What is this tumult?" And there was one of them who said, "Mary has gone forth from her body, and the apostles are singing alongside of her." Then Satan entered into their hearts,[83] and they said, "Arise, let us go and kill the apostles	Our Lord with angels... Going...the bier, and... They were from life, but with mourning that was heard as if from a great crowd, which was... And when the high priests heard the great voice of those who were singing, they were troubled and saying among themselves, "What is this great tumult?" And one of them answered and said to them, "Mary has gone forth from the world, and the apostles are singing before her." And the Lord who said to them, [Satan] entered their hearts, Arise...

82. Ps 113.1 (LXX).
83. Cf. John 13.27.

THE BOOK OF MARY'S REPOSE   113

Ethiopic

and burn the body of the one who bore the deceiver."

73) And when they had got up, they went forth with swords and spears,[84] in order to kill them. †And then the angels in the clouds attacked them, and they smashed their heads into the wall, since they could not see [where] they were going—except for [those who found] the way to go out, to report what had happened to them. And when they drew near to the apostles and saw the crowned bier, the apostles were singing and saying, "A great victory has been accomplished. Behold the Dormition, which has blessed us, the people: how much glory we receive!"†[85] And they got

Syriac

. . . .the body that bore the deceiver.

And immediately they went forth with swords and rods to kill the apostles who were in the cloud. The angels went forth from the cloud at God's command and struck them with hallucinations. And they all became blind and smashed their heads into the walls, because they did not know how to go out. But one of them found the way out, and he went out. And when he drew near to the apostles and saw the crowned bier and the apostles singing, he answered and said to them with great wrath, "Why do you trouble the people with what you have done?" And he rose up with

84. Cf. Mark 14.43.

85. The Jewish attacker's cry against the Virgin, which usually appears here in other early narratives (e.g. see the Syriac, opposite column), must have been just too offensive for some medieval copyist. Subtle changes have been made in the text preserved by both MSS to revise the attacker's outrage so that it becomes praise of Mary's Dormition. The text as it appears in other early witnesses is generally similar to what we find in the earliest Greek narrative, also translated in this volume: "When he approached the apostles, he saw them carrying

114 THE DORMITION AND ASSUMPTION OF MARY

Ethiopic	Syriac
up and went forth with great wrath, and they were wanting to [over] throw the bier and grasp it where the book was. And they pulled and wanted to send it down into a pit. Then one of them touched the bier with his hands, and they were cut off from his shoulder blade. And they remained, and he saw them hanging from the bier, and other [parts] of them remained hanging from their body.	rage and ran to the bier and took hold of it, and he tried to throw it down to the ground. And he took hold where the staff was, in order to throw the body down to the ground. And at once his hands clung to the bier and were cut off from his elbows, and his hands remained hanging onto the bier, and the other half remained on his body.

Ethiopic

74) Then the man wept before the apostles, begging them and saying, "Do not repay me with such torment. Remember, Peter, my father, because he was the doorkeeper and your disciple, and I said to you, 'You are this man's disciple.'[86] How I beseech you now and ask you, do not repay me!"[87] And Peter said to him, "This is not my act, that I will heal you, nor another one of them. Now then, if you believe that Jesus is the

---

the crowned bier and singing hymns. And he was enraged and said, 'Behold, the dwelling place of the despoiler of our people: what glory she receives today!'" (*Greek Mary's Repose 39*).

86. Cf. Mark 14.66–7.

87. The earliest Greek narrative, also translated in this volume, reads here: "O Peter, remember my father, when the doorkeeper, the maidservant, questioned you and said to you, 'You are one of this man's disciples,' and how and in what manner I questioned you" (*Greek Mary's Repose* 40).

THE BOOK OF MARY'S REPOSE   115

Son of God, whom you seized and killed, and those who are
without the law did not believe [then you will be healed (?)]."
And he said, "We didn't believe? Yes, truly we believed that
he was the Son of God. But what shall we do with our[88]
pride, which darkens our eyes.

75) [When] they [our fathers] were about to [die],[89] they
summoned us and said to us, 'Behold children, God has
chosen us from every tribe, so that we would be before his
people with power, so that you would [not?] labor in another
land. This [is your] task: that you will build up the people, so
that you will receive from them tithes, and first-fruits, and every
firstborn that the womb brings forth. But take care, children,
lest the place of their places [i.e. the temple] should be too
abundant for you, and they will rise up and go against it. [Do
not] anger God, but give from what you have to the poor, the
orphans, and the widows of the people, and save the soul of
the blind.' But we did not listen to our fathers' instruction.
When we did not believe [them], the place was very abundant,
and we put the firstborn of all the sheep and cattle and of
all of the beasts on the table of those who sell and buy. And
the Son of God came, and he expelled them all from that
place, and he said to those who were selling doves, 'Take this
out of this place, and do not make my father's house a house
of commerce.[90] You have established it in corruption, you

88. MSS: "their."

89. In this section the words in brackets are supplied through comparison with from the earliest Greek narrative (*Greek Mary's Repose* 41)
and John of Thessalonica's *Homily on the Dormition* 13 (JUGIE, *Homélies
mariales byzantines (II)*, 399–400; trans. DALEY, *On the Dormition*, 65–6),
both of which have better preserved this story: they are absent from
the Ethiopic version.

90. John 2.16.

116 THE DORMITION AND ASSUMPTION OF MARY

who have been accustomed to evil.' And we were plotting in our hearts, and we rose up against him and killed him, knowing that he was the Son of God. But do not remember our evil and ignorance; but forgive us, because our beloved has come, who is from God, so that we will be saved."

76) Then Peter ordered that they put down the bier, and he said to the high priest, "Are you listening now with your whole heart? Go then and embrace Mary's body, saying, 'I believe in you and in the one who came forth from your womb.'" Then the high priest of the Jews blessed Mary in his language for three hours, and he allowed no one to approach her while he was prophesying and bringing forth testimonies from the 100 books of Moses, where it was written about her that God was born in glory, so that the apostles heard the magnificence of what was given by him, which they had not heard at all. And Peter said to him, "Go then and touch her bier with your hands." He touched [it], saying, "In the name of Jesus, the son of Mary, the son of the dove, who was crucified, with goodness my hands have touched your bier."

Ethiopic	Syriac
Then they became as they were before, and they were patient [?]. And Peter said to him, "Arise and take a palm leaf from this book,[91] and go into the city, and you will	...who did as he had been commanded, and they were just as it was before, although something had happened, nothing had changed. And when he had been healed, Peter said

91. The translator's confusion of Greek terms for palm and book is even clearer here. So also in the Syriac we see a branch (here using the Greek word *thallos* as a loan word in Syriac) taken from the staff, which must have included a number of branches. Presumably, the underlying text of the Ethiopic version also described taking a palm branch from this palm staff (*brabeion*).

THE BOOK OF MARY'S REPOSE   117

Ethiopic

find blind people who do not see and do not recognize the way. And tell them what has happened to you, and for those who believe, place the palm leaf on their eyes, and then they will see. And if they do not believe, they will not see."

77) And he went just as Peter ordered him, and he found many people in a crowd, weeping and saying, "Woe to us! What has happened [to us] is as Sodom. Woe to us! It has surpassed [Sodom], because at first he attacked them [with blindness],[92] and after that, he brought down fire from heaven, and it consumed them. Woe to us, because the end has come for us, in the coming fire!"[93] Then that man took the book, the palm leaf, and he spoke with them concern-

Syriac

to him, "Arise and take a branch from this staff and go into the city, and thus you will find blind people, around five thousand, who do not know the way to go out. Speak with them and tell them everything that has happened to you. And the one who believes and places this branch on his eyes, he will immediately see the light again."

And when the high priest heard and did what Peter told him, he found many people, around five thousand, standing and weeping and saying, "Woe to us! What has come up on us is the same as Sodom, which immediately struck them with hallucinations. Fire and brimstone also came down from heaven and burned them all equally. And so also he is doing to all of us and bringing an end to us and burning the sinners with fire." And after these things, the one who was

---

92. Other early narratives again refer specifically to some sort of visual impairment, making the parallel with Sodom more exact.

93. Cf. Gen 19.11, 24.

118   THE DORMITION AND ASSUMPTION OF MARY

Ethiopic	Syriac
ing the faith. And whoever believed, his eyes were opened; and whoever did not believe, his eyes were not opened, but he remained in his blindness.	his son and was carrying the branch spoke with them and said to them, "Whoever is with Christ, since he was born from Mary and he is the Son of God, he has seen the light." And immediately everyone who believed and confessed saw the blind; and immediately everyone who believed and confessed saw the light. And whoever did not believe did not see but was like him the son of evil.

Ethiopic

And the apostles immediately brought Mary to the tomb.

*Paul asks the Other Apostles
to Teach him the Secret Mysteries.*

78) And [94] when they had set her down, they all sat together, waiting for the Lord to come and take Mary's body. Mary was lying down, and the apostles were sitting

Ethiopic	Christian Palestinian Aramaic
at the entrance of the tomb, as the Lord had commanded	. . .at the entrance [95] of the tomb of Mary, as he had com-

---

94. There is also a fifth-century Syriac palimpsest fragment of sections 78 and 79, although it is so badly damaged that there is little point in trying to translate it here. Nevertheless, one can consult

THE BOOK OF MARY'S REPOSE   119

Ethiopic

them. And Paul said to Peter, "Our father, you know that I am a neophyte and this is the beginning of my faith in Christ. For I did not meet the master, so that he could tell me the great and glorious mystery. But I have heard that he revealed it to you on the Mount of Olives. Now then, I beg you to reveal it to me too." And Peter said to Paul, "Paul, my brother, [it is clear][96] that we rejoice now that you have come into the faith of Christ, but we cannot reveal this mystery to you. For we fear that perhaps hearing this, you would be afraid. But be patient, and behold, we will remain here for three days, and our Lord will come

Christian Palestinian Aramaic

manded them. Paul said to Peter, "Father Peter, . . .

. . .the beginning of the faith which is in Christ. For I did not meet our master in discourse to have it revealed, so that he would tell me the great and glorious mysteries. For I have heard that he revealed everything to you on the Mount of Olives. And now I beg you to reveal it again to me too.". . .Peter said to Paul. . .that you have come into the faith of Christ, . . .

. . .lest it is not possible for you to hear. But remain. . .and you. . .

. . .three days. . .

. . .will come, and the angels to

Müller-Kessler's edition and translation to see that indeed this section is also attested by these early fragments: Christa MÜLLER-KESSLER, "Obsequies of My Lady Mary (II): A Fragmentary Syriac Palimpsest Manuscript from Deir al-Suryan (BL, Add 14.665, no. 2)," *Collectanea Christiana Orientalia* 19 (2022), 45–70, 65–6.

95. *bt'rh* in the edition is presumably a typo for *btr'h*.

96. A main verb is missing here; one has been supplied from the earliest Greek narrative.

120 THE DORMITION AND ASSUMPTION OF MARY

Ethiopic	Christian Palestinian Aramaic
with his angels to take up Mary's body, and if he orders us, we will gladly tell you.	take up Mary's body. And if he orders us, then we will reveal...them.
79) †And while they were deliberating	At the door of the tomb, speaking...[97]

Ethiopic

among themselves, behold, two men passed from Jerusalem to Kidron, and when they came to a vineyard, they said, "Let us go inside, {my[98] brothers; if no one answers me, I will plant a vineyard." And Paul said to the apostles, "If you will not reveal our Savior's words to me, you will go, and I will hear the words of those two men, so that I will not tell you how those two men ridicule us, O our father." And Peter said to him, "We have found its interpretation for you, while you were speaking, Paul, the storehouse of wisdom, and you are in this with us." And when he knew that Peter had confessed, humbling himself, he said, "He confessed." And he said, "Forgive me, O our father Peter, because we have not been found wise according to you, but it is given from creation. And now command me to speak." And then all of the apostles answered

97. The Christian Palestinian Aramaic fragment continues for several more lines, but the text is very limited and general and is not easy to correlate with the other extant versions. Perhaps the phrase "There is none, who mocks me so much" correlates somehow with the demons in Solomon's court in the following section.

98. The section in braces is preserved only in manuscript B. Manuscript A, which omits this material, resumes the narrative at the beginning of section 80 below. Perhaps a scribe omitted the passage because it is corrupt; nevertheless, its omission does not much improve the sense of the narrative at this point.

THE BOOK OF MARY'S REPOSE   121

with one voice, and they said to him, "speak Paul, our beloved."
And Paul said, "They are demons who have ridiculed
humans." And Paul said to them, "Listen to me and hear the
end of these words.} †

Solomon Adjudicates a Conflict between a Man and his Son.

80) [There was a time] when Solomon was judging a man
and his son regarding his mother's property.[99] And after she
died, his father took two wives; then his son seized him,
saying, 'Give

Ethiopic	Christian Palestinian Aramaic
me my mother's property.' And together they came and spoke to Solomon in court. And while he was judging them, a demon came into their midst and laughed a great laugh. And Solomon got up from the judge's seat, and he seized the demon in his hand and removed him by himself, so that he could punish him	...me my mother's property.' And as he asked him, they came before King Solomon... ...laughing...

99. A similar, but much briefer, version of what appears to be the same
story is preserved in the *Testament of Solomon* 20 (C. C. McCown, ed.),
*The Testament of Solomon, Edited from Manuscripts at Mount Athos,
Bologna, Holkham Hall, Jerusalem, London, Milan, Paris and Vienna*, (Leipzig, J. C. Hinrichs, 1922), 60*–63*; trans. James H. Charlesworth,
ed., *The Old Testament Pseudepigrapha*, 2 vols. (Garden City, N.Y.:
Doubleday, 1983), 1:982–3.

122   THE DORMITION AND ASSUMPTION OF MARY

Ethiopic	Christian Palestinian Aramaic
because he had laughed. And Solomon said to him, 'What is this that you dare to laugh in our midst, in the midst of the courtroom,	...because he had laughed. And Solomon said to him, 'What is it that you dare too laugh...in the courtroom, ...[100]

Ethiopic

while I am judging all the people?' The demon said, 'Do you want to know why I laughed at this man, who is accusing his son over property? Because another day will not come [before] his son will die.' And Solomon said, 'O unclean spirit, how then do you know what is in the heavens?' And the demon said to him, 'We are condemned angels. God has become angry with us and placed us in the clouds. And we ascend, but we do not reach heaven: we knock on the door, and we see their places, because there are guards at the door, so that we do not enter the heights. And we hear them speaking. Perhaps we hear them saying that they will bring an order from the place of great power, so that they will go to a soul. And the righteous come to the door, and they speak with the doorkeepers, and they say to them, "Open for us, because we are going to a soul." And we go forth ahead of them. And we go and enter the house of that person, and we listen carefully for them. And when we have heard them, we laugh at them, since we know.' And when Solomon realized that this was true, he sent the man and his son to their house, saying to them, 'Come in seven days; go to your house, and in seven days, come and I

100. The verso side of this fragment is badly damaged, and it is not clear how the text correlates with any of the other extant versions. Nevertheless, it does seem that this fragment may preserve a variant version of the demon's conversation with Solomon.

THE BOOK OF MARY'S REPOSE

123

will pass judgment on you and your lawsuit.' And when they entered their house together, the boy became sick. And he wept and looked at his father, and he said to him, 'I am dying, and you have made me sad; and you[101] made me go up to King Solomon so that I would be judged as a child. And you did not remember the good words of my mother,

Ethiopic	Syriac
saying to you herself when she went forth from her body, "Do not act unjustly against my beloved son." And behold now, father, you have made me sad and you have brought me to death.'	'...saying to you, "Do not cause any grief for [my] beloved [son]," when she went forth from the world. And behold, you have made me sad unto death.'
81) And then his father wept, saying, 'I give you everything, my son, because you are a boy; for Abraham gave a sign to Levi, his father, so that he might know God.' And he said to his father, 'I beg of you, my father, if I have found favor before you, bring me a small amount of wealth and give it to those who are drawing out my soul. Then perhaps they will leave me alone.' And then his father went and brought exactly half of his property and placed it before his son. And	And after these things, his father wept over his son, saying to him, '[I give] you everything that I have, [my son]...there was...a boy, from the offspring of Abraham and his father Levi. And he gave his father a sign, so that he might know God.' And the son answered and said to this father, 'I beg of you, my father, if I have found favor in your eyes, bring a little of our earnings and give it to the one who is afflicting my soul, so that perhaps he will leave me alone, and I will not

101. MSS: "he."

Ethiopic

he cried out in a loud voice and said, 'I beg you who are drawing out my son's soul, take all these possessions, and leave my son's soul.' Then his son was severely afflicted. And he said to his father, 'My father, they have not withdrawn from me, while afflicting my soul. Perhaps these possessions are too little; bring then what will be sufficient for them. Because [he saw what] you have placed, he has afflicted me severely.'

82) Then his father got up and brought everything that he had, and he borrowed still more [adding?] to it. And he placed [it] before his beloved son and wept, saying, 'I beg you who are afflicting my son's soul, take everything, but leave me my son.' But the son was afflicted and began to die. And he turned and said to his father, 'You see that neither gold nor silver is ransom for my soul,

Syriac

die.' Then his father brought half of his property, and he placed it before his beloved son. And he answered and said in a loud voice, 'I beg of him who is afflicting my son's soul, take these possessions, and leave me my son's soul.' And after this, the boy was severely afflicted. And again he answered and said to his father, 'My father, the one who is afflicting my soul has not withdrawn from me; perhaps what you have brought him is far too little for him. And because he saw that it is too little for him, he has afflicted me severely.'

And his father got up and brought everything that he owned; and he brought with it other things [that] he borrowed. And he placed it before his beloved son, and said in a loud voice, 'I beg of him who is afflicting the soul of my son, take everything that I have, and leave me only my son.' But the boy was severely afflicted. And when he was near death, he turned to his

THE BOOK OF MARY'S REPOSE

125

Ethiopic

but only a heart that is sincere toward God. Arise then, father, and take these possessions, and give to the poor and orphans, and build houses for strangers, † so that they will not pay me interest † [?]. And we will find rest for our souls.' And saying this, when he had spoken, he died.

83) And his father did as his son had ordered. And eight days passed, and he did not return to King Solomon, according to the agreed time, which gave him seven days. Nine days passed, and he did not come. And Solomon sent for them, saying, 'Why have you not come, so that I will deliver your judgment to you, as I said to you.' And he said to him, 'My lord, do you not know that our agreed time was seven days, and that my unfortunate son is dead? And I gave all my possessions on his behalf, so

Syriac

father and said to him, 'My father, you see that neither gold, nor silver, nor anything else can be given for my life, except for a heart that is sincere toward God. Arise then, my father, and take these possessions, and build with them places for strangers, so that they may enter into them, and dwell and rest in them. And also give from them to the poor and orphans, and we will find rest for our souls.' The son said these things, and his life ended.

And his father did everything that his son had told him. And when eight days had passed, and they did not come to King Solomon, according to the agreement that they had made before him, that after seven days they would go to him. And the eighth [day] passed, and the ninth, and they did not go to King Solomon. The king sent after them, saying, 'Why have you not come, so that I will settle [things] among you, as I said to you?' And the boy's father answered and said, 'My lord,

126 THE DORMITION AND ASSUMPTION OF MARY

Ethiopic	Syriac
that he would not grieve. But I have done everything as he ordered.' And then Solomon understood what he said: 'The demons know what will happen. Because of this, people say, "We are the ones at whom they laugh," not knowing what it is that will come upon them.'"	behold, it is eight days since my son went forth from the world. For if I had known that he was dying, I would have given everything that I had to my son, so as not to cause him grief. But I have done everything that he said to me.' And when Solomon heard this from the man, he said, 'The demons know what will happen. Because of this, humans say, "They are not the ones who laugh at us," because they know the things that are said by them.'"

The Apostles Compare their Preaching.

Ethiopic	Syriac
84) Then the apostles agreed with what had been said by Paul, for they proposed that he speak to them again, so that he would not ask them to reveal the mystery to him. And all the apostles turned to him and said, "Our brother Paul, speak to us with your pleasant words, because God has sent you to us to gladden us for these three days." And Paul answered and said, "Peter,	Then the apostles agreed with what Paul said, for they were asking him to speak with them again, so that he would not press them, and they would not reveal to him the glorious mysteries that our Savior taught. And again all the apostles answered and said to Paul, "Our brother Paul, speak with us in words, because we are listening to you with delight. For our Lord has sent you to

THE BOOK OF MARY'S REPOSE

Ethiopic

[since] you are not willing to reveal the greatness of Christ our Savior to me, tell me, when you go forth to preach, what will you teach, so that I will teach from your doctrine."

85) And Peter said to him, "My brother Paul, this word that you have spoken is good. Because you want to learn about the doctrine that we will teach; listen, and I will tell you. When I have gone to preach, I will say that whoever does not fast every day will not see God." And Paul said to Peter, "Our father Peter, what is this word that you have spoken? For when they hear, they will rise up and kill us, because they worship gods and do not believe in God, nor in fasting." And Paul turned to John and said to him, "Tell your doctrine too, our father John, and we will teach thus."

Syriac

us to gladden us for these three days." And Paul answered and said to Peter, "since you were not willing to reveal the great things of Jesus to me, tell me, when you go forth, what will you preach and teach, so that I too will know how to teach with your doctrine."

Peter said to him, "My brother Paul, this word that you have spoken is good. Since you have asked to know and hear what we are going to teach and preach to people, listen, and I will tell you. When I go forth to preach, I will say that anyone who does not fast all of his days will not see God." Paul said to Peter, "Our father Peter, what is this word that you have spoken? For they will not hear your word, and they will rise up and kill you, because they are wicked and unacquainted with God or fasting." And again Paul turned to John and said to him, "Tell us your doctrine too, our father John, so that I too may teach and preach thus."

128   THE DORMITION AND ASSUMPTION OF MARY

Ethiopic

86) And John said, "When I have gone forth to teach, I will say that if there is anyone who is not continent until his repose, he will not see God." And Paul answered and said to John, "What is this word? For they will not believe this word that you speak, because they are people who worship trees and stones. If they hear this from us, they will stone us." And again Paul turned to Andrew and he said to him, "Tell me your opinion too, our father Andrew: as Peter thinks and believes that he is a great bishop, and John believes that he is a virgin, and because of this, they speak heavy words." And Andrew said to him, "When I have gone forth to preach, I will say that whoever does not leave his father and mother, and his brothers and his children, and his possessions,[102] he has not followed God, and he will not be able to see him." And Paul said to Andrew, "[The words] of Peter

Syriac

John said to him, "When I go forth to teach and preach, I will say that anyone who is not a virgin all of his days will not be able to see God." And Paul answered and said to John, "Our father John, what are these words to people who do not know God? For if people who worship stones and trees hear these things from you, they will throw us in prison and lock us up." And again Paul turned to Andrew and said to him, "Our father Andrew, tell us what your opinion is too, so that I too may teach and preach [thus], lest perhaps Peter should think that he is great and a bishop, and John also be proud that he is a virgin, and because of these things they have spoken grand things." And Andrew said to Paul, "When I go forth to preach, I will say that everyone who does not leave father and mother, and brothers and sisters, and children and houses, and everything that he has, and

102. Cf. Luke 14.26.

THE BOOK OF MARY'S REPOSE

Ethiopic

and John are much lighter than yours, Andrew, because you have separated everyone from the earth in one moment. What is this word of yours? † For at this time there is no one who can bear upon him the burden that he has placed on an infant, Andrew." † [103] And Peter answered, as before, and said, "Paul, beloved of our soul, tell us how you would want us to preach."

87) And Paul said to them, "What you hear from me, this I advise you to do, so that we may ascertain something that will be possible for people to bear, because they are just beginning with these things.[104] Let us say, 'Let each man remain with his wife, because of adultery; and let each woman remain with her husband.' And let us establish a fast for them, [and] they will not fast again in the week.

Syriac

go forth after our Lord, he will not be able to see God." And Paul said to Andrew, "Our father Andrew, the words of Peter and John are light compared with yours, for you have separated everyone from the earth in one moment. For who will hear your words at this time and place a heavy burden on himself?" And Peter and Andrew answered and said to Paul, "Paul, friend of our soul, tell us how you want us to go forth and preach."

Paul said to them, "If you will listen to me, do these things, and let us think of things that they will be able to do, because they are new and do not know the truth. Let us say these things to them: 'Let every man take his wife,' so that they will not commit adultery; and 'let a woman take her husband, that she may not commit adultery.' And let us establish one or two days [of fasting] in the week for them,

103. The sentence is very difficult, and its meaning is unclear.
104. Literally, "because they have them from the beginning."

130 THE DORMITION AND ASSUMPTION OF MARY

Ethiopic

And let us not give them doubt [about] fasting, lest they waver and turn away. But if they have fasted today and are a little weary, they will still persevere, saying, 'Tomorrow we will [not] fast again.' And if they come to mealtime, and they have rested, they will give to the poor, saying, 'Why this fast, which comes,' and they will ponder God in their hearts. And let us also say to them, 'Let the one who is not able fast until the second hour, and the one who is average until the ninth, and the perfect one until evening.' And when we have trampled on their wings a little, we will know that they are able to bear this. And then we can give them milk to drink, and we will tell them the glorious things." Then the apostles murmured, not agreeing with the words in Paul's advice.

88) Reading for the 16th Day: The coming of our Lord

Syriac

and let us not be too hard on them, lest they become negligent and turn away. But if they fast today and are a little weary, they will persevere for the time and say, 'Tomorrow we will not fast.' And if they come to the time when they eat, and they find a poor person and give to him, they will say, 'Why do we fast, if we do not give to the poor,' and they will know God in their hearts. And let us also say to them, 'Let the one who is weary fast until the sixth hour, and the one who is able, until the ninth, and the one who is still able, until evening.' And when we have given them to drink as with milk, and we have turned them to us, then we will tell them the great and glorious things, words that will be useful to them." [105] Then all of the apostles murmured and would not agree with Paul's words.

And as all of the apostles were sitting in front of the en-

105. Cf. 1 Cor 3.2.

THE BOOK OF MARY'S REPOSE   131

Ethiopic	Syriac

to his disciples, so that they would bring the holy one's body into Paradise.[106]

And while Paul was sitting at the entrance and speaking with them, behold, the Lord Jesus came from heaven with Michael. And he sat among the apostles, while they were denouncing Paul's words. And he said, "Greetings Peter, the bishop, and John, the virgin: you are my inheritance. Greetings Paul, who advises good things. Truly I say to you that your advice will not be understood, neither Peter's, nor John's, nor Andrew's, except for Paul's: now all of these words will be understood. And I see the whole world in a net, and that Paul will find them in nets. Then all of your words will be made known on the last day." And our Lord turned to Paul, "My brother Paul, do not be sad because the apostles have not revealed the glorious mystery to you. And to whom has it been revealed in doctrine,

trance to Mary's tomb, disputing Paul's words, behold, our Lord Jesus Christ came from heaven with the angel Michael. And he sat among the apostles as they were debating over Paul's word. And Jesus answered and said, "Greetings Peter, the bishop, and greetings John, the virgin, you who are my heirs. Greetings Paul, the advisor of good things. Truly I say to you, Peter, that your advice was always destructive: yours and Andrew's and John's. But I say to you that you should receive that of Paul. For I see that the whole world will be caught in Paul's net, and it will precede them. And then, after these things, your words will become known at the end of time." And the Lord turned to Paul and said to him, "My brother Paul, do not be sad that the apostles, your fellows, will not reveal the glorious mysteries to you. For to them I have revealed the things that are

---

106. MS A: "The 18th Day: Reading."

132   THE DORMITION AND ASSUMPTION OF MARY

Ethiopic	Syriac
that which I will teach in the heavens?"	on earth; but I will teach you the things that are in heaven.

Mary and the Apostles Visit the Places of the Damned.

Ethiopic	Syriac
89) Then our Lord made a sign to Michael, and Michael answered in the voice of faithful angels. And they descended on three clouds, and the number of angels on a cloud appeared to be ten thousand angels in the presence of the Savior. And our Lord said to them, "Let them bring the body of Mary into the clouds." And when her body had been brought, our Lord said to the apostles that they should come to him. And they ascended into the cloud, and they were singing with the voice of angels. And our Lord told the clouds to go to the East, to the region of Paradise. And when they arrived together in Paradise, they placed Mary's body beside the tree of life. And they brought her soul and placed it in her body. And our Lord sent his angels to their places.	And after these things our Lord made a sign to Michael, and Michael answered in the voice of a mighty angel. And the angels descended on three clouds; and the number of angels on each cloud was 1000 angels, singing praises before Jesus. And our Lord said to Michael, "Let them bring Mary's body to the clouds." And when Mary's body entered the clouds, our Lord said to the apostles, "Come near to the clouds." And when they came into the clouds, they were singing with the voice of angels. And our Lord told the clouds to depart for the gate of Paradise. And when they entered Paradise, Mary's body went to the tree of life. And they brought her soul and made it enter into her body. And immediately our Lord sent the angels away to their places.

THE BOOK OF MARY'S REPOSE

133

Ethiopic	Syriac
90) Then the apostles said to the Savior, "Lord, did you not say to us when you were with us and we besought you that we would see the torments?" And he said to them, "Is this what you want? Then be patient on this day of her body's departure, and I will make you ascend, and I will show it to you."	And after these things the apostles said to our Lord, "Lord, you said to us, when you were with us, and when we persuaded you, that we would see Mary's grave, that it would be good for us. And you said to us, 'If you want to see this, wait until the day of Mary's departure, and I will lead you, and you will see the depths.'"

The terrible place
of torment which
the Disciples begged
our Lord to see.

And while he was speaking with the apostles, our Lord made a sign with his eyes to the clouds, and they snatched up the apostles and Mary and Michael with our Lord. And they led them to where the sun sets, and they left them there. And our Lord spoke with the mighty angels, and the earth leaped up, and Gehenna was opened. And the Lord gave place to the apostles, so that they could see,

And when these things had been said by the blessed apostles, our Lord made a sign with his eyes, and a cloud snatched up the apostles and Mary and Michael and our Lord with them, and it brought them to where the sun sets and left them there. And our Lord spoke with the angels of the pit, and the earth leaped up, and the pit was revealed in the midst of the earth. And our Lord gave place to the apostles,

134 THE DORMITION AND ASSUMPTION OF MARY

Ethiopic	Syriac
as they wanted. And they saw the damned people. And when they saw Michael,[107] they wept with great tears. And they said, "Michael, our angel Michael, Michael our king, Michael our archangel, who intercedes every day on our behalf. Have you forgotten us now forever? Why do you not beseech [the Lord] on our behalf?" And the apostles and Mary fell down from the distress of those in the torments, and they fell on their faces.	so that they could see, as they wanted. And when they approached and looked into the pit, those who were in the pit saw Michael. And there was great weeping and groaning; and they answered and said to Michael, "Michael the archangel, Michael our strength, Michael, the captain of the host, were you victorious today in your struggle on our behalf? For you have forgotten us for all this time. Why do you not beseech the Lord on our behalf, that he gives us a little relief from torment?" And as soon as Mary and the apostles saw, they fell to the ground from the distress of those in the pit.
91) And the Lord raised them up, saying, "My apostles, arise, my disciples; for I told you that you would not be able to endure this, and you were not able to endure this. What if I had brought you to	And our Lord raised them up and said to them, "O you apostles, arise and learn; for I told you before that you would not be able to endure when you have seen these things. For if I had brought you to the

107. Compare sections 90–94, 99–100 with the *Apocalypse of Paul* 43–4 (JAMES, *Apocrypha Anecdota*, 34–6) and also with identical scene in the early Irish Dormition apocrypha and in the conclusion to a single manuscript of the Latin *Transitus Mariae* translated in this volume.

THE BOOK OF MARY'S REPOSE

Ethiopic

the interior place, where no human being is known—what would have happened to you?" Then Michael spoke to those who were in the torments, to those who were weeping, "The Lord lives. He lives who is worthy. He lives who will soon judge the living and the dead. He lives who will judge the damned. And there are twelve hours in the day, and twelve hours in the night, which are the number of psalms [?]. And when each of the psalms is finished, those who offer up the sacrifices fall and worship the good God, interceding on behalf of all creation and all humanity."

92) And the angels of the waters besought, saying, "Have mercy on them, Father, so that the fruit of the waters will be abundant for the sake of the human race, because they are your image and likeness. Because of this, I beseech you to hear me, your angel, that there be mercy upon the waters, that they will be abundant."

Syriac

outer place where there is not even a human breath, and where there are many torments that differ from one another, what would have become of you?" Then Michael spoke to those who were in the pit, and he said to them, "My children, the Lord lives, the Lord lives. He lives who will soon judge the dead and living. He lives who has power over all creatures. For there are twelve hours in the day, and twelve in the night, and these are numbered with praise. The sacrifice ascends to God, and the angels fall down and worship his grace, and they intercede on behalf of all creation and all humanity."

And the angel who is placed over the waters approached and besought God, saying, "Let springs of water be abundant for the sake of the human race, because they are your image and likeness, Lord. Because of this, I beseech you to hear me, I who am your minister. Let your mercy be upon the waters and let them be abundant in all the earth.". . .

136   THE DORMITION AND ASSUMPTION OF MARY

Ethiopic

And the angels of the winds worshipped and said, "We beseech you, the good God, for the sake of humanity, let the winds blow, and let your mercy be abundant upon them, because of the fruit of the trees and because of that which sprouts meat [?]" And the angels of the clouds also worshipped, saying, "We beseech you, the good God, do not abandon humanity, so that the clouds will overshadow them, and we will cease revealing to them. But let your goodness cause us to serve them." And many angels were terrified on account of [these] people.

93) And Michael, who is over every soul, said, "I repeatedly fell down, beseeching at every hour, but all your labor is as nothing, because you did not keep the commandments that were given to you." And Michael went and saw for himself the folly of those who had been seduced, and he too fell before the Lord Jesus and said, "I beseech you Lord, give [108] the people rest from this torment, and do not make me look at them and think that I have condemned them."

94) Then Jesus made Michael rise, saying, "Michael, my chosen one, rest from your weeping. Do you love them more than the one who created them, or will you be more merciful to them than the one who gave them breath? And before you asked on their behalf, Michael, I did not spare my blood, but I gave it for their sake. O Michael, was there not one who remained in pain, having abandoned the pleasure of Jerusalem? I was conceived in the womb for their sake, to give them rest, and I wept before my Father. And you, Michael, for one moment you have besought my Father on their behalf. But my blood has not rested, beseeching the Father day and night on their behalf. And when the Father wants to show them

108. MSS: "Lord who gives..."

THE BOOK OF MARY'S REPOSE   137

mercy from torment, they will be returned to the right hand. And I saw those who are in the interior place, who are immersed in blood, and my mercy has been turned away from them. And the cherubim are disturbed by the weeping and petitions, and they clap their hands together from my petition to the Father on behalf of the souls of those who are in torment. And the Father turned and said to me, 'I desire mercy, and my mercy is great, but what is placed before you is as great as your blood.' Now then, Michael, arise and we will show the apostles what is."

The Punishments of the Damned and Mary's Intercession.

95) And when Michael got up, the Lord said, "Arise, apostles, and see what is."[109] And then they saw a man in whose mouth was a flaming razor,[110] which burned, and he was not able to speak. Then Mary and the apostles cried out, saying, "Who is this man who is in torment?" And he said, "He is a reader, who spoke glorious words, and he did not do [them]. Because of this, he is in great torment." And then they saw another person who had been led from afar, with a great punishment of fire in his hand, and he was not allowed to speak. And young children were biting him on his sides, with many others. And the apostles said, "Who is this one who does not receive mercy, while there is fire in his hands, and they bring him and bite him?"

109. The following section (94–8) should be compared with the *Apocalypse of Paul* 34–6 (James, *Apocrypha Anecdota*, 29–30).

110. Arras suggests "palm" as a translation for this otherwise unknown word: ARRAS, *De Transitu*, 1:101 (Lat). Comparison with the *Apocalypse of Paul* 36 (JAMES, *Apocrypha Anecdota*, 30) very strongly suggests that it is indeed meant to translate "razor."

138   THE DORMITION AND ASSUMPTION OF MARY

96) And the Savior said, "This is the one who said, 'I am a deacon,' and he took the glorious blood and did not care for it as he should have. † And [111] those who eat him are those who perished and did not see; those who did what they should not have, and they returned from the temple and did not have mercy; those who do not sin from now, but who see them who have no sin, because they were serving in sin, and this [will be?] with them until they finish their sin. And for this reason they come and eat here, as they eat them."†

97) And then we saw another person who was bound in torment, and [there were] two [who] kept him in darkness. And they were striking him in his face with round stones as *hobet*,[112] and they did not have mercy on him. And they did not turn away, but they were striking him from the right and the left. And Mary said, "Lord, who is this who has a great punishment, more terrible than the others, and he receives no mercy at all? Why are they beating him with round stones as *hobet*, and his bones do not fall to the earth?" And he[113] said to her, "Every person has sinned: the one whom the two from the darkness beat with rocks in his face, how will they not be as dust? But he knows the affliction of human flesh, and if he gets up from this, a stone will be a great and horrible affliction upon him, and he will not be dissolved."

98) And the Savior said to her, "Mary, know who this is, and then I will tell you how his form[114] is not dissolved. This is a priest whom

111. The remainder of this section is very corrupt and cannot be translated well.

112. This word's meaning is unknown.

113. MSS: "I."

114. Literally, "his beauty/goodness."

THE BOOK OF MARY'S REPOSE   139

Ethiopic	Syriac	CPA[115]

the poor, destitute, and afflicted trusted, and he ate the memorials and first offerings; and not only by himself, but he gave them to those who were not worthy. And because of this they beat him in his face. And if you want to know how his face is not dissolved, it is because he was an infidel from the place of believing. And his soul will not die, and it will be in torment while not dying or being dissolved."

...other[116] men and women, these who did something without humility and justifying something. But the men, however, abandoned the marriage that God had appointed for all human beings and used it in a way that was not natural, because they left their wives, and one by one they went into violent intercourse.[117] And the women...do this [for] which abandoned their work, hatred of pagans, and from them... they were lying down as with their husbands. Because of this they also will receive eternal torment."

...and the poor. And he also ate the memorials and first offerings; and not only by himself, but he gave [them] to another who was not worthy. Therefore, he is hit in his face. And if you want to know how his face is not smashed, it is because he struck from inside the [sacred] place. The soul, which is not destroyed, is in torment on account of its dissolution."

115. i.e. Christian Palestinian Aramaic.
116. The Syriac fragments are highly divergent in this section.
117. Cf. Rom 1.26–7?

140 THE DORMITION AND ASSUMPTION OF MARY

Ethiopic	Syriac	CPA
99) And when Jesus had said this, he gave them a way by which they could arise from the torment. And the Savior looked at Michael, and he separated himself from them, and he left Mary and the apostles, so that they would understand them. Then those who were in the torments cried out and said, "Mary, we beseech you, Mary, light and the mother of light; Mary, life and mother of the apostles; Mary, golden lamp, you who carries every righteous lamp; Mary, our master[118] and	These are the things that Jesus said to them. He gave them a way to pass from this and to be saved, because they saw these things. And Jesus and Michael were each taken away from them. And he left Mary and the apostles on the earth so that they would understand them. And at once those in torment cried out and sought intercession from Mary and said, "Mary light and mother of the light; Mary life and mother of life; Mary lampstand of gold who bears the one bearing all; Mary	When the Lord Jesus said this, he gave them a way to turn away from the torment. And he looked and [gave] a glance, and the Savior and Michael removed themselves and left Mary and the apostles so that they would understand them. And at once those who were in torment were crying out with supplications to Mary and saying, "Mary, light and the mother of light; Mary, life and the mother of life; Mary, lampstand of truth; Mary [master] and the mother of our Master; Mary, queen

118. Although the form here is feminine, "mistress" and "lady" both have connotations in English that make them problematic for translation here. Although "master" is often used as a gendered term in English, it is here employed in a neuter sense. In other words, while "master" most appropriately expresses in English the meaning of the

THE BOOK OF MARY'S REPOSE 141

Ethiopic	Syriac	CPA
the mother of our Master; Mary, our queen, beseech your son to give us a little rest." And others spoke thus, "Peter, Andrew, and John, who have become apostles." For they knew that each of them had been appointed as priests over the cities. And	master and the mother of the Master; Mary queen and the mother of our King and God, intercede on our behalf with your son that he gives us a little rest." And on account of these things they spoke to Peter and Andrew and John and	and the mother of our King, beseech your son to let us rest a little". And others spoke thus to Peter and John and Andrew, the apostles. And they said to them, "Indeed, each of them recognized one who practiced my words in every town." And they

Ethiopic and Aramaic words used here, it should not be taken as suggesting the use of masculine forms in reference to the Virgin in the ancient text. In a recent article, Christa Müller-Kessler has criticized this translation for following the "fashion to be politically correct," maintaining that "The societies at the time of this text translation were not aware of such modern concerns with gender issues." Christa MÜLLER-KESSLER, "Three Early Witnesses of the 'Dormition Of Mary' in Christian Palestinian Aramaic from the Cairo Genizah (Taylor-Schechter Collection) and the New Finds in St. Catherine's Monastery," *Apocrypha* 29 (2018), 69–95, 72 n. 15. Yet this remark largely misses the point. The above translation is not so much inspired by an effort to be "politically correct," but rather to find a translation that in fact captures the meaning of the original language for the readers and producers of these texts. "Lady" in North American English has primary connotations that simply do not fit the notions of such language in Late Antiquity. Indeed, while "master" is certainly not ideal, faute de mieux it stands in effectively for "*despoina*," whose sense is not satisfactorily represented in English by "Lady." Likewise, it serves to highlight that both Mary and her son are called by identical titles, the only difference being the feminine or masculine form of that title.

142   THE DORMITION AND ASSUMPTION OF MARY

Ethiopic	Syriac	CPA
they said to them, "Where did you place our doctrine that we taught you? For the day is still coming when Christ will appear to you; and the Lord has appointed everything. And after everything we fear God and all of his commandments." And they were very ashamed and could not reply to the apostles.	all of the apostles. "What do you say about these things?"	said to them, "You from the apostles, where did you place these doctrines, those that were given to you? For until now there was no time that they could be forgotten on account of us. Until now it is fourteen years from when Christ appeared to us. And see, our Lord appointed them over all. And after these things, we feared God." But these from the majority... were ashamed and could not respond to the apostles.
100) The Savior arose and came to the place of torment, and he said to them, "Where did you place what	And immediately our Savior appeared to them, and he came to the place of torment and he said to them,[119]	Then the Savior rose in it and came to the place of torment, and he said to them, "Where did you bring what

119. Müller-Kessler reads "to you" here, but having studied the manuscript myself—it is extremely difficult to read—I suppose that "to them" is the more likely reading. Indeed, the passage that

THE BOOK OF MARY'S REPOSE 143

Ethiopic	Syriac	CPA
they taught you? Did you not hear everything that they said?	"Where did you proclaim what was taught to you? Did you not hear everything that I denied while they seized me and this saying?	was transmitted to him? They did not hear of what you endured, from being tormented, scorned without lying. Oh, it was not against...

Ethiopic	Syriac
And he did not answer, and they spat at him and did not listen. Am I not able, with a wink of my eye, to smash heaven and earth to pieces, onto the sinners who have sinned against me? But I [120] have not done [this], in order to show you my plan, and so that you will know that you will go just like them. Nevertheless, you have not done this, except for their condemnation, which you have done. You [were] reviled,[121] you persevered, and you were oppressed.	And I was treated with contempt and was not considering it, for was I not able, the Lord, with a wink of the eye, to turn the earth upon its inhabitants and upon the sinners who have sinned against me. But I have not done these things, because it was against them and...their signs thus will come. You will continue this...these things you did not do unless it has come upon your own hearing and brought greatness. Because of this, lo, you will be repaid as you did

follows is very garbled, and this may also reflect difficulties in reading the manuscript, although the Ethiopic here is also corrupt and difficult to understand.

120. MSS: "you."

121. The form here is active, but in light of the following verbs it seems that the best translation is passive.

144 THE DORMITION AND ASSUMPTION OF MARY

Ethiopic	Syriac
Because of this you will be repaid. And what joy have I prepared for you!† Because of the tears of Michael, my holy apostles, and my mother Mary, because they have come and they have seen you, I have given you nine hours[122] of rest on the Lord's day."	to them. Thus, the grace. . .for you. But because of the tears of Michael and my holy apostles and my mother Mary, who have come and have seen you, and she persuaded us on your behalf so that you will have a respite and a day of rest for the day and night of the first day."

Mary and the Apostles Visit Paradise.

Ethiopic	Syriac
101) Then he made a sign to the mighty angels with his eyes, and he made it appear as the earth. And then something unexpected happened, and the apostles came to Paradise, and they sat under the tree of life. And the soul of Abraham was there, and the soul of Isaac, and the soul of Jacob, along with many others [whom] the Savior had brought from death to life by his resurrection and placed in the Paradise of the living. David was there with his harp, making music, and Elizabeth was there with them, although	And after these things, the Lord gave a sign to the angels to open the earth, and they were cast within. The apostles went to Paradise, and they were by the nearby tree of life. And Abraham was there, and Isaac and Jacob with all the others, and after the Savior. . . from among the dead and also hid them in Paradise as they were in their lives. And David was there with his harp, and he was playing on his harp all the time. And also Elizabeth was there, the mother of John the Baptist. . .places for women

122. MS A: "three days."

THE BOOK OF MARY'S REPOSE   145

Ethiopic	Syriac

there was another place for women. And the Magi were there, those who went up because of the Savior, and the little children were there, because of the Savior. And we also saw great and wonderful things, namely, all the souls of the good people who had gone forth from their bodies, all those who went forth and are reclining in the bosom of Abraham, Isaac, and Jacob.

...men who were there.. standing fast because of the Savior, for there were also there small children, who on account of the Lord, on account of the Savior were beholding and seeing how many wonders of the ways he was doing from his [wo]rks, indeed, all the souls of the Christians who have gone forth from this world before all things, those who were reclining in the bosom of Abraham, Isaac, and Jacob. And David offered praise with his harp.

102) And we also saw Enoch and the olive tree, [which was there?] at the time when Enoch cut off [a branch] from its foliage and gave [the branch] to the dove, so that it would take [the branch] to Noah on the ark.[123] For in the days of the

And we also saw Enoch and the branch of the olive tree, ...
...Enoch...

...the dove...

...in the days of the flood...
Noah sent the dove to Paradise

123. Richard BAUCKHAM, *The Fate of the Dead: Studies on Jewish and Christian Apocalypses*, Supplements to Novum Testamentum, 93 (Leiden: Brill, 1998), 344, says the following about this tradition: "The tradition that the olive branch came from Eden is found in rabbinic literature: GenRab 33:6; LevRab 31:10; CantRab 1:15:4; 4:1:2. That Enoch was in Eden at the time of the Flood, from which it was protected, is found in Jubilees 4:23–24. [This] text seems to be unique in connecting these traditions."

146 THE DORMITION AND ASSUMPTION OF MARY

Ethiopic

flood, Noah sent the dove to Paradise to ask his father's ancestor.[124] And God had mercy on the earth and looked upon it. And when the dove went forth, it asked Enoch, and it found his words severe, and it returned to Noah, with nothing. And Noah sent it a second time, and it went and petitioned Enoch, and it found that God had had mercy on the earth. And he cut off a branch from the olive tree and gave [it] to [the dove], saying, "Take the sign to Noah and say to him, 'This olive branch is a sign and is what we saw on a tree.'"

Syriac

and asked for his elder, the father of his father. Our Lord also saved the earth with his hands, because the dove went to the earth which had no earth. And when it went, it asked Enoch, and there...and it returned to Noah, having nothing on it. And Noah sent it again a second time. Immediately it went and asked Enoch. And he saw that God had saved the earth and it remained. That branch from the olive tree was a sign for him. And he said to him, "He brought the dove to him...since he heard them, the trees, that were not with you."

The Devil Demands to Test Paul before he Learns the Mysteries.

Ethiopic

103) And the Lord said to them, "Do not be amazed at this. And if you have prepared yourselves on the earth, then will you find a better inheritance. And again I say to you, remain here with Mary and

Syriac

And he said to the mourners, "Do not be amazed at these things, which you have prepared for yourselves on the earth, and an inheritance of virtues from these things that you did not plant. And again

124. i.e. Enoch: cf. Gen 5.22–9.

THE BOOK OF MARY'S REPOSE   147

Ethiopic

with all those who are here until I have made Paul ascend and shown him everything, just as I told him." And the Lord ascended onto a cloud, and he called Paul to his side, while making him ascend onto the cloud with him. And the Devil cried out in the heights, saying, "Jesus, Son of God, who came into the world and preached before Jerusalem and gave a commandment to your apostles that they preach to the whole earth in Jerusalem, how do you make this one named Paul ascend, before he contends with me, in your greatness, and defeats me? And it is fitting that you have shown everything to the twelve, since they were worthy, and they have contended with me and defeated me. But this one has not contended with me and has not defeated me. How do you make him ascend? Let him come then: first he will contend with me, and if he defeats me, bring him and show him everything."

104) Then our Lord said to Paul, "My brother Paul, prepare

Syriac

he said to us thus, . . .and my whole body. . .and until I bring. . .to him what I said to him." And the Lord ascended onto a cloud, and he called Paul to him. And he made him ascend on a cloud to heaven. And then Satan went to you to the place and said, "O Son, the Son of God, who came into the world and persuaded us. . .preached. . .the goodness. . .in all creation. . .to the Lord in the hands. . .them as. . .

. . .this one named Paul, who. . . before he contends with me. . . is fitting. . .

. . .because they contended. . .

. . .my body. . .and introduce him
And he will contend with me and. . .made him ascend and showed him everything.

And again he went to my brother Paul as he was not

148   THE DORMITION AND ASSUMPTION OF MARY

<table>
<tr><td align="center">Ethiopic</td><td align="center">Syriac</td></tr>
<tr><td>yourself for battle, so that he</td><td>prepared for battle with him…</td></tr>
<tr><td>will find nothing against you."</td><td>found for him…</td></tr>
</table>

Ethiopic

And Paul said, "I do not know him, but I know that I must contend with him." And our Lord said to him, "I will send Peter with you, and he will teach you to fight with him." Then he descended to Paradise, where the apostles were, and our Lord said to Peter, "Arise and go with Paul and teach him to fight with the enemy, because he asked that you fight with him." And Peter said, "Lord, where will we fight with him again: on a mountain or in the middle of a crowd?" And he said, "In the middle of a crowd, so that they will know his affliction and his shame. You will fight with him where the cloud sets you down."

The Contendings of Peter and Paul in Rome.

105) And a cloud took them up and set them down in the midst of the royal palace in Rome, as the eunuchs of the king of Rome were sitting and his concubines and his chamberlain were placed around [him]. And when the king saw them, he was troubled, and he ran and went with his eunuchs and with the scepter[125] that was in his hands. Then the king held forth his scepter over them so that they would not strike them and would not lift their hands against his eunuchs. Then the king said to them, "Who are you and from where have you come and how did you deceitfully enter my palace in this place,

---

125. The word here is unusual and does not clearly reflect anything in the lexica. We have followed here Arras' interpretation, although he does not provide an explanation for this translation, but presumably it is in light of the scepter in the following sentence.

THE BOOK OF MARY'S REPOSE 149

which no person has ever seen? Even my own daughter does not have permission to enter to me unless she asks in advance. But you, however, have entered without cause. Who spoke to you? Tell me, then, the things that I have asked you."

106) Then Peter said, "Would you speak, or should I?" And Paul said, "You speak, my father Peter." Then Peter spoke, saying, "If you want to know who we are, I am the one who swore an oath to be manifest to you." [126] And he said, "This is Paul of Tarsus in Cilicia. And if you want to know who we are, listen and we will teach you about the one who was born for our sake, who did not deceive us, who came into our midst for our sake. We are of Jesus the Son of God, who rules the universe, who does not waver, who destroys every kingdom and is able to save those who hear him and submit to him."

107) And the king said to them, "And how can I know that you have spoken the truth or not?" [127] And Peter said, "Perhaps you have not heard the wonders that he worked in Israel: the lame walked, he made the blind see, he made the deaf hear, he made the mute speak, and he cast out demons and cleansed the lepers, he who turned water into wine and from five loaves of bread blessed and gave to us, and we gave it to the people, and they ate and were satisfied, 5,000 people, and we put aside 12 baskets from pieces that were left over. Our own eyes saw this and our hands also served. And there were other wonders that he worked: he rebuked the winds. And you would have heard of many others and signs."

108) And the king said to them, "Much is great that I have heard from you, and if it is true, I will put you to the test. I have a daughter, and a bird plucked out her right eye. And I brought all the physicians of my kingdom, and they were not able to

126. The meaning of the text is not clear here and is likely corrupt.
127. Literally, "spoken the truth which is not."

150   THE DORMITION AND ASSUMPTION OF MARY

heal her, because the pupil [128] of her eye has been destroyed."
And Peter said to him, "Send and bring her to me."

Ethiopic	Christian Palestinian Aramaic
And then the king sent four of his servants,[129] and they brought her. And her mother also came with her. And when Peter saw the pupil of her eye, he knew in his spirit that the bird had plucked the eye out on account of sin.	And the king sent four of his servants and guards, and they brought the girl and her mother with her. And when Peter saw the pupil of the eye, he knew through the Holy Spirit that sin was in her: on account of it the bird had plucked her eye out.
109) And he said to the king, "Tell me her sin, on account of which the bird plucked out your daughter's eye." And the king was ashamed to tell him, because her mother was standing by his daughter. And he said to Peter, "If you are	Peter said, "Regarding her injuries, for us this is the reason that the bird plucked out your daughter's eye." [130] The king began to speak, because the girl's mother was standing there. And he said to Peter, "If you are a physician, come, and if

128. In Greek, the word for "pupil," *korē*, also means "girl" or "daughter," thus making a pun in the Greek original: both the girl and her eye have been destroyed. I thank Janet Spittler for this observation.

129. The word here is again uncertain and not in the lexica, and so we have followed Arras in translating "servants," which is confirmed in the Christian Palestinian Aramaic.

130. The edition of the Christian Palestinian Aramaic text is a mess here: the footnotes do not match up with the translation above, and as they stand, they appear to make inaccurate comparisons between the Aramaic and Ethiopic versions as well as the Aramaic text.

THE BOOK OF MARY'S REPOSE 151

Ethiopic

going to heal her, then heal her, and if you will not heal her, why am I hearing such words? For I have brought many physicians to my daughter, and I applied many cures, and they have not been able to heal her, and I have not heard such words from them." And Peter said to him, "This is why they have not been able to heal her, because they were not informed, since you did not make it known to them. Our healing, however, is that which was given to us by the master physician. This is his word, which our Savior taught us. Since you did not want to confess her sin to us, behold, I will tell it to you." And when he did not decide, then Peter said to Paul. "Raise your hands to pray." And Peter said, "You have assembled every creature and do not allow them to be scattered, and you made the earth and everything on it with might, you who have called out what is not as that which is, and everything is at your

Christian Palestinian Aramaic

you are not, why am I hearing such words? For I have brought many physicians to my daughter, and they employed every cure, and everything that was requested they did, and they did not heal her. And these are words that they did not say." And Peter said to him, "Therefore, whoever asks, he cannot heal her, because they are also not able to speak. Our healing, however, these were given to us by the master physician. These are the words that our Savior taught us. Since then you are ashamed to confess your sins, behold, make it so that there will be for us what he did not want." And then Peter said to Paul, "Raise your hands to pray, and this is what they will pray." And Peter said, "God, the one who assembled the creatures and does not allow them to be scattered, he who made the earth and everything on it with might and power, the one called out when there was nothing, and everything was done by your

152   THE DORMITION AND ASSUMPTION OF MARY

Ethiopic	Christian Palestinian Aramaic
command. And we alone have remained in your hand, you who search out what is hidden, and there is nothing that is impossible before the mystery of Jesus. Hear us who cry out to you and make this king know that there is nothing that has power over your servants."	command. We remained and filled your hands, from the one who has revealed what is hidden, the one for whom nothing is difficult. Our Lord Jesus, our strength, Jesus our life, Jesus the mystery, hear us: we cry out to you, and when *Phygw*,[131] so that nothing is hidden from your servants."
110) And as they were praying, the bird came that had snatched the eye of the king's daughter, and it was also blind. And it came in the midst . . .	And as they were praying, the bird came that had cursed the eye of the king's daughter, so that it too had become blind. And it came in the midst. . .

Ethiopic

of the royal palace with another bird leading it. And it cried out saying, "What is it, Peter and Paul, ministers of the Lord? Listen to me, what I have done, righteous apostles." And the bird spoke with fear. "Hear me, ministers of the Lord. I have

---

131. As is common with the edition of this fragment, the numbering for the note to this word is not correct, and the note is on the following page, which is even more confusing. Müller-Kessler remarks here that "E1 [*The Book of Mary's Repose*] has here the word for 'king.' The reading and meaning of this word remain obscure." MÜLLER-KESSLER, "Three Early Witnesses," 90–1. Indeed, something remains to be understood about this passage. Nevertheless, in the meanwhile, since the word corresponds effectively with "king" in the Ethiopic version, one wonders if this might have been "Paragmos," as the Roman king is named later in the story.

THE BOOK OF MARY'S REPOSE   153

been sent to tell you all the truth about what you ask me."
And they said to it, "We are here on account of you." "Hear
me then: I will tell you why I committed this offense on the
eye of the king's daughter." And the bird said, "Hear me, if it
is heard by you. It happened on his birthday, when the king of
Rome had finished according to his custom. And when he had
finished everything, there was a virgin. He loosened his belt
and stood up after dinner. He saw a girl who had not known a
man. He seized her and tempted her to corrupt her virginity.
The girl, however, cried out and would not allow him to
loosen her belt. The king became enraged, and he ordered that
she be imprisoned in a certain place and remain there until she
died of thirst and hunger, ordering those men who were dwelling in that place: 'No one will conceal[132] her, and if anyone
gives her bread and water, I will cut off his head with a sword.'"

111) "And when it was the third day when she had not
tasted anything, so that the pupil of her eye dissolved from
hunger, the king's daughter, whom you now see blind, went
up on the roof with pure bread in order to put it in the place
where this girl was, saying in her heart, 'It is good for me that
my father does not find me on this roof and that we both do
not die. For I see that she is dying of hunger.' And when she
went to feed her, I came with wicked rage, and I flew in her
face and took out her eyes. And she turned to me to attack
me. The light leaped on my face and blinded me, and I was
thrown into the bushes until this day, when it was given to me
by you in prayer to come here suddenly." And Peter said to
him, "I speak to you truly, and it is fitting for you that you are

---

132. The verbal form is peculiar here. Arras translates "give to her,"
which seems to better suit the context, but does not match the form
in the text.

154 THE DORMITION AND ASSUMPTION OF MARY

blind. You suffered hunger for bread, and you stopped one who was trying to do an act of charity. Perhaps you are one of those birds about which our Lord said: 'The one who sews went forth to sew, and there was some that fell on the path, and the birds of the air came and ate it.'[133] Therefore it is fitting that you die." Then the bird fell at Peter's feet and died.

112) And he turned and said to Paragmos,[134] whose judgment of divine punishment by those who do not see,[135] "And you did not wish to confess your sin, and so it has been confessed. And you have not confessed and have not decided. But go and have your recompense, for I have been sent to you by God." And he turned to the pupil of her eye and said to it, "Since the light vanished from the midst of the world and was put to shame, those who went forth after were not able to extinguish it, and also those outside have not been extinguished."[136] And he placed his hands on her eyes while saying, "In the name of the Lord Jesus Christ, see." Then the daughter cried out and the people with her, saying, "Truly there is no one who is silent and no forgiveness except only by the name of Christ, the Son of God, who found me worthy, the hidden light, and the one who appeared has bestowed favor on me." And Peter said to her, "You pupil of the eye, if we had come and found you dead, we would have raised you up, so that when we came, we would have found mercy for you."

133. Cf. Luke 8.5–6.

134. The name of the Roman king.

135. It is difficult to know where the quotation should begin: perhaps after Paragmos? "The one whose judgment of punishment..." In general, as Arras notes, this section is often confused.

136. Arras also notes in his translation that this passage seems very corrupt. I have drawn from both manuscripts above to try to bring the most sense possible out of the text.

THE BOOK OF MARY'S REPOSE   155

113) The king, however, and those with him fell at the feet of the apostles, saying, "We beseech you, grant us grace also that we may be as you." And Peter ordered them to bring him water, and he gave them a sprinkling while commanding them to keep the commandment that was given to them, saying, "Abide in this until I come to you in eight days. And on account of this our Lord appeared to us, so that I will spend ten days with the people of Philippi. Therefore, be strong in the faith, and we are going to Philippi." When they said this, they went forth from them.

The Contendings of Peter and Paul in Philippi.

114) And as they were going along the way, Paul said to Peter, "Where is the one who was crying out beneath heaven, saying, 'Send Paul so that I will contend with him'?" And Peter said to Paul, "Are you sad, Paul, that he has not come to us? It is possible for the Lord that none of us will see him until the end of the world. Only be patient: that one does not desist in every contest." And then they went and entered the land of Philippi, and they proclaimed the word of the Lord. And the Lord opened the great way of the city. Immediately they worked great wonders: they made the blind to see, the lame to rise, and the deaf to hear, and they cleansed the lepers, so that the entire city believed.

115) And when the apostles were hiding in the city of Philippi, Satan cried out when he saw the multitude that believed, and he could not find [an opportunity] to contend with Paul. And he rose up and made himself look like the leader of the army in the land of Blacks.[137] And he took with him four

---

137. That is, Ethiopia.

156 THE DORMITION AND ASSUMPTION OF MARY

demons, and he made them look like four soldiers. And they went with him to the land of Rome, and they entered the royal palace. And he said to the doorkeeper, "Announce me to the king, that the king of Enda[138] has come and wants to meet him." And when Paragmis heard that it was the king of Enda, then he rose up quickly and went forth. And when the king of Enda saw him, he fell down at his feet weeping. Then Paragmos raised him up, saying, "Rise up and tell me who you are." And he said, "I am the king of Endon and all the provinces of Ethiopia. And there were two men, and they entered my kingdom: one was Peter and the other was Paul, practicing magic. And they taught my soldiers about their God, saying, 'Jesus is the king of light,' and also 'he will destroy kingdoms.' And all my soldiers believed them and left me alone and with only these four. And when I heard that they had come to your kingdom and land, I came to tell you what happened. Now then, while they are with you, rise up and kill them. And if you do not do this, they will work magic, and your soldiers also will leave you. And you will be left alone, and when you go forth, there will be no soldiers with you." And when the king of Rome heard this, he looked at his quiver of arrows and said to the king of Endon, "I have sharpened and made this thing for the magicians. Therefore, I will have you come here in three days, and you will precede them in my presence. Now then, do not make haste: I know where they are. I heard them say, 'We will go to Philippi to teach there.' Now then, I will send for them and kill them."

116) And Paragamos called 10,200 horsemen and said to them, "Go to the land of Philippi and capture both magicians, Peter and Paul, and lead them forth to me, and I will kill

---

138. Most likely India.

THE BOOK OF MARY'S REPOSE 157

them." Then they went forth immediately and surrounded all the fortifications of the city. And when the people of the city heard the sound of the horsemen, they then went out of the city, and their elders and leaders said, "How have we transgressed against the king, and what have we done that he has encircled the city for a great battle?" Then the soldiers said to them, "Do not fear: you will live. For the king has not sent us against you, nor to destroy your city. He has sent us only for the two magicians, Peter and Paul." Then they deliberated among themselves, saying, "Woe to us! What shall we do? For we do not want to betray these two men who have done good things in our city. If we hand them over, we will sin and go astray. Rather, let us go to the soldiers and say that there are no magicians here." And they went to the soldiers and said, "There are no magicians in our city." And the soldiers said to the people of the city, "We will lead you forth in chains if you do not hand over the two magicians now."

117) And again the people of the city turned away and were discussing with one another, "What shall we do? Let us get up and go to them in the city and let us tell them that Paragamos the king of Rome has sent for them." As they were going into the city, an old man met them who had previously been blind and had been healed by Peter and Paul. And he said to them, "You men of the city, why are you following one another thus?" And they said to him, "Because we have been compelled by the king regarding Peter and Paul. Therefore, we are going to them to seek their counsel: 'What do you want us to do?'" And then the old man said to them, "Come and follow me, and we will go before the soldiers and we will pray to the Lord either to have mercy on us so to change the hearts of the soldiers, or, if they are not willing, we will rise up against them. But, until we are dead, we will not hand over the apostles who have worked great wonders. And

158   THE DORMITION AND ASSUMPTION OF MARY

behold, I say to you that even if the king shut those men up in a fire, they would be able to call upon their Lord, and he would deliver them. But they have been patient in order to see if we would fight on their behalf or if we would not fight." Then the whole city followed the old man, and they turned to the east and prayed that the Lord would turn back the soldiers and they would withdraw.

Reading for the 22nd.

118) And then Peter and Paul went forth from the city and no one saw them. And they began to stand among the people, and they prayed for the faith of the soldiers. And as they were praying, the horses of the soldiers turned themselves to the east where Peter and Paul were praying, and they straightened up their ears and cried out with a thin voice, like someone mourning. And the soldiers grew weary from striking the horses in the face, and they were not able to turn them around as they were bowed down on their knees with the people. And the 10,200 horses bowed down on their knees. And then, when the people got up, the horses also got up. And when one of the soldiers wanted to turn his horse, it did not listen.

119) And one of the horses that was great, named Legion, raised his voice like a human being and spoke and said, "Fools! Now wisdom is in your hearts. I say to the 10,200 soldiers of Paragmos the king of Rome, who were sent here for Peter and Paul, for the two soldiers of Christ, and said that they are magicians: they are not magicians. Rather, they came to destroy every magician and every work of the Devil. Have you not seen and understood what they have done? And if you look with your eyes, you will see them, Peter and Paul, standing in your midst with their king Jesus, riding on a white horse and beseeching on account of you. Have you not seen his sign that occurred on your account? For the animals that

THE BOOK OF MARY'S REPOSE   159

surround you, when they saw Peter and Paul bowing down on their knees and feet to the great king on account of you, and neither they nor you, you could not turn around, before we bowed down on our knees with them, as they were acting in their order. Behold then, they are standing in your midst and writing your names in the book of life. They have received a sign from their King Jesus so that they have become his soldiers, for he has prepared that they will ascend into his kingdom."

120) And when the horse said this, Jesus ascended into heaven in a great light, saying as all were listening, "Do not neglect my neophytes," for they raised their eyes from the people to the animals and saw the savior ascending into heaven. And again when the 10,200 soldiers saw him, they cried out with a great voice, saying, "We beseech you, Peter and Paul, soldiers of your king who is not overcome, reveal to us his deeds, so that we may attain what is good." Then they were revealed to them, and they besought them that they could be soldiers like them. And they said to them, "No one is able to be a soldier of our king with such horses and a shield and a sword and arrows. Rather, our horse is his Spirit and the one who is sent to us where we want to go by his Spirit. Also, our shield is prayer, and our arrows his mighty word, and our two-edged sword is faith and works. You, however, men of the world, how will you be able to become soldiers of Jesus, if you have not first left this behind?" And then the soldiers said, "Come, let us leave this behind us, and truly we will be soldiers for you." And Peter said, "Not just as you say, but rise up and let us go to your king and return to him his weapons and his horses and all of his things. And also let us come into the city, and we will make you our disciples in that place. But after this I say to you, before you go, that there is nothing[139]

139. Or possibly, "no one."

160   THE DORMITION AND ASSUMPTION OF MARY

that will be over you, so that you will believe abundantly, for we have taught[140] you before it will be upon you that unless you will have returned his weapons, he will accordingly be angry with you and will order that they throw you in prison. And he will not trouble your heart, because your king is mighty, and he will come and will save you, for the glory of Jesus is with you."

121) And they mounted their horses, and they went and arrived and stood before Paragmos the king. And when he saw them, he said to them, "Where are the two magicians on account of which I sent you, who are called Peter and Paul?" And they said, "What have you done to them in exchange for the light that they graciously gave to your daughter? You vilify them, while not doing anything good for

Ethiopic	Christian Palestinian Aramaic
them. Nevertheless, they have no desire for any goods from you that will perish. For them, there is only Jesus their king, who sits over them. And we also hope to become soldiers for Peter and Paul." And when they had said this, they took off their armor and threw it in his face, while saying, "Take what belongs to you, for we have found a better king." And when he heard this, he was enraged with great anger	...them. For they have no need for your goods, which will perish. For we also serve Jesus, like Peter and Paul." And when they had spoken, they removed their arms and threw them in the king's face. And they said to him, "Take what is yours, for we have found our king better than yours." And when the king heard these things, he was enraged with anger and ripped his purple [garment]...And

140. Or possibly, "had mercy on."

THE BOOK OF MARY'S REPOSE

161

Ethiopic

and ripped his purple garment, while saying, "Woe is me! What will I do? The king of Endan has spoken to me truly: it is true! For he said that they would bewitch my soldiers, and there is no falsehood in him. And now I have understood my 10,200 soldiers. And if I want, I will kill you, for there are no soldiers among you." And then he ordered that they should be thrown in prison. And again 20,400 foot soldiers went to the land of Philippi to reduce the city to dust to its very foundations

Christian Palestinian Aramaic

they[141] said to him, "Truly, what will he do to us? For the words of the king of Kush are true." Indeed, he said, "They bewitched my soldiers," and it is no lie. For I have been rejected by twelve hundred of my soldiers. What then shall I do to you? If it satisfies,[142] I will kill you, since I know that there is no strength in them." Then the king said, "Let them be thrown in prison. And another two thousand soldiers will go on horses, and they will throw down the city to ground and bring these two

141. Something is wrong with the form of the verbs here. A first-person form is expected, as in the Ethiopic, and the third-person forms here do not match well with the first-person forms that follow. One suspects that the Ethiopic is correct and that something is deficient in the Christian Palestinian Aramaic text as we have it.

142. Müller-Kessler here translates "when things turn bad," explaining this as an interpretation of the literal meaning of the text here, "when it goes down," or "when it descends." Smith Lewis translates, "if he goes down." Nevertheless, in light of the context and comparison with the Ethiopic version, I think it makes better sense to understand *nḥt* as a form deriving from *nwḥ*, which has the meaning of "be satisfied," rather than from *nḥt*, "to descend," which does not seem to fit at all here.

THE DORMITION AND ASSUMPTION OF MARY

Ethiopic

and to bring the two magicians so that he could do to them as he wanted. And they were also prepared[143] to go, and he prepared his weapons for war.

Christian Palestinian Aramaic

magicians, and I will do with them as I want." And when they were ready to go, they exchanged their weapons of war.

Peter and Paul Return to Rome and Confront the Emperor.

Ethiopic

122) And Peter knew in the Spirit that they were coming to destroy the city, and he said to Paul, "My brother Paul, arise and let us go to see Paragmos the king, for if we do not go, he will send and destroy the entire city because of us." And he said to him, "Let us go, my father Peter." And when they left the city, they prayed and both mounted a cloud that descended on them, for it obeyed them as a servant obeys his master, for the Savior had subjugated

Christian Palestinian Aramaic

And when Peter knew in the Spirit that they were coming to destroy the city, he said to Paul, "My brother Paul, let us arise and go and make ourselves known to Paragmos the king. For if we do not go, he will send and destroy the city because of us." And he said, "Let us go now, my father Peter." And when they left the city, they prayed, and both mounted a cloud that descended, for it obeyed them as a servant obeys his master, for the Savior had subjugated...

Ethiopic

all creation to them. And the cloud brought them and set them down in the royal palace before the king and before all

---

143. In some MSS: "And he was also prepared."

THE BOOK OF MARY'S REPOSE   163

those who were standing before him. And Peter said to him, "O Paragmos, turn your anger behind you. Do not destroy the city on account of us, for behold, we are before you."

123) Then the king ordered his soldiers to turn back. And he said to them, "You are Peter and Paul, the two magicians?" And they said, "We are, but we are not magicians. Rather, we have come to destroy magicians, which has hardened sin in your soul." And he said to them, "Indeed, I will bring your sin upon you!" Then he ordered that they should make two iron helmets with nails inside and fill them with potent[144] poison and heat them red-hot and place them on their heads, one for Peter and the other for Paul, and hang them upside down. And he said to Peter, "Prince of the magicians, let your prince and your king help you and come and deliver you from my hand."

124) Then Paul suffered greatly, because he was the last among the apostles and he never suffered flagellation,[145] and Peter did not suffer. And Paul said to him, "O my brother Peter, cry out to our king so that he will come and save us." And Peter said to him, "I know that you are suffering. Hold on a little longer, my brother Paul, and the glory of the Lord will be revealed. For endurance is good, since our Lord is among us to help us." Then Peter turned and said, "Paragmos, king of Rome, which will be destroyed, although we are found in this torment, we will cry out to our king, and he will

144. The lexica have no entry for the root LṬ' or any of the possible spelling variants, as van Lantschoot notes. Arras arrives at the translation "glutenous" since in the Tigre language, which is closely related to Classical Ethiopic (Ge'ez), this root means "to adhere, to keep to." See the discussion in ARRAS, *De Transitu*, 1:103–4 (Lat). We have opted for "potent" faute de mieux

145. Cf. 2 Cor 11.23–25 to the contrary.

164 THE DORMITION AND ASSUMPTION OF MARY

come and save us. And if there was one of your soldiers who was in distress in combat and he cried out to you saying, 'Help me,' would you be able to save him?" And when Peter had said this, he prayed while hanging upside down and said, "Lord, who with a word of your mouth suspended the heavens and by your command suspended the earth and the mountains and abandoned that which shakes into the abyss, which you alone made, the tree in paradise and also paradise, who is the Father of the light which is from light, wellspring of the rivers of life, wisdom that is hidden in you, hear your servant and by coming show your glory."

125) And when Peter was saying this, so that it became silent, Paragmos the king was hung upside down on a cloud: himself and his servants and all those who were standing before him were suspended, while no one saw the one who was suspending them and taking hold of them. And then Paragmos wept and cried out, saying, "My Lord Peter, cry out for me and save me from this great torment, for from now on I will not be an infidel. But do not let the king of Andon find

Ethiopic	Syriac[146]	CPA[147]
rest, and let his kingdom be destroyed, since he corrupted my heart against you. Cursed is every person who speaks evil against you. I beg		...rest, and let his kingdom be destroyed, since he is the one who made my heart doubt you. Cursed is the person who speaks evil

146. The Syriac fragment here is very piecemeal and often seems rather different from the other two versions. Nevertheless I have done my best to correlate it with the other two better preserved versions.

147. i.e. Christian Palestinian Aramaic.

THE BOOK OF MARY'S REPOSE

Ethiopic	Syriac	CPA

you, make me come down, and as a servant I will serve you." And Peter said, "By Living God my Lord, you will not come down from that cross unless you first send word to the prison and release the 10,200, having said, O Paragmos king of Rome, 'Let no one free them,' since you are the one who threw them into prison, and there is no one who will release them." And the king turned to his daughter and spoke to her about all of this, saying, "Alas, alas, my daughter! Go quickly and bring them as the apostles ordered, but do not tarry, lest I die on this cross

against you. I beg you, make me come down, [and] as a servant I will serve you." Peter said to him, "By the Living God, you will not cease[148] from...unless you first send to the prison and bring the twelve hundred soldiers." And he said, "Paragmos King of Rome is not the one who released you; he is the one who placed you in prison. But Jesus is the one who released you." But the king turned to his daughter and spoke these words and said, "My daughter, go quickly and bring them and say what you heard, but do not tarry, lest I die in my

---

148. Smith Lewis reads here *'tšlm* instead of *'tšl'*, which leads her to the translation "not be released," which also would make sense.

THE DORMITION AND ASSUMPTION OF MARY

Ethiopic

and in my faithlessness. For I know, my daughter, that many have died hanging thus." And Peter said to him, "Even if you remained here hanging for ten years, you would not die, for you have been suspended by the order of God. For they were outside in this Gehenna and from the seventh generation[150] upon the earth and did not perish, because they were from the Lord."

126) And the daughter opened the prison and brought them, as they had ordered: for she alone re-

Syriac

...I am hanging. For I beg of my daughter, since many have died hanging on account of this name...

Peter said to Paragmos, ...

CPA

wicked faith. For I know, my daughter, that many have died by hanging in this name.[149] Peter said to him, "If you spent ten years, you would not die, for you have been suspended by the order of God. For there is...in Sheol from the day that a person was born on the earth, and they did not die, because they were from God.

And she, Lapita,[151] opened the door of the prison and brought them, as he had ordered her, for she alone

149. Instead of "in this name," Smith Lewis read "in these years," which seems to make slightly better sense.

150. Or possibly, "human generation."

151. Smith Lewis reads here "Luhith," which is the same name that appears in the later Arabic version of this legend.

THE BOOK OF MARY'S REPOSE — 167

Ethiopic	**Syriac**	**CPA**

Ethiopic
mained unsuspended. And when they arrived, the king said, "O Peter, behold, they have released them, and make me also come down." And Peter said to him, "By the Living God my Lord, as you have rebuked the apostles with your mouth, if you do not take pen and ink and write saying, 'There is no other God

Syriac
...Paragmos persuaded Peter, ...

...And Peter said to him, "He is the one knowing God, because she opened her mouth and blasphemed the word of Jesus but did not hold back at all. He confessed...

CPA
remained unsuspended. And when they arrived, the king said to Peter, "My master Peter, behold, [they] have been released. Say that I shall also be released." And Peter said, "By the Living God, against whom your mouth blasphemed, if you do not take pen and ink and write and say, 'There is no other God...

Ethiopic
and Lord except only Jesus, since he is King of the entire universe,' and saying, 'I am on an impure throne,' and order that it be proclaimed in the middle of the city." Then the king ordered that they bring him ink and a pen and paper, and he wrote while hanging upside down, "There is no God and Lord except Jesus; he is King of the entire universe. I, however, am a king on wooden with gold and silver

Syriac
...forever. And you confessed that he will make known about...

168 THE DORMITION AND ASSUMPTION OF MARY

Ethiopic	Syriac
of impure fame." And they brought the writing to the middle of the city, and when they read it, he was brought down. Then he ran with those who were with him, and when they went, they fell down at their feet, saying, "Do not be angry with us because we did evil against you and I was angry with you. Rather, forgive us and forgive our madness, which has possessed us up to this moment." And he remained instructing them and led them into a newly constructed tower.	...and after they went...to the city...
	...and he came... ...when they fell at Peter's feet and said, "Do not...something... ...against you...and we were considering you...
127) As for the 10,200 soldiers, he baptized them and gave them statutes of the word from the Law and, to those who were the best of them, priestly ordination. And they departed and went to the land of Philippi to visit those who were neophytes there, for they left them in a troubled state.	...And they went to Philippi. When he came, he awoke......
And they said to the king and those who were with him, "Behold then, you have understood that there is no King but Jesus. Remain then in his law so that, when you have	And he said to the king and to those who were with him, "You know there is a king... ...authority...

THE BOOK OF MARY'S REPOSE   169

Ethiopic

come into the great day of torment and you have cried out to him, he will save you. Behold then, we are going to Philippi to visit those there who are our brothers. Perhaps in the next days, if God wills, we will return to you and visit you." And after giving peace, they went forth.

Peter and Paul Defeat the Devil.

Ethiopic

128) And the Devil also went forth with them and was following the apostles. He took the appearance of an Ethiopian nobleman, and he cried out, saying, "My fathers Peter and Paul, wait for me so that I may speak with you: I have been sent to you." And they turned around, and he came before them and sat,

Syriac

... And he said, "Our fathers Peter and Paul, wait. He did not speak to you because I was sent to you earlier to give the agent." And when they stopped, he went and sat down...

Ethiopic

having the appearance of a human being. And he said to them, "My lords, allow me to rest a little and I will tell you what they sent me to give. Whence did we find the one whom they call Paragmos? Who corrupted his heart against you again, for again he says that you are magicians. Behold indeed, you are not magicians. Therefore, come with me for

170 THE DORMITION AND ASSUMPTION OF MARY

ten days, so that your works will be known. Do not look, apostles of the Lord, and do not see my nakedness. And do not say, 'This man is shameful.' I am not in fact one who is shameful, but I am ashamed of what I will tell you. But what shall I do? For when you left his heart grew fat, and he said to me, 'I know that your feet are light, and if you run, you are as swift as a horse.' And he called me and said to me, 'If you follow those two men and bring them to me, I will find you and I will find you all.' And I went forth in sorrow and was following you. I say to you with a heavy heart: I left behind my breastplate and threw away my clothes, for I said in my heart, 'It would be better for me to die at the hand of Paragmos.' And therefore you see me naked. And if you did something good for me, come with me, so that they will not kill me on account of you."

129) Then Peter understood in the Spirit that this was the Devil. And he drew a sign in the dirt, and he stood on it and said, "Living God my Lord Jesus Christ! He who slandered you in your work and humiliated your intermediary [152] and made you an object of derision: you may not pass this where I have drawn unless you reveal yourself, who you are." Then he leaped at Paul, wanting to stab him. Paul was afraid, and he ran and embraced Peter. And Peter said to him, "Do not fear, my brother Paul, for I am with you in this fight. But you, grab one of his horns, and I [will grab] the other, and the glory of the Lord will be revealed and, moreover, the cross made manifest." And when they grabbed him to lay hold of him in order to split him in two, then he adjured, saying, "I adjure you by Jesus your king, I adjure you by the right hand of the Father, who is the Son, I adjure you by the dew of heaven and the expanse of the earth with its fruit, I adjure you

152. Van Lantschoot suggests this is a reference Paragmos.

THE BOOK OF MARY'S REPOSE   171

by the one who gave you the crown in the land of inheritance, that you do not destroy me before my days have arrived. Only give me a way by which I can go past this sign, and from now on I will not attack you. Behold, I have promised you." And he placed the small finger of his hand on another that was the largest, saying, "Behold, I have revealed my sign to you, so that I have no power with you, only release me." And then they gave him the sign so that he could go past that sign. And then Peter and Paul went to the city of Philippi.

130) The Devil came to them again and called out to Peter, saying, "Peter and Paul, you two seducers, look at me then. Does it look to you like I am afraid to contend with you? I have sworn to Tatrakos,[153] who with me is an angel of damnation, that I will not cease contenting with you and with those who are like you until the end of the world." And Peter said, "Previously you came to us, and you were put to shame. Now you have come to us again, and the Lord will make you fall at our feet. Go then now, in the name of Christ." And when he left, they entered Philippi and visited the neophytes there.

131) Then the Lord spoke to them, saying, "Dawn has come outside the gates of the city." And then the apostles blessed them from the least of them to greatest of them. And when day broke on the land, they went outside and were there early in the morning. And behold, the horses that were there went forth from the east like fire yoked to chariots of fire. And they took up Peter and Paul and flew them into a cloud. And the people stood while looking on, and they cried out, saying, "We bless you and we bless the place to which you went." And Peter said to them from the chariot of fire, "And you also, if

153. Arras identifies this as the name *Tartarouchos*, "the custodian of the Tartarus."

172 THE DORMITION AND ASSUMPTION OF MARY

you keep the commands that we have given you and remain in purity, when you go forth, eagles of light will take you up on their wings and will lead you up just like this chariot of fire." And saying this, they disappeared into the heights, and then the people could no longer see them, and so they turned back and went into the city while praising and singing glory.

The Apostles Behold God in the Seventh Heaven.

132) And then we apostles arrived in Paradise, with our companions the apostles, and we greeted them, telling them everything that happened to us. And then our Lord brought us to a white river and he washed us together with Mary. And he led us up to the seventh heaven, where God sits. And we wanted to enter into him, so that we could embrace him, and we were afraid, because [God was] entirely fire. But we saw two seraphim standing, each one having six wings: with two they covered their feet, and with two they flew.[154] And they did not touch the face of God, because [God is] completely perfect: for they could not see the face of God, because [God was] entirely fire. And the other two wings of the seraphim covered their faces, both of them covering. And with two they were suspending the feet of God, lest they make an impression on the heights and on the earth; for at that moment, when his feet touch the earth, [that will be] the time of the world's consummation. †For [there is] still a little [time?], and they will touch the earth, because from twelve days he comes in twelve, except for a little.

133) Our Savior hurried, intending to show us[155] everything, as we came to announce everything, saying "God is the

154. Cf. Isa 6.2.
155. MSS: "you (pl)."

THE BOOK OF MARY'S REPOSE 173

beginning of knowledge." But we were not able to go into the Father, since there is no one who speaks with another seraph, who has six wings, who appeared to us from our Savior, saying, "This then is what is appropriate for the just in the days of his kingdom; and he will cover you with his wings, and he will gather you to him." And we wanted to worship and embrace him, but we were not permitted, saying, "It is difficult now: wait a little longer[156] and embrace my hands, because the one who has embraced my body will not die." And Mary, because she has gone forth from her body, she has embraced him. And we saw our Lord Jesus Christ and Mary sitting at the right of God. And we saw every sign of God that was on his side, and the sign on his hands, which was on that day when we were with him.†

134) And Peter asked our Lord, saying, "This is marvelous: the body is similar to the spirit." And Peter said to him, "Have you not healed the wound of that spear, the stab of the sword? Are you unable to heal it? Until you teach us this and tell us this teaching, I will not rest." And he said to us, "Until the day of judgment, when he will rebuke the children of Israel, if there is someone who wants to deny this sign, [let him know that?] it was revealed, because he wanted to send his son at every time. And if there are some people from the city who want to rise up against him and beat him and tear his purple garment, the son will show his father and he will protect him. And on that day, when the king wanted to bestow delights on every city, then he ordered that nothing would be given to that city. And the people of that city will speak, saying, 'Why have we not found delights?' And he will answer them, saying, 'Why did you rise up against my son?' Then they will deny, saying, 'We have not risen up against him, and we did not

156. Literally, "reside again."

174   THE DORMITION AND ASSUMPTION OF MARY

know him.' Then his father will order that the purple garment be brought, and the son will show his father the evidence of their rebellion. Thus, then it will be for the children of Israel."

The Apostles Are Returned to Earth to Proclaim What They Have Seen.

135) And after these words, our Lord turned his face to a seraph that had two wings, and he made a sign to him. And the seraph left two words, which no one could understand. Then a great gathering of angels came with a pure, adorned throne, and there was no end to its glory. Myriads of angels were surrounding it, each one on his own throne. Then they said to us, "Go to the earth and proclaim everything that you have seen." And they brought another throne for Mary, and there were 10,000 angels and three virgins surrounding it. And she sat [on it] and went into Paradise, and they remained in the third heaven, singing.

136) But Michael made us descend, so that we would inhabit the earth. And we saw other wonders, because we saw every power. And we also saw the sun and its light, while eagles were circling and carrying the sun. And a light appeared in the eagles' midst, so that we asked Michael and said to him, "How is the light of the sun different here, and it appears different on the earth?" And he taught us, saying, "Light is upon all creatures. And when the first sin took place, when blood was shed on the earth, a seventh part of the sun's light was removed from it. And because of this the eagles remain here, surrounding the light at this part." And we also saw the powers of the stars. And when we saw these great wonders, we came together with Michael to the Mount of Olives, by the order of our Lord, to whom be glory and power, unto the age of the age. Amen.

The *Six Books Apocryphon*
The Book of the Departure
of My Lady the Virgin Mary, the Theotokos

[The First Book].

Liturgical Invocation.

(1.1) The peace of God [5ᵃ] who sent his Son and came into the world; and the peace of the Son, who migrated from heaven and dwelt in Mary; and the peace of the Holy Spirit, the singer who sings and the Paraclete who is praised; and the peace of the Lord of created beings, the glory of whose divinity the created beings are unable to comprehend; who left the adorned chariot in the highest heights and descended and dwelt in the Virgin Mary's womb; be with us and with all of our assembly, and bless the crowns of the priests, our fathers, who sit at the head of their flock, unto the ages of ages, Amen.

(1.2) Open, O Lord, the gate of heaven to our prayer at this hour; and let sweet incense ascend from our assembly to the heavenly ranks; and let the trumpets of the archangels sound in heaven; and let the choirs of heavenly beings stand in ranks; and let there be praise in heaven before the glorious king; and from all the dwellings of the Father's house, let the voices of the watchers sing; and let the soldiers stand before

176 THE DORMITION AND ASSUMPTION OF MARY

the soldiers, ranks with ranks, armies before armies; and let there be praise and sweet incense unto God, and thanksgiving and worship unto Christ, and praise and glorification to the Holy Spirit.

(1.3) The departure of my Lady Mary from this world we call to memory before you, our brothers. Command, Lord, a blessing and a good reward for the ministers, that they may glorify; [5^b] for the rich, that they may praise; for the poor, that they may become rich; for the old, that they may give praise; for the young, that they may bless. And answer the women, the daughters of Eve, when they call upon you in prayer, O Lord, for from them was chosen the holy and virgin woman, whom God chose from all creation. And from her was born the Lord of glory, the Son of the exalted God, to whom be glory, and to her may there be a good commemoration, unto the ages of ages, Amen.

(1.4) Blessed be your grace, O God who died; the king's son who humbled himself; the immortal one who willed and died; who migrated from the Father to Mary, and from Mary to the manger, and from the manger to the circumcision, and from the circumcision to growing up, and from growing up to the flagellation, and from the flagellation to the humiliation, and from the humiliation to the cross, and from the cross to death, and from death to the grave, and from the grave to the resurrection, and from the resurrection to heaven. And behold, he sits at the right hand of the one who sent him. Stretch forth your right hand, O Lord, from the exalted throne of your glory at this time, and bless, O Lord, our congregation, which glorifies the commemoration of your mother, my Lady Mary and her departure from this world, unto the ages of ages, Amen.

(1.5) O you faithful listeners, listen carefully and discerningly to the coronation of my Lady Mary, so that everyone

THE SIX BOOKS APOCRYPHON   177

who believes in the undivided Father will speak the truth, confessing that God sent his Son [6ᵃ], and he was born of the Virgin Mary without intercourse. As the prophet Isaiah said, the most glorious of the prophets, "He arose like an infant before him, and like a root from the dry earth";[1] and the prophet also says, "Behold, a virgin will conceive and bear a son, and they will call his name Emmanuel,"[2] which is translated, "our God is with us." For my Lady Mary was also holy and chosen by God from when she was in her mother's womb; and she was born from her mother in purity and holiness. And she purified herself from all bad thoughts, so that she could receive Christ, who came to her, so that by being born from her, he could give life to the people who believe in him. It is fitting that we observe this woman's commemoration. This is the one blessed among women,[3] from whom was born the Savior of all creation. This is the land of blessing, from which was born the husbandman of joys, so that by going forth into the world, he could root out the thorns, and burn the tares, and defeat error, and abolish and chase Satan away, and make tranquility reign, and spread peace over all of creation.

Monks from Mount Sinai Seek
the Book of Mary's Departure.

(1.6) Now then, we will recall in your presence about this book of my Lady Mary, how it was revealed at this time. The blessed men on Mount Sinai, Saint David the presbyter, Saint John the presbyter, and Saint Philip the deacon were greatly

1. Isa. 53.2.
2. Isa. 7.14.
3. Cf. Luke 1.42.

178   THE DORMITION AND ASSUMPTION OF MARY

concerned, because these [6ᵇ] three blessed men were at the sanctuary that was established on the summit of the mountain, Mount Sinai.[4] And these blessed men wrote letters and sent them to Cyrus,[5] the bishop of Jerusalem, that my Lord might take great concern for your holiness. And they asked there about the book of my Lady Mary's departure, how she departed from this world, "For we have a great desire to know with what glory she was crowned."

(1.7) And when the letter was written from Mount Sinai, brothers came and brought it to Jerusalem. And it was read before all of the people. And they sought the book of my Lady Mary and did not find it. But they found a book that was written by the hand of James the bishop, "I James, the bishop of Jerusalem, have written with my own hands in this volume, that in the year 345[6] my Lady Mary went forth from this world. And six books were written concerning her, and each book was written by two of the apostles. And I, James, attest [concerning] these books that were written that John the younger was carrying them. And Paul, and Peter, and John the younger know where they are, because they went with them from Jerusalem."

4. The British Library manuscripts add here: "where the thorn bush was, from which the Lord spoke with Moses. The blessed men were there at the sanctuary and were serving as caretakers of the church of the martyrs that had been built there."

5. This Cyrus is seemingly to be identified as Cyriacus, as indicated directly in the Arabic version of this text. For more on this figure, see Stephen J. SHOEMAKER, "'Let Us Go and Burn Her Body': The Image of the Jews in the Early Dormition Traditions," *Church History* 68.4 (1999), 775–823, at 802–3.

6. Of the Seleucid or Greek era, i.e. 33/34 CE.

THE SIX BOOKS APOCRYPHON   179

(1.8) And when the bishop of Jerusalem sought the book of my Lady Mary, and they did not find it, they wrote [7ᵃ] a letter to Mount Sinai, "From Cyrus, bishop of Jerusalem, and all the holy clergy who are with him, to our brothers, the priests and our fathers who are on Mount Sinai, much peace. We have received the letter that came from you; and we have made inquiries in all of Jerusalem concerning the book of my Lady Mary but did not find it. Nevertheless, we have found an autograph [note] of Bishop James written thus: 'John the younger was carrying with him the books that were written when my Lady Mary died, and Paul and Peter and John the younger know where they are, because they went with them from Jerusalem.'"

The Book's Miraculous Discovery in Ephesus.

(1.9) And the letter went from Jerusalem to Mount Sinai, and the brothers who were dwelling on Mount Sinai read it. And they wrote letters to Rome, Egypt, and Alexandria. And the brothers went and made an inquiry of the bishops of remote regions, and they did not find it. And they came to Ephesus and spent the night in Ephesus at the shrine of Saint John. And they prayed and offered incense and said, "Our Lord Jesus Christ, Son of the living God, who loved Saint John the apostle more than his fellow apostles,[7] if, Lord, it is pleasing to your divinity that the wonders and glories that you performed before my Lady Mary, who bore you, should be revealed to the world, [7ᵇ] let Saint John the apostle appear to us and speak with us this night." And the brothers fell on their faces, and while praying they fell asleep and slept. And Saint John the Apostle stood among the blessed men and said to them,

7. Cf. John 13.23.

180   THE DORMITION AND ASSUMPTION OF MARY

"Do not be sad, O blessed men, because Christ will reward your feet, in as much as you have walked in the lands. Arise and take the book of the mother of my Lord, and go to Mount Sinai, and inquire concerning the welfare of our brothers. And tell them, 'John has sent this book to you so that there will be a commemoration of my Lady Mary three times in the year.'" [8] We saw this sign, and we trembled and were afraid and in great fear. And the Blessed one departed from among us, and we were bowing down and praying.

(1.10) And morning broke, and the sacristan opened the door and entered [the place] where the grace of Saint John goes forth; and there he found a written volume, placed on the opening of the place from which the grace goes forth. And he picked it up and went forth before the whole people; and he opened it and found that it was written in Hebrew, Greek, and Latin. And there was written in it thus, "This Jesus Christ, who was born of the Virgin Mary, he is God in heaven and on earth." And this volume was translated from Greek into Syriac in Ephesus. And it was copied and sent to Mount Sinai; and from Mount Sinai it was copied [8ª] and sent to Jerusalem. May our Lord Jesus Christ, who came from his holy heaven and prepared his mother for burial with great glory, remove the scourge of anger from the face of the world, and bring peace, and let peace reign over all creation, unto the ages of ages, Amen. Here ends the first book.

8. The British Library manuscripts add: "because, if humankind will celebrate her memory, they will be delivered from wrath."

THE SIX BOOKS APOCRYPHON   181

The Second Book.

Mary Regularly Prays at Golgotha and the Tomb of Christ.

(2.1) In the year 345,[9] in the month of the latter Tishrin,[10] my Lady Mary went forth from her house and went to Christ's tomb, because every day she used to go and weep there. But immediately after the death of Christ, the Jews closed the tomb and piled great stones over the door.[11] They placed guards at the tomb and at Golgotha and ordered them that if anyone should come and pray at the tomb or Golgotha, he or she should die immediately. And the Jews took our Lord's cross and the other two crosses, and the spear with which our Savior was wounded,[12] and the robes of mockery that he wore, and they hid them, because they were afraid that one of the kings or princes might come and ask about Christ's murder. And every day they saw [8ᵇ] my Lady Mary when she came to the tomb carrying fire and incense and prayed there. And the watchmen came in and said to the priests, "Mary comes to the tomb and Golgotha in the evening and at dawn and prays there." And there was a great tumult in Jerusalem on account of my Lady Mary. And the priests went to the governor and said to him, "My lord, send and order Mary not to go and pray at the tomb of Christ and Golgotha."

9. Of the Seleucid or Greek era, i.e. 33 CE.

10. i.e. November.

11. Cf. Matt 27.66.

12. The British Library manuscripts add: "and the nails that they had fixed in his hands and feet."

182   THE DORMITION AND ASSUMPTION OF MARY

King Abgar of Edessa Seeks Vengeance against the Jews.

(2.2) And while they were thinking, letters came from Abgar, the king of the city of Edessa, to Sabinus the procurator who had been appointed by the emperor Tiberius.[13]   And Sabinus the procurator had authority as far as the river Euphrates.   And because the apostle Addai, one of the seventy-two apostles, had gone down and had built a church in Edessa and healed king Abgar's disease, King Abgar truly loved Jesus Christ and was constantly asking about him.   And when Christ was dead, and King Abgar heard that the Jews had murdered him on the cross, he was very upset.   And Abgar rose up and rode, and he came to the river Euphrates and was wanting to go up against Jerusalem and destroy it, because it murdered Christ.   And when Abgar came and reached the river Euphrates, he thought [9ᵃ] to himself, "If I cross over, there will be enmity between the emperor Tiberius and me."   And Abgar wrote letters and sent them to Sabinus the procurator, and Sabinus sent them to the emperor Tiberius. Abgar wrote thus to Tiberius, "From Abgar, king of the city of Edessa, much peace to your majesty, our lord Tiberius.   So that your sovereignty would not be violated by me, I did not cross over the river Euphrates; I was wanting to go up against Jerusalem and destroy it, because it murdered Christ, the wise physician.   But you, as a great king who rules over the whole earth and over us, send and grant me a judgment against the people of Jerusalem.   For Your Majesty should know that I want you to grant me a judgment against the crucifiers."   And Sabinus received the letters and sent them to the emperor Tiberius.   And

13. Compare the events mentioned briefly in this paragraph to the much fuller development of this legend in the *Doctrina Addai* (George HOWARD, trans.), *The Teaching of Addai*, Society of Biblical Literature Texts and Translations 16, Early Christian Literature Series 4 (Chico, CA: Scholars Press, 1981), ܐ (Syr) & 13 (Eng).

THE SIX BOOKS APOCRYPHON   183

when he read them, the emperor Tiberius was enraged and was going to destroy and kill all of the Jews.

The Jewish Priests Prevent Mary from Praying at Golgotha.

(2.3) And the people of Jerusalem heard this and were disturbed. And the priests went to the governor[14] and said to him, "My lord, send and order Mary not to go to pray at the tomb and Golgotha." And the governor said to the priests, "Go and order her and admonish her, however, you want." And the priests went to my Lady Mary and said to her, "The governor orders you not to go to pray at the tomb and Golgotha. [9^b] And now Mary, we say to you, remember the sins that you committed before God, and do not lead people astray and say that he who was born from you is the Messiah. Heaven and earth bear witness that he is the son of Joseph the carpenter. For if you wish to pray, enter the synagogue and hear the laws of Moses, and we will call out to God and he will have mercy on you. But if you will not accept these terms, then leave Jerusalem and go to your house in Bethlehem. We will not allow you to pray at the tomb and Golgotha."

Mary Leaves her Jerusalem House
for her House in Bethlehem.

(2.4) The Jews said these things to the Virgin, and she did not agree to them. Afterwards my Lady Mary became sick, and she sent and called all of the women of the neighborhood

14. Literally "judge," here and elsewhere. Nevertheless, the text frequently uses this term interchangeably with the word for "governor," and since the Roman governor is clearly intended, for clarity I have consistently translated both terms as "governor."

184 THE DORMITION AND ASSUMPTION OF MARY

where she lived and said to them, "Farewell now, for I am going to Bethlehem, to the house that I have there, because the Jews will not allow me to pray at the tomb of Christ and Golgotha. But, whoever of you wishes, let her come with me to Bethlehem. For I entrust myself to my Lord, whom I have in Heaven, who, whenever I call on him, fulfills my wish." And when my Lady Mary said to the daughters of Jerusalem that whoever wished should go to Bethlehem with her, [10ª] the virgins who were serving her drew near and said to her, "Whoever wishes to go with you, Lady Mary, will receive a blessing from God. But we will not leave you until we die, because we have left our parents and brothers and all that we have for your sake. And we will come with you and serve you, and we want to die with you and to live with you."

The Three Virgins who Were Mary's Servants.

(2.5) And my Lady Mary's virgins were with her day and night and were serving her. And they were daughters of wealthy men and leaders of Jerusalem. These were their names: Calletha, Neshra, and Tabetha. Calletha was the daughter of Saint Nicodemus, the friend of Christ, who by the name Calletha [the bride] symbolizes the glorious church. And the next one, whose name was Neshra, was the daughter of Gamaliel, the head of the synagogue of the Jews; and by the image of Neshra [the eagle] is represented Christ the King, who carries and bears on his wings the holy church, which was betrothed to him before the foundations of the world. And she whose name was Tabetha [the good] was the daughter of Tobia, a *comes*.[15] This Tobia was from the people of the house of King Archelaus,

15. An office of varying importance in the administration of the later Roman Empire.

THE SIX BOOKS APOCRYPHON   185

and this Archelaus was from the family of Caesar Nero, the one who crucified [10ᵇ] Simon the chief of the apostles. And the interpretation of these names is thus: Calletha is the Catholic church, which is in the heavenly Jerusalem. And this church that we have on the earth is the image of the one that is in heaven, and on it is established the throne of the glorious God. And Neshra is the Christ, who sits at the right hand of his Father on the chariot of the Seraphim. And Tabetha is the Holy Spirit, by whom life is given to all human beings. These were the names of the virgins who were serving my Lady Mary. And these virgins and my Lady Mary arose and went forth to Bethlehem on Thursday, and they spent the night in Bethlehem.

John Arrives in Bethlehem in Answer to Mary's Prayer.

(2.6) And on that Friday my Lady Mary was distraught, and she said to them, "Bring me a censer of incense, because I want to pray to Christ, my Lord who is in heaven." And they brought her a censer, and she prayed, saying, "Lord Jesus Christ, hear the voice of your mother and send to me Saint John the younger, whose blessing is great, so that I may see him and rejoice. And send to me his fellow apostles, so that I may see them and praise your grace, which helps me. And you hear me when I pray to you."

(2.7) And when [11ᵃ] my Lady Mary prayed thus, John was living in Ephesus. And he went forth to go to the church of Ephesus, and the Holy Spirit stood before him and said to him, "Enter the sanctuary so that I may speak with you." And he entered and bowed down to pray before the altar. And the Holy Spirit said to him, "The time has drawn near for the mother of your Lord to depart from this world. Go to Bethlehem to greet her." The Holy Spirit said these things to John, and he came to his disciples and commanded them to

186   THE DORMITION AND ASSUMPTION OF MARY

continue worship of the Lord at the appropriate time. And John went out from Ephesus to go to Bethlehem. He bowed down to pray and said, "Lord Jesus Christ, hear the voice of your servant and give my feet strength to go quickly to Bethlehem, on account of that which the Holy Spirit revealed to me before the glorious altar."

(2.8) John prayed thus, and a cloud of light caught him up and brought him to the door of the upper room in Bethlehem. And John opened the door of the upper room, and he entered and found the Blessed one lying on a bed. And he approached and kissed her on her breast and on her knees. And he cried out and said to her, "Peace to you, the mother of my Lord! Peace to you, Theotokos! [11^b] Do not be sad, because you will go forth from this world with great glory." And my Lady Mary rejoiced greatly that Saint John had come to her. And the virgins approached and bowed down before him. My Lady Mary said to him, "Set up a censer of incense and pray." And Saint John set up a censer and prayed. And a voice was heard saying, "Amen: assemble yourselves, all of you." And John listened and obeyed the voice. And the Holy Spirit said to him, "Did you hear the voice that called out from heaven?" John said, "I heard it." The Holy Spirit said to him, "This voice is a messenger to your fellow apostles, who are coming here today." And John was praying, and the Holy Spirit made known to the apostles, wherever they were, that they should sit on adorned steeds and clouds of light and go to my Lady Mary in Bethlehem.

The Other Apostles are Miraculously Brought to Bethlehem.

(2.9) It informed Simon Cephas in Rome, as he was going in to offer the oblation in the church where the oblation of strangers was. And he was bowed down and praying before the

THE SIX BOOKS APOCRYPHON   187

altar, and the Holy Spirit said to him, "The time has drawn near for the mother of your Lord to depart from this world. Go to Bethlehem to greet her." And it informed Paul in the midst of Rome, in the city called Tiberias. And it found [12ᵃ] Paul while he was contending with the Jews, who were debating with him, abusing him, and saying to him, "Your words, which you preach concerning the Messiah, are not accepted. Because you are from Tarsus and are the son of harness makers, and because you are the son of poor people, you take hold of the name of the Messiah and go about with it." And the Holy Spirit said to him, "The time has drawn near for the mother of your Lord to depart from this world. Go to Bethlehem to greet her."

(2.10) And in India the Holy Spirit told Thomas, who had gone to visit the son of the sister of Ludan, the king of India.[16] And he was sitting by his bed and talking with him. And the Holy Spirit said to him, "The time has drawn near for the mother of your Lord to depart from this world. Go to Bethlehem to greet her." And the Holy Spirit told Matthew, "The time has drawn near for the mother of your Lord to depart from this world. Go to Bethlehem to greet her." And Matthew was at Yabus. And the Holy Spirit told James in Jerusalem, "The time has drawn near for the mother of your Lord to depart from this world. Go to Bethlehem to greet her." And the Holy Spirit informed Bartholomew in the Thebaid, "The time has drawn near for the mother of your Lord to depart from this world. [12ᵇ] Go to Bethlehem to greet her."

(2.11) Now, none of the apostles had died yet, except Andrew, the brother of Simon Cephas, and Philip, and Luke, and Simon the Canaanite: these were dead. And on that day the Holy Spirit informed them in their graves, and they arose

16. Cf. *Acts of Thomas* 2, where the king's name is Gundaphorus.

188 THE DORMITION AND ASSUMPTION OF MARY

from Sheol. And the Holy Spirit said to them, "Do not suppose that the resurrection has come; but inasmuch as you have risen from your graves today, it is so that you will go to greet the mother of your Lord, because the time has drawn near for her to depart from the world." And the Holy Spirit informed Mark, "The time has drawn near for the mother of your Lord to depart from this world. Go to Bethlehem to greet her."

(2.12) The Holy Spirit revealed these things to the holy apostles. And while the apostles were wondering in the countries where they were, how they would come to my Lady Mary, their Lord sent them chariots. And a cloud of light descended and caught up Peter, and he was standing between heaven and earth, waiting for his fellow apostles to come to him. And immediately the Holy Spirit caught up all of the apostles [13ª] on chariots, and they came to Peter. And powerful winds blew, and heaven and earth shone with a bright light. And the apostles sat on eleven thrones, and the thrones were placed on chariots of light. And the Holy Spirit led these chariots, and they came between heaven and earth, and the apostles arrived in Bethlehem.

(2.13) And the Holy Spirit said to John in Bethlehem, "Go out and welcome your fellow apostles, who have come." And John went out and bowed down to them. And Peter said to him, "Is the mother of our Lord dead, my brother John?" John said, "She is not dead yet." And a censer of incense was set up, and a sweet smell spread through the entire region of Bethlehem. And the apostles went into the upper room to my Lady Mary, and they kissed her on her breast and on her knees. And they stood before the Blessed one and said to her, "Do not be afraid, Blessed one, and do not be sad. The Lord God who was born from you will lead you forth from this world with glory to the glorious mansions of the blessed God, over which your son rules, and in which he makes the just who love him joyous."

The Apostles Explain their Miraculous Journeys.

(2.14) And my Lady Mary raised herself up and sat on the bed and said to [13ᵇ] the apostles, "Now I am certain that my Lord will come from heaven, and I will see him. Afterwards I will die, as you have come and I have seen you. And now I want you to tell me, who told you that I am about to die, and from what places you have come to me, that your coming was so sudden. Make known to me and tell me, for I know with certainty that the one who was born from me is the son of the glorious God, and I believe in him and worship him because according to the lowliness of his handmaid he has dealt with me." Peter said to his fellow apostles, "Let each one of us tell the Blessed one how the Holy Spirit spoke with him and from where he has come."

(2.15) The apostles said, "John came first; let him explain for her how he came." John said, "The Holy Spirit told me in Ephesus and said to me, 'The time has drawn near for the mother of your Lord to depart from this world. Go to Bethlehem to greet her.' And a cloud of light caught me up and brought me to the door of the upper room." Peter said, "The Holy Spirit told me in Rome and said to me, 'The time has drawn near for the mother of your Lord to depart from this world. Go to Bethlehem to greet her.' And a cloud of light caught me up, and I was standing between heaven and earth, and I saw the chariots of all the apostles, [14ᵃ] which were flying and coming toward me." Paul said, "I was in the city called Tiberias, and the Jews were contending with me there. And the Holy Spirit said to me, 'The time has drawn near for the mother of your Lord to depart from this world. Go to Bethlehem to greet her.' And a cloud of light caught me up and brought me to you."

(2.16) Thomas said, "The Holy Spirit told me in India, when I had gone in to visit the son of the sister of Ludan, the

190   THE DORMITION AND ASSUMPTION OF MARY

king of India. And the Holy Spirit said to me, 'The time has drawn near for the mother of your Lord to depart from this world. Go to Bethlehem to greet her.' And a cloud of light caught me up and brought me to you." Mark said, "I was performing the service of the third hour, and as I was praying, a cloud of light caught me up and brought me to you." James said, "The Holy Spirit told me in Jerusalem and said to me,[17] 'The time has drawn near for the mother of your Lord to depart from this world. Go to Bethlehem to greet her.' And a cloud of light caught me up and brought me to you." Matthew said, "I have given and am giving glory to God, because while I was sitting on a ship, storms rose up against me to destroy the ship. And a cloud of light caught me up and brought me to you."

(2.17) Philip said, "I was dead [14ᵇ] and lying in the grave, and I heard a voice that called me: 'Philip, arise from there.' And a cloud of light caught me up and brought me to you." Simon the Canaanite said, "I too have risen from the grave. And I saw a right hand that grabbed me and raised me up from the house of the dead, among whom I was lying. And a cloud of light caught me up and brought me to you." Luke said, "I too have risen from the grave. A sound struck my ears like the sound of the seraphim's trumpet, and a light shone throughout the tomb in which I was lying, and I thought that the resurrection had come. And a cloud of light caught me up and brought me to you." Andrew answered and said, "I too have risen from

17. The British Library manuscripts have here instead a rather peculiar passage that is not paralleled in any of the other versions that I am aware of: "I was in Jerusalem, and was sitting in the church of Zion, and we were wrapping up some of the vessels of the Lord's house. And before I went forth from Jerusalem to Bethlehem, the Holy Spirit came in to me and said to me."

THE SIX BOOKS APOCRYPHON   191

the grave. The voice of the son of God struck my ears and said to me, 'Andrew, arise from there and go with your companions to Bethlehem. I am coming to you with the assemblies of angels, because the time has come for Mary to be crowned [and depart] from the world.' And a cloud of light caught me up and brought me to you." And Bartholomew said, "I was in the Thebaid and was preaching about the grace and peace of our Lord Jesus Christ. And I saw the Holy Spirit coming like lightning from heaven, and it set me on a cloud of light and brought me to you."

(2.18) The holy apostles spoke these things before my Lady Mary, and each one of them explained [15ᵃ] how he had come to her. And when my Lady Mary had heard these things from the holy apostles, she stretched forth her hands to heaven and prayed and said, "I worship while praying and glorifying [God] that I am not a mockery to the nations of the gentiles, and that the words of the Jews, who said that they would burn me with fire when I am dead, are not true. But I believe and am certain that the one who was born from me is the son of the glorious God." [18]

(2.19) And after my Lady Mary had prayed, the apostles set up a censer of incense and prayed. And thunder sounded in heaven, and it came like the sound of racing wheels striking the surface of the sky. And a great host of angels descended from heaven in ranks and orders without number. And with their wings they covered the upper room in which my Lady Mary was lying. And a voice like that of a human being speaking was heard in the midst of the chariot of the seraphim, who were standing over the Blessed one's upper room. And the people of Bethlehem went in and told the governor and

18. The British Library manuscripts have instead: "The one who was born from me is the ruler of heaven and earth."

192   THE DORMITION AND ASSUMPTION OF MARY

the priests of Jerusalem everything that they had seen and heard. Here ends the second book.

The Third Book.

Mary Works Miracles in Bethlehem.

(3.1) And men from Bethlehem, when they saw the signs that were done, went to my Lady Mary while she was lying in the upper room. And[19] [15b] the people of Bethlehem arose and were beholding them. And the people of Bethlehem saw the first vision, when the apostles came and were ministering to her in the upper room. And they saw when the heavens were opened and the hosts of angels of the Lord descended. And they saw the clouds coming and dropping sweet dew over all of Bethlehem. And they saw the entire assembly of Christ while it was sitting with her and holding a censer of incense to honor the Blessed one. And the people of Bethlehem saw the stammering, the dumb, the blind, the deaf, the sick, the afflicted, those beset by unclean spirits, and everyone who had an illness coming and placing their heads on the door of the upper room and on the wall and on the rock, and crying out and saying, "Lord Jesus Christ, have mercy on me." And at the

---

19. From this point until the end of the paragraph, the text in the British Library manuscripts is very different, reading instead: "And the people of Bethlehem saw the disciples when they came and were ministering in the upper room. And they saw the clouds coming and dropping sweet dew over all of Bethlehem. And they saw the sun and the moon, which came and worshipped before the upper room. And they saw the stammering, the dumb, the blind, the deaf, the sick, the afflicted, those beset by unclean spirits, and everyone who had an illness going to her and being healed."

THE SIX BOOKS APOCRYPHON 193

very moment when one was healed, the people of Bethlehem saw these signs and were unwillingly giving praise to God.

(3.2) And women were coming to her from the cities and from distant regions, and from Rome and from Alexandria, and from Egypt and from Athens, the daughters of kings and daughters of procurators and prefects. And they were bearing gifts and offerings, and they were coming and venerating my Lady Mary. And they believed in Christ, who was born from her, and she was healing each woman who had [16ª] an illness. And there came to my Lady Mary a woman from Beirut who had a demon that was continually strangling her. And she prayed over her, and immediately she was healed.[20] And there came to her Yuchabar from Alexandria, the daughter of Nonnus the procurator, who was completely covered with leprosy. And she came and bowed down before my Lady Mary. And she took water and made the sign of the cross over it. And she sprinkled it over her body, and immediately she was healed. And there came to her Abigail the Egyptian, the daughter of Gershon, the king of Egypt, who had the illness strangury. And she prayed over her, and she was healed. And there came to her Flavia from Thessalonica, whose right eye Satan had destroyed. And immediately she made the sign of the cross over her, and she was healed. And there came to her Malchu, the daughter of Sabinus the procurator, and she had two demons, one that tormented her by night, and another that came upon her in the daytime. And[21] she petitioned my Lady Mary,

20. The British Library manuscripts have: "The blessed one prayed over her and cursed the demons in the name of our Lord Jesus Christ, and immediately the demons came out of her."

21. In the British Library manuscripts, this episode concludes simply with "and she was healed." Following this, they skip directly to "And there was a festival..." at the beginning of the next section.

194 THE DORMITION AND ASSUMPTION OF MARY

and she prayed over her and placed her hand upon her head and said to her, "In the name of my Lord who is in heaven, I adjure you at this time concerning this soul, so that she will be healed." And immediately these demons came forth from the woman. And they were wailing and crying out, saying, "You and the child who was born from you, you have dispersed Legion with his hosts."[22] Then [16ᵇ] my Lady Mary prayed and cursed these demons in the name of Christ, and immediately they were cast into the sea and were strangled. And there came unto my Lady Mary a boy from Egypt, the son of a descendant of Sophron the King of Egypt, and he had elephantiasis on his head. And he wept before my Lady Mary, and she prayed over him, and he was healed. And those who were coming and were sick and taking refuge in my Lady Mary the Theotokos were immediately healed from their sufferings.

(3.3) And there was a festival in Jerusalem, and many people gathered for it. And the sick and afflicted who had come asked, "Where is my Lady Mary?" And they said, "She is in Bethlehem." And innumerable people set out and went to Bethlehem. And they knocked at the door of the upper room, but the apostles did not open the door. And when the door was not opened, those who were ill were crying out and saying, "My Lady Mary, Theotokos, have mercy on us." And my Lady Mary heard the voice of the people crying out to her, and she prayed and said, "Lord Jesus Christ, hear the voice of the souls that are crying out to you." And a great force of healing went forth from the Blessed one to all the sick. And at that moment two thousand eight hundred souls were healed, men, women, and children. And there was great praise on that day, [17ᵃ] because as soon as they were healed, these sick went to the

22. Cf. Luke 5.9.

THE SIX BOOKS APOCRYPHON   195

praetorium, and in the presence of the governor and the priests, they told what my Lady Mary had done through her prayers.

The Jews Seek to Expel Mary from Bethlehem.

(3.4) And the priests disturbed the governor and were saying to him, "Glorious governor, give an order concerning this woman, that she may not remain either in Bethlehem or in the entire jurisdiction of Jerusalem." The governor said to them, "I am not about to send and drive a woman from her house." They said to him, "Send men with clubs, and let them bring us the disciples of the deceiver, and let them bring her, the very same one with a great dishonor." And as soon as they cried out and troubled [him] greatly, saying, "By the life of the emperor Tiberius, if you do not do our will, then we will make it known to him," the governor then ordered a chiliarch[23] to go with thirty men to Bethlehem and to bring the disciples and my Lady Mary. And they set out and went.

Mary and the Apostles Miraculously Return to Jerusalem.

(3.5) And the Holy Spirit said to the apostles, "Behold, men are coming against you from Jerusalem. Arise, go forth from here, and do not be afraid: I will carry you and make you pass through the air of heaven and above the men who are coming against you. You will pass over and they will not see you, because the power of the adored Son is with you. And the apostles arose[24] and went forth from the upper room.

---

23. A captain of a thousand men.
24. Beginning at this point, there is great divergence between the Göttingen manuscript and the British Library manuscripts that comes to an end only at n. 26 below. The Göttingen manuscript presents a

196 THE DORMITION AND ASSUMPTION OF MARY

And Paul was bearing a pole on the bier of my Lady Mary, and Peter was bearing [17ᵇ] a pole, and John was bearing a pole, and Thomas was bearing a pole. And the rest of the angels and the apostles were ministering and going before her. And while the apostles were carrying the Blessed one, the Holy Spirit carried the apostles and the Blessed one, making them pass over the men who were coming against them, and they did not see them. And when the men were going along the Jerusalem road, they heard a great tumult that passed above them. And they stood, gazing at the sky and saying, "What is this wonder?" And when the apostles arrived in Jerusalem, the Holy Spirit said to them, "I have brought all of you to Jerusalem, so that the Jews will not think that in taking flight you fled from them and the strength of your Lord did not aid you."

(3.6) And when the men reached Bethlehem, they crept on their hands and their knees[25] so that they might open the door of the upper room suddenly, so that not one of our Lord's disciples might escape from their hands. And when they opened the door of the upper room and entered it, they found nothing,

much fuller account of these events that is occasionally similar to, but not identical with, the other early version edited by Agnes Smith Lewis. The version of these events preserved in the British Library manuscripts is as follows: ". . .and carried my Lady Mary's bier, and they went forth from the upper room. And they passed above the men who were coming against them, and they did not see them. And when the men came to Bethlehem, they opened the door of the upper room and entered, and they found nothing in it, neither the disciples nor my Lady Mary. The men were enraged, and they seized the people of Bethlehem and said to them, 'Will you not come and say to the governor and the priests, "We found nothing there"?' And the people of Bethlehem went with the men, and they said, 'We have found nothing there.' And the priests said. . ."

25. Literally, "feet."

THE SIX BOOKS APOCRYPHON   197

neither the disciples nor my Lady Mary. And immediately the men were enraged, [18ª] and they seized the people of Bethlehem and said to them, "Did you not come and say to the governor and the priests of Jerusalem that the disciples of Jesus came to Mary, and that the powers of the Lord did not cease descending and ascending to heaven? Come and go with us to Jerusalem and persuade the governor and the priests of Jerusalem as you like." And the people of Bethlehem went to Jerusalem, and these men with them, and they said before the governor and the priests that they found nothing. Then the priests[26] said to them, "The disciples of the deceiver have made some incantations and blinded your eyes, and you did not see them." And the governor said to the people of Bethlehem, "If you hear any news of them anywhere, seize them and bring them to us."

The Jews Discover Mary has Returned to Jerusalem and Complain to Governor.

(3.7) And after five days, the angels of the Lord were seen, entering into and coming forth from my Lady Mary's house in Jerusalem. And people from many neighborhoods gathered and cried out and said, "Holy Virgin, Theotokos, plead with Christ, whom you have in heaven, to send us healing, because we are afflicted." [18ᵇ] And[27] the people of Jerusalem were afraid with great fear. And the priests sent [some men] in the morning and said, "Go and ask who lives in that neighborhood." And when they asked, the people of that neighbor-

26. Beginning here, the text of the Göttingen manuscript is again more or less equivalent with the British Library manuscripts.

27. The passage "And the people. . .told the priests" is absent from the British Library manuscripts, which resume at n. 28 below.

198   THE DORMITION AND ASSUMPTION OF MARY

hood told them, "My Lady Mary the Theotokos has come to her house, and these hymns have come before her." And those who were sent came and told the priests. And [28] the priests and Sadducees arose, and they cried out in the *praetorium*, saying, "Governor, there will be great destruction here in Jerusalem on account of this woman." And the governor said, "And what shall I do for you now?" The people of Jerusalem said to him, "Let us take fire and wood and go and burn the house where she lives." The governor said to them, "Go and do whatever you want." And the people of Jerusalem gathered, and they took fire and wood and went to the house where my Lady Mary was living. And the governor was standing at a distance looking on.

(3.8) And the people of Jerusalem came to the house, and the doors of the house were closed. And they laid their hands on them to break them down. And immediately an angel of the Lord struck their faces with his wings, and fire blazed forth from the doors with no one casting it. And it burned the faces [19ª] and hair of the people who had come and approached the door of the house, and many of the people died. And there was great fear in all of Jerusalem.

The Governor Confesses Christ as Son of God and Rebukes the Jews.

(3.9) And when the governor saw this sight, he raised his hands to heaven and said, "Truly this deed that I have seen is that of the Son of God, who was born from the Virgin Mary and is worshipped and glorified in her." And on the next day

28. The British Library manuscripts resume here.

THE SIX BOOKS APOCRYPHON

199

the governor gave orders and sent for the people of Jerusalem, the priests, the elders, and the Sadducees. And he said to them, "O wicked people, people that crucified the God who came to it, you are people with bitter souls and stiff necks and doers of the desires of their own souls. And I give thanks to God that I am not from your country,[29] but the emperor Tiberius made me governor and sent me [to be] over you, because you are wicked and a perverted people. And I read [in] the letter of Pilate, something that his wife wrote to him, how she saw in a dream at night this Christ whom you killed, and how in this letter Pilate made known that he washed his hands of his blood and said, 'I have sinned greatly, because this man whom the people of Jerusalem have killed was righteous, while I, Pilate, did not have a hand [19b] in his blood.'[30] And[31] now, people of Jerusalem," said the governor, "none of you may come near the house of this holy woman."

(3.10) Then drew near Caleb the Sadducee, who believed in Christ and in my Lady Mary. And he whispered to the governor and said to him, "Your Highness, make them swear this oath which I tell you: 'By God who brought Israel up

29. The British Library manuscripts omit "but the emperor Tiberius. . .hand in his blood." Both resume at n. 31 below.

30. For various letters and other writings attributed to Pilate, see the discussion and texts in J. K. ELLIOTT, *The Apocryphal New Testament: A Collection of Apocryphal Christian Literature in an English Translation* (Oxford: Clarendon Press, 1993), 164–225, although I have not found an instance where this exact quotation appears in the above form; see also Wilhelm SCHNEEMELCHER, ed., *New Testament Apocrypha*, trans. R McL. WILSON, rev. ed., 2 vols. (Louisville, Ky.: Westminster/ John Knox Press, 1991–2), 1:501, 526–7.

31. The British Library manuscripts resume at this point.

200 THE DORMITION AND ASSUMPTION OF MARY

from Egypt, and by the holy books of the Law, these which were written by the hands of the living God, if you do not tell me what you think of Mary's son. Do you call him a prophet? Do you regard him as a righteous man? Is he the Messiah, the Son of God? Is he a son of man from among the sons of men? Tell me so that I may know, because you are readers of the Law.'"

The Governor Supervises a Debate between the Jews and Christians.

(3.11) Then the governor ordered that all of Jerusalem be assembled. And when it was assembled according to the governor's order, he came and stood on his tribunal, and he made them swear as Caleb had instructed him, by the God of Israel and the holy books of the Law, "Let everyone who believes in my Lady Mary and the child born from her, that he is the Messiah, the Son of God, separate himself and stand by himself; and whoever does not believe, let him show himself as an unbeliever." Then the people were divided into two groups, and those who believed in Christ separated themselves [20a] to one side. And the governor said to them, "What do you say? Do you believe in this child, who was born from Mary?" They said to him, "We believe in him, that he is the Messiah, the Son of the living God, and he is the one who by his command rules heaven and the earth." The unbelievers said to the governor, "My lord, according to our books, the Messiah has not yet come." The governor said to them, "Tell me: this one who has come, what do you think of him?" They said to him, "He is a deceiver, who is not even good like one of the righteous."

(3.12) The lovers of Christ said to the unbelievers, "Show us the miracles and signs that the ancient, the intermediate, and the latter [prophets] did, and we will show the signs that Christ did, that they are greater than all created things."

THE SIX BOOKS APOCRYPHON   201

The unbelievers said, "How will you show us that the son of Mary is the Messiah?" The lovers of Christ said, "We are showing it." The governor said to them, "You will not speak your words against each other with shouting and uproar; instead, speak to each other in a gentle voice from your books, for I too wish to see and know what your doctrines are."

(3.13) And the lovers of Christ said to the unbelievers, "Our father Adam, when [20b] he was dying, commanded his son Seth in his testament and said to him, 'My son Seth, behold, offerings have been placed by me in the cave of treasures, gold and myrrh and frankincense, because God is about to come into the world. And he will be seized by evil and wicked men, and he will die, and by his death make a resurrection for all the children of Adam. And behold, the Magi will come from Persia, and they will carry these offerings and go and bring them to the Son of God, who is born from the Virgin Mary in Bethlehem of Judea.'[32] And so it was: the Magi came and brought offerings. And we are not ashamed of anything that we are saying. What do you say?"

(3.14) The unbelievers said, "Surely Christ is not greater than Abraham in the eyes of God, who opened heaven and spoke with him as we are speaking with each other?"[33] And the lovers of Christ said, "You see that you know nothing! For we who are lovers of Christ know that the son of Mary created Adam. And before Abraham was formed in his mother's womb, Christ was before all created things.[34] And

32. *Testament of Adam* 3.7 (Stephen Edward ROBINSON, ed.), *The Testament of Adam: An Examination of the Syriac and Greek Traditions*, Society of Biblical Literature Dissertation Series 52 (Chico, Calif.: Scholars Press, 1982), 64–5.

33. Cf. John 8.52 and Gen 15 and 16.

34. Cf. John 8.54–8.

202   THE DORMITION AND ASSUMPTION OF MARY

this is what you have said, that God spoke with Abraham from heaven: it was Christ who spoke with him!"

(3.15) The unbelievers said, "Surely, [21ª] Christ, of whom you are so proud, is not greater than Isaac, who became an offering, and the fragrance of his offering ascended and pleased God above in the exalted heights, and heaven and earth delighted in it?"[35] The lovers of Christ said, "That Isaac was not killed on the altar, when Abraham offered him, was entirely because Christ, who was born from Mary, was about to come and die for all creatures, and by his death the entire world was to be delivered from error. For if Isaac had died, he would have been called a single offering. But when Christ died, an offering of all created things was offered in him to God."

(3.16) The unbelievers said, "Surely Christ is not greater than Jacob, the like of whose vision human beings have never seen, who went up and slept on the mount of Gilead, and God opened the heavens and spoke with him and stretched a ladder from heaven to earth, and the angels descended to greet him?"[36] The lovers of Christ said, "Jacob, the angels, and the ladder that he saw pointed to the coming of Christ and the mystery of his death."

(3.17) The unbelievers said, "The ascent of Elijah to heaven refutes you, because everything that he says in heaven is heard and everything that he wills on earth is done."[37] The lovers of Christ said, "Elijah ascended in a whirlwind to the heaven in which the sun and the moon are fixed, and no one worshipped him in his ascent, except Elisha his disciple. But

35. Cf. Gen 22.
36. Cf. Gen 28.10–17.
37. Cf. 2 Kgdms 2.1–12.

THE SIX BOOKS APOCRYPHON 203

Christ, when he ascended into heaven, ascended not to a single heaven, but [21ᵇ] above all the heavens. And when Christ ascended into heaven, all the creatures above and below bowed their heads and worshipped him, and behold, they worship and glorify him forever."[38]

(3.18) The unbelievers said, "Let Moses come, and his signs, with which he scourged the Egyptians and delivered Israel. And when Pharaoh wanted to prevent us from reaching the sea, Moses lifted up the dry staff that was in his hand and piled up the waves of the sea in heaps."[39] The lovers of Christ said, "Jesus too, who was born from Mary, rebuked demons, and they were scattered before him.[40] And to Simon Peter, when the sea sought to swallow him, he stretched out his hand and raised him up, and he did not sink.[41] And if Christ was not the ruler of the sea and land and all created things, why would all these created things obey him when he commands them?"

The Christians Prevail and Demand
to Know Where the Cross is Hidden.

(3.19) Then the governor gave an order, and four men from the unbelievers were scourged with severe beatings.[42]

38. Cf. Luke 24.50–3.

39. Cf. Exod 14.

40. e.g. Matt 8.28–32, 9.32–3.

41. Cf. Matt 14.28–33.

42. Beginning at this point, the parallels between the Göttingen manuscript and the British Library manuscripts temporarily cease, and the Göttingen manuscript instead includes an episode that is found more completely in Smith Lewis's version. The British Library manuscripts resume with a text comparable to the Göttingen manuscript at note 43 below.

204 THE DORMITION AND ASSUMPTION OF MARY

And after they were scourged, the lovers of Christ said to the unbelievers, "Since you seek to be free from blame, we will show you what we will do with you, and we will reveal all of the deceits that have occurred in Jerusalem in the presence of this distinguished governor, whom God has sent to seek vengeance against you for the ignominy of Christ, whom you killed." And the governor said to them, "Say everything that you wish, and do not be afraid." And they immediately said, [22a] "Where is the wood hidden, on which Christ was crucified, and the crown of thorns, and the spear that wounded him, and the nails that fastened him by his hands and feet, and the garments of disgrace with which you clothed him? Tell where they are hidden!"

(3.20) The governor said to them, "Speak and reveal everything that they say to you." The unbelievers said, "My lord, they too know everything that we know." And when the governor saw this, he stood on his tribunal, and he adjured them and said, "By Christ who was born from the virgin Mary, in whom you believe, and in whom I too believe, reveal and tell everything that you know about Christ." Then the lovers of Christ called out with one voice and said, "O wise judge! Woe to us because of the judgment of Christ on the last day! Woe to us because of your judgment, O son of Mary, whom we killed! Woe to us, how much we have wronged you! And not only have we wronged you, but also the Father who sent you into the world!"

(3.21) The governor said to them, "Reveal to me where the wood is on which you crucified Christ, and the spear, and the nails, and the garments of disgrace with which you clothed him." And they went and they showed him. The governor said to them, "Great is this thing that was hidden among you. And now that you are angry with each other, you have revealed it. And if the emperor were to hear, he would cut off

THE SIX BOOKS APOCRYPHON 205

all of your heads!" [22ᵇ] And[43] the day ended, and the governor spent the night enraged in his *praetorium*.

Mary Heals the Governor's Son.

(3.22) And when the cock crew, the governor went forth, he and his two servants and his son with him, because his son had dysentery and strangury. And he knocked at the Blessed one's door, and her handmaid came out and answered him. The governor said to her, "Go in and tell your Lady: 'The governor of the city Jerusalem wants to venerate you.'" Then my Lady Mary ordered that the door should be opened for him. And he entered and bowed down and venerated her, and he cried out and said to her, "Peace to you, Theotokos, and peace to Christ who was born from you, and peace to the heavens, which bear the throne of your son's Godhead, the Son, Christ, who arose from you! Mouth and tongue are too feeble to tell the glories of you and your son, the holy child! The earth on which you walk will become heaven; the heaven that beholds you will give a blessing to the human beings that believe in you. The healthy who see you will receive joy; the sick who come to you, you will give them healing. I venerate you, my Lady Mary. Stretch out your right hand and bless me, me and this my only son that God has given me. And pray for the souls that I have in the city of Rome, that I may go forth in peace and see them, and bear gifts and offerings, and come and venerate you."

(3.23) Now my Lady [23ᵃ] Mary was standing and praying, and a censer of incense had been placed before her. And when she heard the governor's words, she turned around

43. At this point, the British Library manuscripts resume with a text that is comparable to the Göttingen manuscript.

206   THE DORMITION AND ASSUMPTION OF MARY

and prayed, and she stretched forth her hands and blessed him and his son and said to him, "Sit down." Now the twelve apostles of our Lord were there with my Lady Mary. And when she said to the governor, "Sit down," he did not want to sit, but he ran and fell immediately at the feet of the apostles and said to them, "Peace be with you, chosen ones who were chosen by God before all creatures! And peace to Christ who chose you to be his preachers in the world!" The apostles said to him, "We have heard what you have done to the crucifiers and have prayed much for you." The governor said to them, "The disgrace that they have become before God and humanity is enough for them." The apostles said to him, "Indeed, what have they done that they should not be a disgrace!" Thus the apostles spoke to the governor when he went and venerated them. And he was dismissed and went forth from Jerusalem and went to his house in the city of Rome, because he was from there. And when he went to Rome, he went before the emperors and the nobility of Rome and told them of the miracles that my Lady Mary was working [23ᵇ] in the world. And the disciples of Paul and Peter, whom they had in the city of Rome, also went and wrote these holy words which they heard from the governor.

Apparitions and Miracles of the Virgin Mary.

(3.24) And their disciples wrote to the apostles, "When you have prepared my Lady Mary for burial, bring with you to the city of Rome the book of her death, how she went forth from this world, for, behold, all places are full of the glories of the Blessed one, and since we have believed in her here, she has often appeared to the people who believe in her prayers. For she appeared here on the sea when it was raging and stormy and about to destroy the ships that were sailing on

THE SIX BOOKS APOCRYPHON   207

it. And the sailors called on the Blessed one's name and said, 'My Lady Mary, Theotokos, have mercy on us!' And she rose above them like the sun and delivered these ships, which were ninety-two in number. And she saved them from destruction, and nothing was lost from them. And she appeared in the daytime at the moment when thieves fell upon some men and were going to kill them, and the men cried out and said, 'My Lady Mary, Theotokos, have mercy on us!' And she rose above them like a flash of lightning and blinded the eyes of the thieves, [24a] and they were not seen by them. And the men escaped, and none of them was harmed. And she appeared to a woman, a widow whose son went to look into a well of water and fell into it, and there was no one near her to bring him up. And the woman cried out at the mouth of the well and said, 'My Lady Mary, Theotokos, have mercy on me!' And my Lady Mary appeared to her and immediately snatched the young man up, and he was not drowned. And she gave him to his mother alive. And she appeared to a man who was sick for sixteen years, and the physicians were unable to offer any help in all this length of years. Then he brought a censer and placed incense in it and called to mind the Blessed one and said, 'My Lady Mary, Theotokos, heal me!' And immediately she came to him and healed him and sent him to the church of Rome before all the people. And she appeared to a man, a merchant, who had borrowed a thousand dinars and went to trade with them in another place. And he was going along the road, and the purse fell from him and was lost. And after he had journeyed for a long time, he sat down to eat bread and changed his clothes. And he looked for [24b] the purse and could not find it. And he was weeping and moaning, and going along the road and praying, 'My Lady Mary, Theotokos, have mercy on me.' Then my Lady Mary had mercy on him and took him and brought him to the purse of dinars, and

208 THE DORMITION AND ASSUMPTION OF MARY

he took what was his and did not lose anything. And she appeared on the road to Egypt to two women, who were attacked by a large snake, and it ran after them to devour them. And they called on her name and said, 'My Lady Mary, Theotokos, have mercy on us.' And my Lady Mary appeared to them and struck the snake on its mouth, and it was split in two. And the women were delivered and did not perish."

The Apostles Carry Mary to Her Grave and the Jews Attack Her Body.

(3.25) And while my Lady Mary was performing these miracles and signs in Rome and in all places, the apostles were with her. And when the apostles and my Lady Mary were in Jerusalem and Friday had dawned, the Holy Spirit said to the apostles, "Tomorrow morning take my Lady Mary and go out from Jerusalem on the road that leads to the head of the valley. Behold, there are three caves there and a raised seat of clay. Bring the Blessed one and place her on the seat and attend to her until I tell you."

(3.26) And when it was morning, [25ª] the apostles arose and carried the Blessed one and went forth from Jerusalem. And the Jews were standing and mocking and saying to each other, "Behold, the disciples of the deceiver are carrying Mary and going forth." And the Blessed one was looking at them. And there was there a mighty Jewish man, whose name was Yuphanya [Jephonias], who was tall in stature and outstanding in strength and powerful in might. The scribes of Israel said to him, "Come near, Yuphanya, and blow on Mary, and she will fall from her bier, for behold, the disciples of the deceiver think that they have conquered Jerusalem." And Yuphanya went and cast both of his arms on two poles of the bier and hung on them so that the bier might break and fall down, and

THE SIX BOOKS APOCRYPHON   209

the Jews might seize it and burn it in a fire. Yuphanya placed his hands [on the bier],[44] and the angel of the Lord struck him with a sword of fire and cut off both of his arms from his shoulders, and they hung like ropes from the bier. And he was weeping and coming after the apostles who were carrying the Blessed one and said, "Lord Jesus Christ, have mercy on me! Apostles of Jesus have mercy on me!" And the apostles said to him, "Why do you call on us? Call on my Lady Mary, she whose bier you sought to break, and she will answer you." [25b] Yuphanya said, "My Lady Mary, Theotokos, have mercy on me." And my Lady Mary said to Peter, "Give Yuphanya his arms, which are hanging from the bier." And when Peter had spat on one of them, he said, "In the name of my Lady Mary, the Theotokos, cleave to your place." Then Peter made the arms cleave to their places. And Peter took up a dry staff and gave it to him and said, "Go and show the power of the Son of God to all of the Jews. And tell of my Lady Mary, what she has done for you with her prayers."

Priests Dispatch Romans to Mary's Grave
& the Romans are Destroyed.

(3.27) And[45] when the apostles went to the cave at the head of the valley, they entered the three caves. And they placed the Blessed one's bier on the seat. And a great service of angels and apostles on her behalf lasted for five days. And the Jews in Jerusalem heard and sent the chiliarch and the

44. The passage in brackets is from the British Library manuscripts and helps with the sense of the passage.
45. Beginning here, the Göttingen manuscript includes a passage that is not found in the British Library manuscripts. The text of the British Library manuscripts resumes below at n. 46.

210   THE DORMITION AND ASSUMPTION OF MARY

Romans with him, because at that time there was no governor in Jerusalem, but it was something that the priests ordered. And when the priests had sent the Romans against the apostles, they ordered them thus, "Go to the three caves at the head of the valley and bring wood and fire and fill the caves. And bring great rocks and pile them up at the entrance of the cave. And set the disciples on fire [26ᵃ] and Mary with them." And the men went and wandered in the valley for three days. And the Holy Spirit darkened their eyes, and they did not remain at the mouth of the cave. And they came and sat at its mouth. And while they were speaking with each other, the entrance of the cave was opened before them, and they saw the bier laid down, and a woman sitting on it, and the apostles and angels ministering before her. And three men from them were bold, and they entered. They went in a little, and immediately fire consumed them, and the earth swallowed them up.

(3.28) And their associates, who were outside the mouth of the cave, fled out of their fear to Jerusalem. And they said before all the people everything that had happened to them. And the priests gave much gold to the men that they had sent and said to them, "Do not say before anyone that a single one of you died there, lest the people go astray, and the people would say thus: 'Perhaps Mary is something in the presence of God.'" And the men spoke as they were commanded by the priests. For the Jews had a custom that as soon as anyone went to my Lady Mary and was healed, they took gold and gave it to him and said [26ᵇ] to him, "Do not say that Mary healed you," because [46] the Jews hated my Lady Mary greatly. And they were also saying, "If now while she is alive she prevails over us, when she is dead and we see where she is buried, we will go and take her corpse and burn it with fire." But Christ who was born of the Virgin

46. The text of the British Library manuscripts resumes at this point.

THE SIX BOOKS APOCRYPHON   211

Mary gathered the Blessed one, his mother, from this world, from before the race of crucifiers, who were thirsting after her like ravenous wolves to devour her, the blessed sheep. For let no one who loves God and my Lady Mary who gave birth to him be a friend or companion of the Jews, for if he is, the love of Christ is separated from him. Here ends the third book.

The Fourth Book.

(4.1) And while the apostles were ministering to my Lady Mary in the cave, the Holy Spirit revealed to the apostles in the cave where they were ministering, "In the sixth month, the angel Gabriel was sent to the mother of your Lord, my Lady Mary, and he greeted her and told her about the holy child that was to be born from her for the salvation of the world (and the sixth month [27ᵃ] is Nisan) on the first day of Nisan, which was Sunday, while my Lady Mary was sitting, and lying before her were the dyed fabrics of the curtains, which she was making for the house of the Lord." [47] And again the Holy Spirit said to the apostles, "Thus believe and thus confess that on Sunday your Lord was announced and came into the world. And on Sunday he was born in Bethlehem. And on Sunday the people of Jerusalem went forth unwillingly and glorified him with heavenly and earthly hosannas. And on Sunday he rose from the grave and put to shame all his crucifiers. And tomorrow too, which is Sunday, he will come from heaven, and with all creatures that are above and below before him he will glorify his mother who gave him birth. And those who did not believe in his coming into the world will be put to shame."

47. Cf. Luke 1.26–38 and *Protev.* 10.

212 THE DORMITION AND ASSUMPTION OF MARY

Biblical Matriarchs and Patriarchs Assemble for Mary's Death.

(4.2) And the Sabbath Day declined, and the angels and apostles were ministering before her. And the morning of holy Sunday arose. And Eve, the mother of all human beings came, and my Lady Mary's mother, and Elizabeth, the mother of Saint John the Baptist. And the mother of my Lady Mary drew near and placed her mouth on her breast and kissed her and said to her, "Blessed be God, who chose you [27ᵇ] for himself, so that you would be a dwelling place for his glory, because from the time when you were formed in my womb, I knew that the God of heaven would come and dwell in you."

(4.3) And Peter drew near and moved these women aside, and they stood at the Blessed one's head, because the chariots of the patriarchs were seen coming. And our father Adam came, and Seth his son, and Shem and Noah, who was the leaven of the world. And they worshipped the glorious one. And other chariots appeared coming, [those] of Abraham, Isaac, and Jacob, and of Saint David the Psalmist. And they worshipped before the Blessed one. And the chariots of the prophets were seen coming, and with censers in their hands they worshipped before the Blessed one. And creatures without number went forth from the gate of heaven to descend to the earth: assemblies [48] of watchers, and hosts of angels, and ranks and orders of seraphim, divisions and thousands of fiery angels. And hosts of spirituals were standing at the

---

48. Beginning at this point, the Göttingen manuscript includes a passage not found in the British Library manuscripts. The British Library manuscripts continue at n. 49 below, and in place of this passage, they have: "Then the great king appeared, coming and holding the sign of the cross."

THE SIX BOOKS APOCRYPHON 213

door of heaven and beholding the coronation of the Blessed one and the glory that she had. Then Enoch, Isaiah, and Moses appeared, sitting on three chariots of glory. They came and remained between heaven and earth. And they were expecting that Christ the king would appear.

Christ Appears to Receive his Mother's Soul.

(4.4) And the Holy Spirit said to the apostles, "Set up [28ᵃ] a censer of incense, because Christ your Lord is coming from heaven unto you." And twelve legions of angels and great angels appeared, whose number was 120,000. Then the person of Christ the king appeared on a chariot that seraphim were carrying. He[49] descended and stood beside her, and all the creatures blessed and worshipped him. And the Lord Jesus Christ called to his mother and said to her, "Mary!" And she said to him, "Here I am, Rabbuli" (which means "Teacher"). And[50] the Lord said to her, "Do not grieve: arise and see the glory that my Father has given me and that I have come to show you." And the holy virgin looked at it and beheld the glory of which no human mouth is able to speak. The Lord said to his mother, "Is everything that I told you true, Mary?"

49. At this point the text in the British Library manuscript again parallels the Göttingen manuscript.

50. Beginning at this point, the Göttingen manuscript again includes a passage not found in the British Library manuscripts, which continue at n. 51 below. In its place, the British Library manuscripts have: "And my Lady Mary said to her son, 'Stretch forth your hands and place them on my eyes and bless me.' And Christ stretched forth his hands and placed them on his mother's eyes. And she took them and kissed them and said, 'I worship these holy hands, which made heaven and earth.'"

214 THE DORMITION AND ASSUMPTION OF MARY

And she said to him, "Yes, truly, Rabbuli, everything that you said to me is true." Then he said to her, "I will bring your body to the Paradise of Eden, and it will be there until the resurrection. I will also give angels for your honor, and they will serve you and minister to you."

Mary Intercedes for the World She is Leaving.

(4.5) Then[51] the apostles drew near and said to my Lady Mary, "Leave a blessing for the world from which you are going forth, [28ᵇ] so that those who make a commemoration and an offering to you, and believe in God who sent his Son and dwelt in you, and confess that the son who was born from you is the Messiah, and glorify the Holy Spirit who escorts you, will be delivered from severe afflictions."

(4.6) Then my Lady Mary prayed and spoke thus in her prayer, "May God, who willed from his own will and was reconciled in his love and sent his Son from heaven and dwelt in the palace of my members, have mercy on the people who call upon him." And again she prayed and said, "Christ my son, king of heaven, Son of God who does not pass away, receive the prayers of the people who call upon and remember the name of your mother in your presence, and make misfortunes pass away from them, and make difficult times cease from the earth." And[52] again she prayed and said,

51. At this point the text in the British Library manuscripts again parallels the Göttingen manuscript.

52. Beginning here, the Göttingen manuscript diverges significantly from the text in the British Library manuscripts, which again become comparable below at n. 53. The British Library manuscripts have instead: "And give a crown to old age, and growing up to youth, and help the souls that call upon you. And make bad times cease from the

THE SIX BOOKS APOCRYPHON
215

"Lord Jesus Christ, may what you will be accomplished in heaven and on the earth. This I ask of you my Lord, that wherever people gather and make a commemoration of me and present me with offerings, accept, my Lord, their offerings, and receive the prayer that ascends before you. And[53] make death and captivity, the sword and famine, all malignant illnesses, and every suffering that befalls humanity pass away from the land in which they make offerings. Make them cease from the people who make [29ᵃ] offerings before you.[54] May the lands be delivered by these offerings from the locust, so that it will not destroy them, and from blight, that it might not be upon them, and from hailstones, that they might not descend on them from heaven. Let everyone who is sick be healed; and whoever is afflicted, let him be relieved; and whoever is hungry, let him be satisfied; and whoever is poor, let him have abundance; and whoever is vexed by a spirit of Satan and calls on my name, let him be sent a healing; and whoever is in bondage through an injustice by human beings, let his bonds be lost; and those who are traveling on the sea, and storms rise up against them, and they call upon the name of the Lord, let them be delivered from harm; and those who are in remote places and call upon my name, let them come safely to their homes. And the fields that give an offering in my honor, let them be blessed and bring forth the seeds that

earth, when human beings, my Lord, hold a commemoration of my body and spirit, which have gone forth from the world."

53. At this point, all three manuscripts again preserve a comparable text.

54. Instead of "Make them cease from the people who make offerings before them," the British Library manuscripts have: "Make pestilence cease from the land in which offerings are made to me. And bless the garland of the year."

216 THE DORMITION AND ASSUMPTION OF MARY

are buried in the furrows; and the vines from which wine is pressed in my name, let them bear bountiful clusters. And let the people who make offerings to me from their possessions be blessed.[55] And may there by concord on kings, peace on governors, and blessings and joy on the face of the earth unto the ages of ages, Amen." My Lady Mary said these blessings and words of joy before Christ her son who came to her.

(4.7) Then the Lord Jesus Christ said to his mother, [29ᵇ] "Everything that you have said to me, I will do to please you. And I will have mercy on those who call upon me in your name.[56] And those who commemorate and make offerings to you, their prayers will be received before the glorious throne of my Father in heaven and before your son Jesus Christ and before the Holy Spirit and before all the companies of angels. And blessings and joys will come upon people who commemorate and make offerings to you because of your greatness, unto the ages of ages, Amen." And all the creatures answered, and they arose there and said, "Amen."

55. In place of "And let the people who make offerings to me from their possessions be blessed," the British Library manuscripts have the following: "And let there be peace and harmony on all creatures who call upon you. And Lord, let the garland of the years and months be blessed before you. And when the priests make offerings, receive their tithes with gladness. And make their churches thunder with thanksgiving and let the Holy Spirit sing with them."

56. Beginning here, the Göttingen manuscript includes a passage absent from the British Library manuscripts. This passage ends at n. 57 below, at which point all three manuscripts preserve a comparable text.

THE SIX BOOKS APOCRYPHON 217

Mary's Soul Departs from Her Body.

(4.8) And[57] the Lord signaled Peter and drew near to him and said to him, "Now is the time; raise a psalm and let the creatures sing Alleluia." And while all the created beings sang with the voice of Alleluia, the Lord Jesus Christ prayed, and the holy angels gave glory. And immediately the soul of the Blessed one went forth from her, and he sent it to the mansions of his Father's house. And as she was dying, my Lady Mary said to her son, "Farewell, Rabbuli, for behold, I am looking for your coming, which is at hand." And Simon Peter ran, and John the younger, and Paul, and Thomas. And immediately John placed his hands on her eyes and closed them. And[58] Paul and Peter stretched out her arms and feet.

57. At this point, the text of the British Library manuscripts is again comparable with the Göttingen manuscript.

58. Beginning here, the Göttingen manuscript includes a passage that is not in the British Library manuscripts. The manuscripts only become comparable again at n. 61 below. The British Library manuscripts have instead: "And our Lord ordered them to place the blessed one in a chariot of light. And the twelve apostles bore it as it went to the Paradise of Eden.

[Sections 9, 10, and the first part of 11 are absent.]

(11) And the apostles ordered that there should be a commemoration of the blessed one three times in the year. [The first is] on the twenty-fourth of the first Kanun [December]. And because it is not possible that there should be a commemoration of her on the Nativity, we order that the commemoration of her will take place two days after, so that by her pure offerings the seeds that the farmers have borrowed and sown will be blessed.

(12) And the apostles said that there should be a commemoration of the blessed one in the month of Iyar [May], on account of the seeds that were sown, and on account of the flying and creeping locusts, that they might not come forth and destroy the crops, and then there

218 THE DORMITION AND ASSUMPTION OF MARY

[30ª] And they did not remove her garment from her but enshrouded her in it. And outside of the woolen garment that

would be a famine and the people would perish. And the Holy Spirit said to them: 'They are buried in the earth until the day appointed for them, and they come forth to fulfill the will of their Lord. And when they are created, in one hour they are created, and wherever they go to destroy, in one hour they make the land desolate.' And the apostles also ordered that on the Wednesdays, Fridays, and Sundays of every month of the year there should be prayers, and that these three days should be observed and no work should be done on them.

(13) And the apostles also ordered that there should be a commemoration of the blessed one on the thirteenth [or B: the fifteenth] of the month of Ab [August], on account of the vine-bearing clusters and the trees bearing fruit, so that the clouds of hail, which bear stones of wrath, will not come and break the trees and their fruit and the vines with their clusters.

(14) And the apostles also ordered that an offering that have been offered in the name of my Lady Mary should not remain over the night, but that at midnight of the night immediately preceding her commemoration, it should be kneaded and baked. And in the morning let it go up onto the altar, while the people stand before the altar with psalms of David. And let the New and Old Testaments be read, and the book of the departure of the blessed one. And let everyone be before the altar in the church, and let the priests make the offering and set up a censer of incense and light the lights, and let the entire service be concerning these offerings. And when the entire service is finished, let everyone take his offerings to his house. And let the priest speak thus: 'In the name of the Father, and of the Son, and of the Holy Spirit, we celebrate the commemoration of my Lady Mary.' Thus let the priest speak three times; and with the words of the priest who speaks, the Holy Spirit will come and bless these offerings. And when everyone takes away his offering and goes to his house, great aid and the blessing of the blessed one will enter his dwelling and sustain it forever."

THE SIX BOOKS APOCRYPHON 219

she was wearing, the Holy Spirit enshrouded her in a garment of light over all of the Blessed one's bier.

Mary's Body is Brought to Paradise in the Company of the Apostles.

(4.9) And the twelve apostles were carrying her, and clouds of light were carrying the twelve apostles. And the sounds of the seraphim's trumpets were sounding before the Blessed one's bier as she went to the Paradise of Eden with great glory. And my Lady Mary went to the Paradise of Eden with great glory. And they placed her in unending light among the glorious trees that were in the Paradise of Eden, whose sweet fragrance was greater than sweet spices. And all the creatures returned and came to greet my Lady Mary.

(4.10) And finally the twelve apostles went forth from Paradise, and Paradise was closed. And the apostles turned and went to the Mount of Olives on the clouds on which they were sitting, and no one of them was separated from his companion. And they set up incense and prayed and said, "As you deemed us worthy, Lord, to behold the departure of your mother from this world, and to assemble us on clouds of light to be blessed by your holy mother, then Lord Jesus Christ bring us, even us, into your Father's kingdom, and give us a crown of glory, and we will be [30ᵇ] your children, and you will be our God. And as your holy mouth promised us, and you said, give us authority, Lord, at the last day, on which you came, to sit on twelve thrones and to judge the twelve tribes of Israel,[59] because they do not believe in you, nor in the mother that bore you."

59. Cf. Matt 19.28.

220 THE DORMITION AND ASSUMPTION OF MARY

The Apostles Establish Three Annual Feasts in Mary's Honor.

(4.11) And when they had prayed, they said, "Let us write everything that we have seen in 'The Departure of the Blessed One': 'In the year three-hundred and forty-five, my Lady Mary went forth from this world. And we the apostles have written that there will be a commemoration of the Blessed one three times in the year, because if people observe the commemoration, they will be preserved from wrath, and peace will reign over all the regions of the earth, and all bad afflictions will be prevented from going forth over the earth and harming it.'" And the apostles ordered that there be a commemoration of the Blessed one in the second Kanun [January], two days after the Nativity, so that by her offerings and prayers, the locusts that hide in the lands will be killed, and seeds that the farmers have borrowed and sown will be blessed. And the fragrance of her offering will ascend and persuade Christ, so that one of the kingdoms will not be stirred and wage war with the others, and the blood of many people be shed [31ª] upon the earth, because when there are wars, heaven and earth are in mourning over people killing each other. And the air is disturbed, and the smell of the air is changed from people's corpses, as in the days of Noah, so that smell of corpses spreads from end to end of the earth.

(4.12) And the apostles ordered that there be a commemoration of my Lady Mary in the month of Iyar [May], on the fifteenth, on account of the seeds that were sown, and on account of the beard of wheat, so that from them there will be an offering to the Lord and the Blessed one. And the apostles ordered that for the entire month of Iyar, people should draw near to the presence of God with weeping and mourning and prayers.

(4.13) And the apostles ordered that there be a commemoration of my Lady Mary in the month of Ab [August], on

THE SIX BOOKS APOCRYPHON

221

the thirteenth, on account of the vine-bearing clusters, and on account of the trees bearing fruit, so that the clouds of hail, which bear stones of wrath, will not come, and the trees and their fruit be broken, and the vines and their clusters be diseased, and those eating them suddenly become ill, and there will be a fearful pestilence on everyone, and it will kill parents in front of children and children in front of parents.

Bread Offerings for Mary's Annual Commemorations.

(4.14) And the apostles ordered that there will be a commemoration of the Blessed one [31b] in these three months, so that people will be delivered from hard afflictions and a plague of wrath will not come upon the earth and its inhabitants. And the apostles ordered that offerings that have been offered to the Blessed one should not remain overnight, but in the evening let flour of the finest wheat flour [60] come to the church and be placed before the altar. And let the priests make the offering and set up censors of incense and light the lights. And let the entire evening service [vespers] be concerning these offerings. And when the service is finished, let everyone take his offering to his house. Because as soon as the priests pray and say the prayer of my Lady Mary, the Theotokos, "Come to us and help the people who call upon you," and with the priest's word of blessing, my Lady Mary comes and blesses these offerings. And when everyone takes his offering and goes to his house, great aid and the blessing of my Lady Mary will enter his dwelling and sustain it forever.

60. Presumably, this imitates the flour offerings of the Hebrew Bible: e.g. Lev 5.11. The British Library manuscripts identify the offering as "kneaded and baked," thus indicating bread.

222   THE DORMITION AND ASSUMPTION OF MARY

(4.15) And[61] the apostles arose and took censors of incense and drew near to the Lord to ask him that the years and their garlands be blessed. And the apostles prayed and said, "Lord Jesus Christ, hear the voice of our prayers, and bless the garlands of the years that are coming to the world, and bless the twelve months. [32a] Let Nisan come, bearing the buds of the flowers of blessing, so that it may perfume the altars of the Lord with glorious flowers. Let Iyar come, bearing blessed ears of corn, from which an offering may be made to the Lord. Let Haziran come, bearing tables of newly rubbed corn from the ears, and carrying dishes full of new bread, which the Lord will bless and give to the people. Let Tamuz come, giving thanks for people who sing on the threshing floors, which are full of rejoicing. Let Ab come, giving worship to God, who has blessed and given unripe and ripe fruits. Let Ilal come, worshipping and praising Christ, who has blessed the months and years. Let [the first] Teshrin come and its good things, which heard the voice of the farmer who has sown with the plow of the cross. Let [the second] Teshrin come, and its joys with it, fragrant dew that comes from heaven, anointing and blessing the earth and its inhabitants. Let [the first] Kanun come, and its joys with it, thick clouds, and lightning, and rain that pours out on the face of the earth. Let [the second] Kanun come, and with it snow and ice, which please the earth. Let Shebat come, bearing on its shoulders good things that give birth to joys. Let Adar come, bearing gifts for the Lord, the best lambs and sheep, giving thanks."

(4.16) Thus the apostles prayed and said, "Yea Lord God, who sent his Son [32b] to us to save the world from error, let

---

61. At this point, the texts of all three manuscripts are again comparable.

THE SIX BOOKS APOCRYPHON   223

your blessing be upon the earth and its inhabitants when [62] an offering is made to my Lady Mary, the Theotokos." Then the voice of the apostles' prayer ascended to heaven. And the Lord Jesus Christ came to them on a luminous cloud and spoke with them and said to them, "Be strong and take courage, and be valiant and do [63] not be afraid. Everything that you seek will be given, and everything that you cry out will be heard, and your wish will be constantly with your Father in heaven." Then the apostles bowed their heads and were blessed by the Lord Jesus Christ.

The Apostles Write the Six Books Apocryphon.

(4.17) And the apostles arose, and they prayed and said,[64] ["Come, let us go down from the Mount of Olives to the cave at the head of the valley, and let us write there how my Lady Mary was crowned with the cloud of light." And the apostles went down from the Mount of Olives to the cave at the head of the valley and set out incense and commanded that this book should be written as follows, "We all, the apostles, testify before God, and before our Lord Jesus Christ, and before the Holy Spirit, that our Lord Jesus Christ did these miracles

62. Beginning here, the Göttingen manuscript differs significantly from the British Library manuscripts. The texts again become comparable below at n. 63. In place of the passage above, the British Library manuscripts have: "inhabitants, and let your grace come to us and be revealed to us at this time. Then our Lord Jesus came to them and said to them."

63. At this point all three manuscripts are again comparable.

64. A lengthy passage from the British Library manuscripts is lacking here in the Göttingen manuscript, and we have restored it from the British Library manuscripts, as indicated by the brackets.

224   THE DORMITION AND ASSUMPTION OF MARY

before his mother when she was departing from the world." And six books were written about her, each book by two of the apostles, [containing] all the signs and all the miracles which my Lady Mary did. And this book was written in Hebrew and Greek and Latin, and the apostles deposited it with Saint John, whose blessing is great. And the apostles prayed and called on the Lord Jesus to come and bless them, so that each of them might go to the country from which he had come. And they prayed for a long time, and the Lord came to them and blessed them and ascended into heaven.]

(4.18) [And [65] the twelve apostles asked Paul and Peter and said,] "Because we are twelve apostles, it is fitting that the book of the Blessed one be written in twelve copies, and that a copy should go forth with each one of us." And Peter said, "The apostles from among us who were dead, who, behold, are going to their graves, shall we write the book of my Lady Mary for them?" The apostles said to Peter, "What do you command should happen?" Peter said, "Let each of us, when he has gone to the place from which he has come, write and preach to the people to whom he has gone whatever the Holy [33ᵃ] Spirit puts in his mouth." And they spoke thus, "Let him teach the world unto which he is going, so that there will be a commemoration of my Lady Mary three times in the year, because if the people observe the commemoration, they will be delivered from wrath."

(4.19) And John the younger took the book of the departure of the Blessed one. And Paul and Peter called to John, and the apostles Paul, Peter, and John talked among themselves and discussed dividing the book. And when they were about

65. The initial phrase in this section is inserted from the British Library manuscripts, continuing the insertion made in the previous section.

THE SIX BOOKS APOCRYPHON   225

to have an argument about it, a voice came to them from heaven, which said to them, "Go in peace, blessed ones; be looking for and expecting my coming, which is coming." And lightning and thunder appeared to them coming from heaven, singing before the apostles and going to the places from which they had come. And those who were dead returned to their graves, and the blessed ones slept and were at rest.

(4.20) Through the prayers of the prophets and apostles and martyrs and confessors, may everyone who believes in the Father and in the Son and in the Holy Spirit and in my Lady Mary the Theotokos, receive a blessing from our Lord Jesus Christ, who was born of the Virgin Mary. And may everyone who observes the commemoration of the Blessed one be remembered in heaven and on earth. And may our Lord Jesus Christ have mercy and compassion on all our congregation, [33b] which has heard these holy words, unto the ages of ages. Amen. Here ends the fourth book.

The Fifth Book.

Christ Leads Mary on a Tour of Heaven.

(5.1) And when the Blessed one was placed in the Paradise of Eden and was crowned with great glory, and the apostles had departed in all directions, the Lord Jesus Christ came to her in the Paradise of Eden[66] with assemblies of heavenly

66. Beginning at this point, the Göttingen manuscript differs significantly from the British Library manuscripts. The British Library manuscripts are again comparable with G starting at the beginning of the following section 2. In place of the above, the British Library manuscripts have: "And chariots of spiritual beings descended from heaven in endless numbers. And the Paradise of Eden was covered,

226 THE DORMITION AND ASSUMPTION OF MARY

beings. For the Paradise of Eden is on earth and a great mountain. And its foundations are placed on the earth, and it is much higher than all mountains. And four rivers go forth from it: Gihon and Pishon and Euphrates and Tigris.[67] And when there was a flood, the waters went up as far as the lower parts of the mountain of Paradise, and immediately a command held it back. For the flood did not dare to disgrace that holy mountain.[68] For the Lord of the flood made his glory to dwell over the Paradise of Eden, and he stood and beheld the flood that was scourging humanity.

(5.2) And when our Lord Jesus came to my Lady Mary, he called out and said to her, "Mary, arise!" And immediately [34ª] she was restored to life and she arose and worshipped him. And the Lord Jesus said to her, "I have come to you to show you the glory of my Father's house." Then Mary said to him, "It is well, Rabbuli." [69] And the Lord said to her, "Mary, look and see what I have prepared for the righteous who love me." And the Blessed one saw the resting places of the righteous, how they were built and beautified and adorned. And she beheld the tabernacles of the children of light. And she saw the banquet hall of the martyrs. And she saw the glorious resting place in which the righteous will dwell.[70] And she saw

and all the mountains that surrounded it. And the sound of nothing was heard except the voice of those saying, 'Holy!, holy!'"

67. Cf. Gen 2.10–14.

68. Although cf. Gen 7.19.

69. The British Library manuscripts add: "And Elijah the prophet came to our Lord and to my Lady Mary, and Enoch and Moses and Simon Peter. They came at the command of our Savior to the Paradise of Eden."

70. Or "were dwelling." The tense is not clear from the grammatical form.

THE SIX BOOKS APOCRYPHON   227

the lovely trees of Paradise: how beautiful was their appearance, and how fragrant the smell of their branches, and how the perfumes were scattered among the tress, and how the fragrant aroma wafted among the branches. And Christ picked some of the fruit from the lovely trees and gave it to her, so that she might taste some of the fruit that was raised by the Holy Spirit. These things my Lady Mary saw in the Paradise of Eden.

(5.3) And immediately the cherub of the sword cried out and spoke.[71] And the Lord said to his mother, "Come, ascend and see the heaven in which is the splendor of my Father. And you will ascend and see the heaven of heaven, and you will observe and see [34ᵇ] marvels that do not see you. And you will ascend above the waters of heaven and see the glory that is above them.[72] And from the waters you will ascend above and see the decorated Jerusalem, the palace of my Father, in which he dwells. And you will see and glorify God who chose you from all creatures." And the command of the Lord made a sign, and the sun came, and its course stopped at the gate of heaven, and its other head was fixed in the middle of Paradise.[73] And the Lord Jesus Christ was sitting on a chariot of light, he and my Lady Mary. And they ascended on wheels of fire that overpowered the sun, and they entered the lowest heaven. And my Lady Mary saw there all the storehouses of God: the house of ice and snow and frost; the house of rain and dew and heat; the house of dark clouds and whirlwinds, servants of

71. Cf. Gen 3.24.

72. Cf. Deut 28.12.

73. The British Library manuscripts omit: "And you will see and glorify God who chose you from all creatures.' And the command of our Lord made a sign, and the sun came, and its course stopped at the gate of heaven, and its other head was fixed in the middle of Paradise." The expression "its other head" is a little odd.

228 THE DORMITION AND ASSUMPTION OF MARY

God that proclaim him. And she saw there wrath and tranquility when a command went forth to the creation. And she saw the place where the prophet Elijah stood and prayed, because it was in this lowest heaven. These things my Lady Mary saw in the heaven that was outside.

(5.4) And she ascended to the heaven of heaven that is above the waters of heaven. And she saw above the waters ranks of angels spreading their wings. [35ᵃ] And the gaze of their eyes was watching over their Lord. And they were not able to cease the sound of their crying out and saying, "Holy, holy, holy, Lord of hosts!" [74] And she ascended and saw the heavenly Jerusalem, in which the Father and his Son and his Holy Spirit are secluded. And she saw that it had twelve walls and twelve gates named after the twelve apostles. And an apostle was standing on each gate with angels and archangels who were standing and glorifying. [75] And over the outer gate of Jerusalem were standing spiritual beings without number, glorifying with their trumpets, and Abraham, Isaac, Jacob, and Saint David the Psalmist. And they drew near and worshipped before the Lord and my Lady Mary as she entered to see the heavenly Jerusalem. And she entered the first gate and was worshipped by angels. And she entered the second gate, and the prayer of the cherubim was offered to her. And she entered the third gate, and the prayer of the seraphim was offered to her. And she entered the fourth gate and was worshipped by the family of chiliarchs. [76] And she entered the fifth gate, and

74. Isa 6.3.

75. Cf. Apoc 21.12.

76. The British Library manuscripts have: "family of archangels," which seems to make more sense.

THE SIX BOOKS APOCRYPHON

the thunders and lightnings spoke praises before her. And she entered the sixth gate, and they cried out, "Holy, holy, holy!" before her. And she entered the seventh gate, and fire and flame worshipped before her. And she entered the eighth gate, [35b] and rain and dew worshipped before her. And she entered the ninth gate, and Gabriel and Michael worshipped her. And she entered the tenth gate, and the lights worshipped her. And she entered the eleventh gate, and all the apostles worshipped and glorified her. And she entered the twelfth gate, and the child who was born from her strengthened her and guarded her.

(5.5) Thus my Lady Mary entered the heavenly Jerusalem and worshipped before God the Father. In that hour my Lady Mary saw the holy Father and the beloved Son and the Holy Spirit, the Paraclete. Then our Lord Jesus Christ drew near and took his mother and showed her secret and terrible things. And he showed her the dowry of the church, his bride. And he showed her what eye has not seen nor ear heard and that has not entered into the human heart: what God has prepared to give to those who love him on the day of the resurrection.[77] And he took her and came within the extreme limit of all created things. And he showed her and said, "This is the place where Enoch dwells, and to this place I have removed him, and this is the place where he prays." Here ends the fifth book. [36a]

---

77. Cf. 1 Cor 2.9; also Isa 64.4.

The Sixth Book.

Mary Beholds the Heavenly Dwelling Places of the Just and the Wicked.

(6.1) And the Blessed one lifted up her eyes and saw the two worlds, the one that passes away, and the one that does not pass away. And she saw in the world that does not pass away many lights shining brightly and resting places without number. And among the resting places there was a scent of perfumes, and trumpets were sounding over the dwelling places. And she saw the tabernacles of the just and multitudes standing on this side of the tabernacles and gazing at the tabernacles. My Lady Mary said to Christ, "My Lord Rabbuli, what are these?" Christ said to the Blessed one, "These are the tabernacles of the righteous, and these lights are shining in their honor. And from a distance they behold their happiness. For not until the time has come will they receive their glory." [78]

(6.2) And again my Lady Mary saw another place, and it was extremely dark, and great smoke was going up from it. And the smell of sulfur was rising up all around it, and a strong fire was blazing in it. And the fire's sound was going like heavy thunder when it is in heaven. [79] And many people were standing on this side of the darkness and [36ᵇ] weeping and sad as they stood at a distance. My Lady Mary said to Christ, "My Lord Rabbuli, what are these?" And our Lord said to his mother, "This which is roaring is Gehenna, which

78. The British Library manuscripts have instead, "until the day of the resurrection, when they will take possession of their dwelling places."

79. The British Library manuscripts have "when it is above in the heavens and is listened to with fear: thus was the coming of the sound of the fire, which was burning for the wicked."

THE SIX BOOKS APOCRYPHON   231

burns for the wicked, and those who are standing and looking at it are the sinners. And from a distance they behold their torment and know for what they are reserved at the last day. For the day of their judgment has not yet come. And at the last time, all those who neglected my commandments, which I commanded them, and have not listened to me will be tormented in Gehenna."

Mary Intercedes for Sinners and Returns to Paradise.

(6.3) And as my Lady Mary was standing, and our Lord Jesus beside her, she heard the voice of the righteous, "Glory to you God, who gives a good reward to the righteous, who call on your name on the last day." And the wicked also cried out beside the darkness by which they were standing and said, "Have mercy on us, Son of God, righteous judge, when you come to destroy heaven and earth." Then when my Lady Mary heard the voice of the righteous, she was glad; and when she heard the voice of the wicked, she was sad. And she petitioned Christ and offered a prayer for the sinners, and she spoke thus, "Rabbuli, have mercy on the wicked when you judge them on the day of [37ª] judgment, for I have heard their voice and I am sad."

(6.4) And[80] our Lord Jesus came in order [to show] Lady Mary all these things. And they were sitting on clouds of light. And the throne of their glory was settled on the decorated, flaming throne. And wheels of fire bearing their chariots were placed on the back of cherubim. And on clouds and lightning was the glory of our Lord and my Lady Mary led forth. Then

80. This folio is slightly damaged in the Göttingen manuscript, although the text is easily restored through comparison with the British Library manuscripts, as indicated in brackets.

232   THE DORMITION AND ASSUMPTION OF MARY

the Lord Jesus Christ took his mother and came to the Paradise of Eden with multitudes of heavenly beings.

Mary Summons John and Tells him of her Heavenly Journey.

(6.5) And my Lady Mary called to Saint John the younger and told him everything that our Lord Jesus Christ had shown her. And she said to John, "Keep safe these things that your Lord has shown me, when they are to be revealed and I tell you, these words and the books of my glorious deeds will go forth, so that people will make commemorations and offerings to me. Because, at the time when afflictions will be abundant among humanity, and they will call upon [my] name in prayer and be delivered [from] destruction, when [there will be tremendous] and powerful signs, and [there will be] wars, and there will be [famines], and the earth will tremble [from] the sin of wicked, [37b] who are destroying it with immoral deeds. At that time the affliction of humanity will increase; the air of heaven will become dark; and the winds and whirlwinds will blow; and the times will be unfortunate; and in the night, visions will be seen; and there will be destruction of humanity, one by another; and bitter plagues will be sent upon creation; and the Son, Christ, will come, and on the face of the earth he will not find faith prevailing in the mouth [of] humanity."

(6.6) These things, [and] there are more than these, [which] human [beings] are not able to tell, the Lord Jesus Christ [revealed] to his mother, [my Lady] Mary, and my Lady Mary revealed them to Saint John the younger. And the Lord Jesus Christ [said] to my Lady Mary, "You are blessed Mary, because of what your eyes have seen and [what] you are about to see, because in the time when afflictions will abound among humankind, and they will call upon your name in prayer and

THE SIX BOOKS APOCRYPHON   233

will be delivered from destruction." And my Lady Mary said
to Christ, "Your words are true, Rabbuli, because they are
from the holy mouth of your Father. And everything that you
said to me when you were on earth is true and has been fulfilled. And everyone who believes in you will inherit eternal
glory with you, which the children of light will inherit and
the righteous will expect, who praise you [38ᵃ] [and[81] your
Father and your Holy Spirit in heaven and on earth." Here
ends the sixth book.

> Here ends the narrative in this volume,
> the Six Books of the departure of
> my Lady Mary from the world.
>
> Glory to the Father and to the Son
> and to the Holy Spirit unto
> the ages of ages, Amen.]

81. The final folio of the Göttingen manuscript is lost except for
"and"; the remainder of the text has therefore been supplied from the
oldest of the British Library manuscripts, which is contemporary in
age with the Göttingen manuscript.

The Greek Revision
of *The Book of Mary's Repose*

A Narrative by Saint John, the Theologian and Evangelist, concerning the Dormition of the All-holy Theotokos and How the Undefiled Mother of Our Lord Was Translated.

1) Great and worthy of amazement, above all discourse and beyond all understanding are the affairs of Mary, the holy and ever-virgin mother of our true God and Lord, Jesus Christ: the seedless conception, the uncorrupted birth, and God's incarnation from her, coming forth into the world in the form of a human being. But no less so is the mystery of her glorious and wondrous Dormition.

A Great Angel Informs Mary of her Death.

2) When Mary heard from the Lord that she was to come forth from the body, a great angel came to her and said, "Rise Mary, and take this palm staff,[1] which was given to me by the

1. Although the Greek word in question generally translated as "palm" in the early Dormition narratives, its more usual meaning is "prize" or "a wand or baton," and this latter meaning is occasionally clear in other linguistic traditions, such as in the fifth-century Syriac fragments of the *Book of Mary's Repose* most importantly. For more details, see

236   THE DORMITION AND ASSUMPTION OF MARY

one who planted Paradise, and deliver it to the apostles, so that while holding it they may sing before you, because in three days you will lay aside the body. For behold, I will send all the apostles to you, and they will bury you and will not leave you until they have carried you to the place where you will soon be in glory."

3) Mary answered and said to him, "Why have you brought only this palm staff to me and not one for each of the apostles, lest it be given to one, and the others will murmur? And what do you want me to do, or what is your name, so that if they should ask me, I can tell them?"[2] And the angel said to her, "Why do you seek my name?[3] For it is wondrous, and you cannot hear it. But when I am about to ascend, I will tell it to you, so that you may share it with the apostles secretly, so that they will not repeat it to others and will know the power of my authority. Only do not hold on to[4] the palm staff, because many miracles will come to pass through it, and it will be a test for all the people of Jerusalem. To the one who believes then, it will be revealed, and to the one who does not believe, it will be hidden.[5] Go to the mountain then, and there you will learn my name, because I will not speak it inside of Jerusalem, lest it be completely devastated. But you will hear it on the Mount of Olives. Yet you cannot tell it to

the discussion of this object in the notes to that translation (§71). I have adopted "palm staff" as a translation in order to reflect this.

2. Cf. Exod 3.13.

3. Cf. Gen 32.29.

4. The Greek verb used here is a little peculiar, and other related texts generally instruct Mary not to have any concerns or worry with regard to the palm staff.

5. Cf. Mark 16.16.

THE GREEK BOOK OF MARY'S REPOSE   237

the apostles,[6] as I am about to tell you, because the time has come for you to put off the body."

Mary Recognizes the Great Angel as the Lord Jesus.

4) Then Mary, holding the palm staff in her hand, went to the Mount of Olives, with the angel's light shining ahead of her. And when she came to the mountain, it rejoiced greatly, along with all of its trees, so that its trees bowed their heads and venerated the palm staff that was in her hand.

5) When Mary saw this, she thought that it was Jesus and said, "Lord, are you not my Lord?" Then the angel said to her, "No one can work miracles except the Lord of Glory. For just as my Father sent me for the salvation of humanity, to convert those whom he has entrusted to me, so also [he has sent?] from the trees, so that my friends will eat from them and receive the likeness, which he has entrusted to me.[7] And not only do I transfer trees, but I also carry people who humble themselves before God; I transfer them to the place of the just on the day that they come forth from the body. And so when you come forth from the body, I will come to it myself on the fourth day: because our Savior was resurrected on the

---

6. As WENGER notes (*L'Assomption*, 213 n. 2), this strangely seems to contradict the angel's previous statement that she is to share his name with the apostles in secret.

7. The rather cryptic reference to the trees here is presumably a remnant from the story of a date palm from which the Holy Family fed during their flight into Egypt, as related in the *Book of Mary's Repose* 5–10. Although this episode has been dropped from this version of the text, this otherwise peculiar mention of trees and their transfer to paradise is almost certainly a vestigial reference to this missing episode, a lingering trance of its imperfect excision from this version.

238   THE DORMITION AND ASSUMPTION OF MARY

third day, so I will raise you up also on the fourth day. And not only you, but I also transfer all who observe the commandments of God to the sweet-smelling Paradise, because they have kept themselves perfect on earth."

The Soul's Departure from the Body and the Secret Prayer.

6) Mary said to him, "Lord, how do you come to them, or who are those that you transfer? Do they distinguish themselves and offer sweet-smelling sacrifices, and thus you come to them? Or rather do you come to the righteous or to the elect? Or, when you are sent, do you come to those who call upon your name while praying? You must tell me about this, so that I too can do thus, and you will come and take me up."

7) And he said to her, "What's the matter, mother?[8] When I am sent to you, I will not be alone, but all the hosts of angels will come, and they will sing before you. I have been sent to you now so that you will know[9] [what to do?], in order that you will share [this] with the apostles in secret. Now, you want to know what you will do. When I was sent to you, I received a prayer from the Father, as I was coming to you, and now I am telling it to you so that you will say it when you go forth from the body at the rising of the sun, for thus [the prayer] is offered up. And what I tell you, share with the apostles, because they too are coming. No friend of the world, who loves the world, is able to speak this prayer."

8) When he had said these things, the angel ordered her to share this prayer with the apostles, "For they are coming to

8. This could also mean, "what are you thinking?"

9. The verb here, "know," is not what one would expect: instead, a verb meaning "be made to know" seems more appropriate, as we find, for instance, in the *Book of Mary's Repose* 17.

THE GREEK BOOK OF MARY'S REPOSE 239

you, as I have told you, and they will sing before you and they will bury you. Therefore, take this palm staff." And when Mary had received the palm staff, the angel became as light, ascended into the heavens.

Mary Returns Home and Prays.

9) Then Mary returned to her house, and at once the house trembled on account of the glory of the palm staff in her hand. And after the tremor, she went into her secret, inner room and put it away in fine cloth. And when she had undressed, she took water and washed, and she put on different garments while blessing, saying,

10) "I bless you, sign that appeared from heaven on the earth, while you chose me and dwelt in me. I bless you and all of my relatives, those who will receive me,[10] who came forth invisibly before you, in order to bring you along. I bless you because you gave me a measure of virility for the parts of your body, and [because] I have been found worthy of the kiss of your bridal chamber,[11] as you promised me before. I bless

10. The word here, *paralēmptōras*, is unusual for a number of reasons. The word is rather uncommon in Greek usage, although it occurs often as a Greek loan word in Coptic texts, particularly in gnostic and other early Christian esoteric texts, such as those discovered at Nag Hammadi. In these contexts, it seems to be a "gnostic" technical term for heavenly powers that meet the soul at its separation from the body and guide it safely past the Demiurge, the creator god, and his minions to return to its place of origin in the spiritual realm, the Pleroma or the "Fullness." Here the idea seems to be that Mary's relatives will fill this role when she goes forth from the body.

11. The Valentinian gnostic initiation ritual known as "the bridal chamber" prominently features a sacred kiss: perhaps this is a reference to this ritual practice. See, e.g. Einar THOMASSEN, *The Spiritual Seed: The*

240   THE DORMITION AND ASSUMPTION OF MARY

you so that I will be found worthy to partake of the perfect Eucharist and your sweet-smelling offering, which is an abundance for all the nations."

11) "I bless you so that you will give me the garment that you promised me, saying,[12] 'By this you will be distinguished from my relatives,' and [so that] you will cause me to be taken to the seventh heaven, so that I will be found worthy of your perfect fragrance with all of those who believe in you, so that you will gather them together with me in your kingdom. For you are hidden among the hidden, observing those who are not seen. You are the hidden race, and you are also the Pleroma;[13] you are the Pleroma, and I have painfully given birth first to you and then to all of those who hope in you."

12) "Hear the prayer of your mother Mary crying out to you. Listen to my voice and send forth your favor on me, so that no power will come to me in that hour when I go forth from my body; but fulfill what you said when I was weeping before you, saying, 'Let me pass by the powers that will come upon my soul.' And you made a promise to me, saying, 'Do not weep, O Mary my mother: neither angels nor archangels,

---

Church of the "Valentinians," Nag Hammadi and Manichaean Studies 60 (Leiden: Brill, 2006), esp. 333–414; Herbert SCHMID, *Die Eucharistie ist Jesus: Anfänge einer Theorie des Sakraments im koptischen Philippusevangelium (NHC II 3)* (Leiden: Brill, 2007), esp. 83–109.

12. Reception of a heavenly "garment" is another common theme in gnostic accounts of the soul's salvation. See again, e.g. THOMASSEN, *Spiritual Seed*, esp. 348–55.

13. The Pleroma, which means the "Fullness," is a common technical term for the spiritual realm in early Christian gnostic and esoteric traditions, such as those found at Nag Hammadi in particular. The "hidden race" is also a term used in gnostic texts to describe the Gnostics themselves.

THE GREEK BOOK OF MARY'S REPOSE   241

nor cherubim nor seraphim, nor any other power will come upon you, but I will come myself to your soul.' But now pain has come upon her who gives birth. I bless you and the three servants sent by you for the service of the three ways. I bless you and the eternal light in which you dwell. I bless every plantation of your hands, which will endure unto the ages. Holy, holy, you who rest among the holy ones, hear the voice of my supplication." [14]

Mary Summons and Addresses her Friends and Family.

13) When she had said these things, she went forth and said to the maidservant of her house, "Go out and call all of my relatives and acquaintances, saying, 'Mary calls you.'" The maidservant went out and called them, just as Mary had ordered her. And when they had come, Mary said, "Fathers and brothers, let us help ourselves through good works and faith in the living God. For tomorrow I will go forth from the body and will depart for my eternal rest. Arise then and do a great act of kindness with me: I ask you neither for gold nor silver, because all of these things are vain and corruptible. But I ask you only for piety [15] that you keep what I say to you and remain with me for these two days and nights. Each of you, take a beautiful lamp, and do not let them go out for the

14. Ps 27.2 (LXX).

15. This is another difficult word whose lexical meaning is not clear, and the above translation seems to be the best guess based on the nearest lexical forms. In other closely related texts, including the *Book of Mary's Repose*, Mary asks for "*philanthrōpia*," although in the early Irish version she asks for "constant prayer," which seems to offer the best parallel in this case.

242   THE DORMITION AND ASSUMPTION OF MARY

three days, so that I can tell you my thoughts before I depart this place." And they all did as she commanded them.

14) The report was spread to all of Mary's acquaintances and friends, and Mary called all those closest to her and said to them, "Arise and let us pray." And after the prayer they sat down, discussing with one another the mighty works of God, signs and wonders that he worked through his mother.

John Arrives at Mary's House.

15) As Mary was praying and saying Amen, behold, suddenly the Apostle John arrived on a cloud. And he knocked on Mary's door, opened it, and went in. When Mary saw him, her spirit was disturbed, and sighing, she did not have the strength to restrain her tears, nor could she keep silent her great lamentation. She cried out in a loud voice and said, "Father John, remember the words of the master, what he advised you for my sake on that day when he went forth from us and I wept, saying, 'You are going away; with whom do you leave me and with whom will I live?' And he said to me, while you stood and listened, 'John is the one who will take care of you.' Now then, father John, do not forget what has been commanded to you regarding me. Remember that he loved you more than the others.[16] Remember that, while you were reclining on his breast,[17] he spoke to you alone the mystery that no one else knows, except you and I, because you are a chosen virgin, and he did not want me to grieve, because I am his dwelling place. Then I said to him, 'Tell me what you said to John.' And he told you the very things that you imparted to me. Now then, father John, do not abandon me."

16. Cf. John 19.26–7.
17. Cf. John 13.23.

THE GREEK BOOK OF MARY'S REPOSE   243

16) When she had said these things, Mary wept in a quiet and desolate voice. But John could not bear it: his spirit was troubled, and he did not know what to say to her. For he did not know that she was about to go forth from the body. Then John cried out in a loud voice, "Mary, my sister, who became the mother of the twelve branches, what do you want me to do for you? For indeed, I left behind my servant to provide you with food. You do not want me to transgress the command of my Lord, which he commanded us, saying, 'Go throughout the whole world, until the sin of the world is abolished'?[18] Now then, tell me what you need."

17) She said to him, "Father John, I have no need for the things of this world, but tomorrow I will go forth from the body. I ask you, father John, to do an act of kindness for me: watch over my body and place it in a tomb. And guard me with your brothers, the apostles, on account of the high priests. For with my own ears I have heard them say, 'When we find her body, we will commit it to fire, because from her that deceiver came forth.'"

18) When John heard her say, "I will come forth from the body," he fell at her knees and wept, saying, "Lord, who are we that you have shown us these tribulations? For we have not yet forgotten the previous ones, so that we can endure yet another tribulation. Why, O Mary, do I not go forth from the body, so that you might watch over me?"

Mary Shares the Secret Prayer
and Book of Mysteries with John.

19) When she heard John weeping and saying these things, she asked those present to be quiet, and she restrained John,

18. Cf. Matt 28.19.

244 THE DORMITION AND ASSUMPTION OF MARY

saying, "Father John, be patient with me in [your][19] weeping for a moment, so that I may tell you what the angel imparted to me." Then John wiped away his tears, and Mary said to him, "Come with me, and tell the crowd to sing psalms." And while they were singing psalms, she brought John into her inner chamber and told him the prayer that had been given to her by the angel.

20) And she brought forth a small case that contained a book and said, "Father John, take this book in which is the mystery. For when he was five years old, the teacher revealed all the things of creation, and he also put you, the twelve in it."[20] And she showed him her funeral garments and every preparation of her dwelling,[21] saying, "Father John, you know everything that I have in this big house except my funeral garments and two tunics. There are two widows here: when I go forth from the body, give one to each.

21) After she said these things, she brought him to where the palm staff was, which had been given to her by the angel, so that the apostles would take it. And she said to him, "Father John, take this palm staff, so that you may carry it before me, for this is why it was given to me." Then John said to her, "Mary, my mother and sister, I cannot take this by myself, without my fellow apostles being present. Otherwise, when they come, murmuring and resentment will arise among us: for

19. Although the text reads "my weeping," clearly, in light of the sentence that follows, "your weeping" must be understood, as found in the *Book of Mary's Repose* 44 and other closely related versions of this text.

20. The odd phrase, "and he also put you, the twelve," is also present in the *Book of Mary's Repose* 44, which reads almost identically at this point in the text.

21. Or, "of her body" (i.e. her corpse).

THE GREEK BOOK OF MARY'S REPOSE   245

there is one among us who has been appointed the superior. But when we come together, the approval of our Savior will be upon us."

The Miraculous Arrival of the Other Apostles.

22) After these things they both came out, and while they were coming out of the inner chamber, behold, suddenly there was thunder, so that those in that place were disturbed. And after the sound of the thunder, behold, suddenly the apostles descended on a cloud, from the corners of the world to Mary's door. Being eleven in number, they were seated on clouds. First Peter, second Paul—he was also carried on a cloud and numbered among the apostles; for at that time, he had the beginnings of the faith of God. After them the rest of the apostles also met one another in the clouds at Mary's door. And they embraced one another, gazing at each other and marveling at how they suddenly came to meet in the same place.

23) Peter answered and said, "Brothers, let us pray to God, who has gathered us together, especially because our brother Paul, the joy of our souls, is with us. Truly brothers, the scripture and the word of the prophet have been fulfilled which says, 'Behold, how beautiful and pleasant it is for brothers to dwell together!'" [22] Paul said to Peter, "You have found the appropriate testimony: for I was separated, and now I have been brought into the community of the apostles." Then Peter encouraged them to say a word of prayer. And the apostles raised their voice, saying, "Yes, let us pray that it be made known to us why God has brought us together." When those nearby realized that they should pray, they said to Peter, "Father Peter, you have been appointed over us: therefore, you pray

22. Ps 132.1 (LXX).

246   THE DORMITION AND ASSUMPTION OF MARY

for us!" And Peter said, "God our Father and our Lord Jesus Christ will glorify you, just as my ministry has been glorified. Therefore, bless me in this, if it is pleasing to you."

Peter's Prayer.

24) Then Peter stretched out his hands and said, "Lord God, who is seated upon the chariot of the cherubim,[23] who is seated in the heights and looks upon the lowly,[24] who dwells in unapproachable light[25] in eternal rest, the hidden mystery in which the saving cross was revealed. We do this very same thing when we raise our hands in the image of your cross, so that by recognition of this we will receive rest: for you are rest for the weary limbs; you loosen the hard labors;[26] you are the one who reveals hidden treasures; you have planted your goodness in us. For who among which of the gods is as merciful as your Father? And you do not remove your benevolence from us.[27] Who is as merciful as you, just as your Father is very merciful, because he saves those hoping in him from evil."

25) "Your will has conquered every desire; your faith has crushed falsehood; your beauty has vanquished comeliness; your humility has cast down every arrogance. You are the living one and the one who has vanquished death, our rest that has uprooted death, the glory of your mercy, which was sent from the Spirit of the Father of truth. Emmanuel, Emmanuel, Maranatha, from now unto the ages of ages. Amen."

23. Cf. 4 Kgdms 19.15.
24. Ps 112.6 (LXX).
25. 1 Tim 6.16.
26. Cf. Matt 11.28; Isa 45.3.
27. Cf. 2 Mac 6.16.

THE GREEK BOOK OF MARY'S REPOSE   247

Mary and John Greet the Apostles.

26) When they said Amen, Peter and Andrew embraced one another, and John was in their midst, saying, "Bless me, all of you." Then they all embraced each another, according to the proper order. After embracing, Peter and Andrew said, "John, beloved of the Lord, how did you come here, and how many days have you been here?" John answered and said, "Listen to what happened to me. It happened when I was in the city of Sardis, with twenty-eight disciples, who believed in the Savior: I was raised up on a cloud from their midst! It was the ninth hour, and behold, when the cloud descended upon the place where we were, it snatched me up and brought me here. When I knocked on the door, they opened it for me, and I found a great crowd around our mother Mary, who was saying, 'I will come forth from the body.' I did not remain among those surrounding her, but my grief weighed down on me."

27) "Now then, my brothers, when we go in tomorrow, do not weep, lest she be troubled—for this is what our teacher taught me when I reclined on his breast at the supper—lest the crowd around her, seeing us in tears, should be divided in their hearts, saying, 'They also fear death.' But let us encourage each other with the sayings of the beloved."

28) Then, when the apostles went into Mary's house, they said with one voice, "Mary, our sister, mother of all the saved, the grace of the Lord be with you." [28] When she saw them, she was filled with joy and cried out, saying, "And grace be with you. How have you come here together? For I see you gathered together." And they said, each one, how, in an instant, they were gathered together from every land by clouds; for each one told the country from which he had

28. Cf. Luke 1.28.

248   THE DORMITION AND ASSUMPTION OF MARY

been brought. Then they all greeted her, from Peter to Paul, saying, "May the Lord, the savior of all, bless you."

Mary Prays to the Great Cherub of Light and Prepares for Death.

29) Then Mary rejoiced in spirit and said,[29] "I bless you, the master of every blessing. I bless the dwelling places of your glory. I bless the great cherub of light, who dwelt for a time in my womb. I bless all the works of your hands, which obeyed with complete submission. I bless your love, with which you loved us. I bless all the words of life that come forth from your mouth and give us the truth. For I believe that the things that you told me have happened to me. You said, 'I will send all the apostles to you when you go forth from the body'; and behold, they have been brought together, and I am in their midst, just like a fruit-bearing vine, just as when I was with you, and you were like a vine in the midst of your angels, binding the enemy in chains, with all of his workings. I bless you with every blessing, because the things that were spoken to me have happened. For you said, 'You will be able to see me with the apostles when you come forth from the body.' Behold then, Lord, they have been gathered together."

30) When she had said these things, Mary called Peter and all of the apostles, and she brought them into her inner chamber and showed them her funeral garments. And after this, she went out and sat down in their midst. The lamps were still lit, and they did not allow them to be extinguished, just as Mary had commanded them. When the sun set on the second day, at the beginning of the third day, on which she

---

29. Cf Luke 1.47.

THE GREEK BOOK OF MARY'S REPOSE   249

went forth, Peter said to the apostles, "Brothers, let the one having learned discourse speak throughout the night, until the sun rises, exhorting the crowd." And the apostles said to him, "Who is wiser than you? We would be delighted to hear your learning."

Peter Offers an All-Night Discourse.

31) Then Peter began to speak, "Brothers and all you who have come here at this hour for the benevolence of our mother Mary, you who have lit the lamps that shine with the fire of the visible earth, you have performed a noble service. But I also desire that each virgin will receive her lamp in the immaterial firmament of heaven.[30] This is the three-wicked lamp of the more glorious human being, that is, the body, the mind, and the spirit. For if these three shine with the true fire, for which you are struggling, you will not be ashamed when you enter into marriage and rest with the bridegroom. So it is for our mother Mary: the light of her lamp has filled the world and it will not be put out until the end of the age, so that all those wishing [to be saved][31] will take courage from her, and you will receive the blessings of rest. Now then, brothers, struggle, recognizing that we will not remain here forever."

32) After Peter had said these things and exhorted the crowd until dawn, the sun rose, and Mary got up and went outside, and she recited the prayer that the angel had given her. And after praying, she went in and laid down on her bed,

30. Cf. Matt 25.1–13.

31. Something seems to be missing here, and the addition above is supported by the *Book of Mary's Repose* 55 and also the Dormition homily of John of Thessalonica (JUGIE, *Homélies mariales byzantines [II]*, 390).

250   THE DORMITION AND ASSUMPTION OF MARY

and she fulfilled the course her life.[32] Peter sat at her head, and
John at her feet, and the others were in a circle around her bed.

Christ Returns to Receive Mary's Soul.

33) And at about the third hour of the day, there was a
great thunder and a sweet-smelling fragrance, so that everyone
was driven off to sleep by the exceedingly sweet smell, except
for only the three virgins.[33] He caused them to remain awake
so that they could testify concerning the funeral of Mary the
mother of our Lord and her glory. And behold, suddenly the
Lord Jesus arrived on clouds with an innumerable multitude
of holy angels.[34] And he entered into the inner room, where
Mary was, along with Michael and Gabriel, while the angels
sang hymns and remained standing outside of the inner room.
And as soon as the Savior entered, he found the apostles
gathered around Mary, and he embraced them.

34) And Mary opened her mouth and gave thanks, saying,
"I bless you, because you have done what you promised, and
you have not grieved my spirit. You promised me that you
would not allow angels to come to my soul, but that you would
come to it. And it has happened to me, Lord, according to your

32. Note, however, that this passage does not seem to refer to the
moment of her death: see below.

33. Regarding the witnesses to Mary's Dormition in this text, and
the matter of just who was put to sleep and who remained awake for
the Virgin's Dormition according to the early tradition, see Stephen
J. SHOEMAKER, "Gender at the Virgin's Funeral: Men and Women as
Witnesses to the Dormition." *Studia Patristica* 34 (2001): 552–8. It
would appear that different traditions have been merged to secure the
witness to this event under male, apostolic authority.

34. Cf. Matt 24.30–1; 26.64.

THE GREEK BOOK OF MARY'S REPOSE   251

word. Who am I, a lowly one, that I have been found worthy of such glory?"[35] And when she had said these things, she fulfilled the course of her life, with her face smiling at the Lord.

35) The Lord embraced her, and he took her holy soul and placed it in Michael's hands, wrapping it in indescribably splendid skins. And we, the apostles, beheld the soul of Mary as it was given into Michael's hands: it was perfect in every human form, except for the shape of male or female, with nothing being in it, except for a likeness of the complete body and a sevenfold whiteness.

Mary's Funeral Procession.

36) And the Savior said to Peter, "Guard Mary's body, my dwelling place, diligently. Go out from the left side of the city, and you will find a new tomb.[36] Place the body in it, and remain there until I speak to you." When the Savior had said these things, Mary's body cried out, saying, "Remember me, king of glory; remember that I am your creation; remember that I guarded the treasure that was entrusted to me." Then the Lord said to the body, "I will not abandon you, my pearl, the inviolate treasure: by no means will I abandon the treasury that was sealed until it was sought." And when he had said these things, the Savior suddenly ascended.

37) Peter, John, and the others were vigilant,[37] and the three virgins attended to Mary's body and placed it on a bier. After that, they woke up the apostles. Then Peter took the palm staff and said to John, "You are a virgin, John, and you

35. Cf. Luke 1.38, 48.
36. Cf. Matt 27.60.
37. Or possibly, "were awake."

252   THE DORMITION AND ASSUMPTION OF MARY

must sing hymns before the bier while holding this." John said to him, "You are our father and bishop; you must be before the bier until we bring it to the place [of burial]." And Peter said to him, "So that none of us will grieve, let us crown the bier with it." And the apostles got up and carried Mary's bier. And Peter said the hymn, "Israel went out of Egypt, alleluia."[38]

The Jewish Attack on Mary's Body.

38) And the Savior and the angels were in the clouds, invisibly singing hymns before the bier at a distance. One heard only the sound of a great crowd, such that all of Jerusalem came out. And when the high priests heard the clamor and the sound of the hymns, they were disturbed and said, "What is this tumult?" And someone told them, "Mary has gone forth from the body, and the apostles are gathered around her, singing hymns." And immediately Satan entered into them,[39] saying, "Let us get up and go out, and kill them and burn the body that bore that deceiver." And they got up immediately and went out with weapons and shields[40] to kill them.

39) And immediately the invisible angels struck them with blindness, and they smashed their heads into the walls, since they could not see where they were going—except for only one among them, who took the road that went out [from the city], in order to see what was happening. When he approached the apostles, he saw them carrying the crowned bier and singing hymns. And he was enraged and said, "Behold, the dwelling place of the despoiler of our people: what glory she receives today!" And in his rage he came upon the bier, wanting to

38. Ps 113.1 (LXX).
39. Cf. John 13.27.
40. Cf. Mark 14.43.

THE GREEK BOOK OF MARY'S REPOSE   253

overturn it, and he took hold of it where the palm staff was. And instantly his hands clung to the bier, cut off from his arms. And they remained hanging from the bier.

40) Then the man cried out and begged the apostles, saying, "Do not abandon me in such great pain. O Peter, remember my father, when the doorkeeper, the maidservant, questioned you and said to you, 'You are one of this man's disciples,'[41] and how and in what manner I questioned you." Then Peter said, "I do not have the power to help you, nor does anyone here. Therefore, believe that Jesus is the Son of God, the one against whom you rose up, whom you imprisoned and killed, and it will put an end to this lesson at once."

41) Jephonias answered and said, "It's not that we didn't believe: yes, truly we know that he is the Son of God. But what are we to do, since avarice darkens our eyes? For our fathers, when they were about to die, summoned us and said, 'Behold children, God has chosen you from all the tribes to build up this people and to take tithes and first fruits. But take care, children, lest the place be increased by you, and you go into business for yourselves; do not anger God but give your surplus to the poor and orphans.' But we did not listen, and when we saw that that place was extremely abundant, we set up[42] tables in the temple for buying and selling. And when the Son of God came into the sanctuary, he threw them all out, saying, 'Do not make my Father's house a house of commerce.'[43] But considering only the practices that he had abolished, we

41. Cf. Mark 14.66–7.

42. Here the text reads "we forgot," but I follow Wenger's suggested emendation (*L'Assomption*, 237, n. 2), which he has taken from John of Thessalonica's homily and which is confirmed by the *Book of Mary's Repose* 75.

43. John 2.16.

254 THE DORMITION AND ASSUMPTION OF MARY

plotted evil among ourselves and killed him, knowing that he is the Son of God. But forgive our ignorance and pardon me: for this has come upon me, I who am loved by God, in order that I might live."

42) Then Peter had the bier set down and said, "If now you believe with your whole heart, go and kiss Mary's body, saying, 'I believe, O Virgin Theotokos, pure mother, in the one who was born from you, our Lord and God.' Then, raising his voice, the high priest spoke in the Hebrew language, and while weeping, he blessed Mary for three hours. And he did not allow anyone to touch the bier, while he brought forth testimonies from the holy scriptures and the books of Moses that it was written about her that she will be called the Temple of God and the Gate of Heaven, such that the apostles heard great and wonderful things from him.

43) And Peter said to him, "Go and join your hands together." And Jephonias ran and said eagerly, "In the name of the Lord Jesus Christ, the Son of God and of Mary the pure dove, the one hidden in his goodness, let my hands be joined together without defect." And immediately they became as they were before. And Peter said to him, "Rise up and take [a branch] [44] from the palm staff, which I will give you, and when you enter the city, you will find a great crowd that cannot find their way out. Tell them what happened to you, and for whomever believes, place this branch on that one's eyes, and immediately that person will see again."

44) And when Jephonias went back, just as Peter had commanded him, he found a great crowd weeping and saying,

44. Something seems to be missing here, and other early narratives, including the *Book of Mary's Repose* 76 and John of Thessalonica's homily (JUGIE, *Homélies mariales byzantines [II]*, 401), support the addition above.

THE GREEK BOOK OF MARY'S REPOSE 255

"Woe to us, because what happened to the Sodomites has also happened to us. For first he struck them with blindness, and then a fire fell and consumed them. Woe to us, for behold, we have been blinded: next, the fire will come." [45] Then Jephonias took the branch and spoke to them about the faith, and whoever believed saw again.

Paul asks the Other Apostles
to Teach him the Secret Mysteries.

45) The apostles brought Mary to the tomb, and after they placed her inside, they sat down to wait for the Lord together, as he had commanded them. And Paul said to Peter, "Father Peter, you know that I am a neophyte, and that this is the beginning of my faith in Christ Jesus. For I did not gain possession of the teacher, so that he could tell me the precious mysteries. But I have heard that he revealed everything to you on the Mount of Olives. Therefore, I implore you to reveal them to me." Then Peter said to Paul, "It is clear that we rejoice greatly that you have come to the faith of Christ, but we cannot reveal these mysteries to you: you are not able to hear them. But wait, for behold, we will remain here for three days, just as the Lord told us. For he will come with his angels to take up Mary's body, and if he orders us, then we will gladly reveal these things to you."

46) And while they were seated at the doors of the tomb, debating with each other about doctrine, faith, and many other things, behold, the Lord Jesus Christ came from the heavens, and Michael and Gabriel with him. He sat in the midst of the apostles and said to Paul, "Paul, my beloved, do

45. Cf. Gen 19.11, 24.

256 THE DORMITION AND ASSUMPTION OF MARY

not be distressed that my apostles have not revealed the glorious mysteries to you. For I revealed them to them on earth: I will teach them to you in the heavens."

Christ Takes Mary's Body to Paradise and She is Resurrected There.

47) Then he nodded to Michael, [and Michael spoke] [46] in a truly angelic voice, and the clouds descended to him. And the number of angels on each cloud was a thousand angels, and they uttered praises before the Savior. And the Lord told Michael to take the body of Mary up onto the cloud and to set it down in Paradise. And when the body was taken up, the Lord told the apostles to come closer to it. And when they came onto the cloud, they were singing with the voice of angels, and the Lord commanded the clouds to depart for the East, to the regions of Paradise.

48) And when they came to Paradise, they placed the body of Mary under the tree of life. And Michael brought her holy soul, and they placed it in her body. And the Lord returned the apostles to their places for the conversion and salvation of humankind.

46. Once again, something seems to be missing here, and Wenger suggests the above restoration, which is supported by the *Book of Mary's Repose* 89.

The Latin Revision
of the *Book of Mary's Repose*

Here Begins the Assumption of the Holy Virgin Mary and Inviolate Mother of the Lord Jesus Christ.

Christ Informs Mary of her Impending Death.

1. While Holy Mary the Mother of God was remaining in Jerusalem after the Ascension of our Lord into heaven, Christ appeared to her and said to her, "Mary my mother, go to the Mount of Olives, and there you will receive a palm from the hand of an angel, which I entrust to you, and tell everyone that after three days you will set aside your body. And I will send all of my apostles to you, and they will encourage you and see your glory. But I will also come to receive you and the entire host of the angels will give praises before you."

2. When the Lord Jesus Christ said these things, he became like a light ascending into heaven.

3. The Blessed Mary got up and went forth to the Mount of Olives. And behold, the angel of the Lord stood before her, having the palm in his hand. And all the trees bowed their heads and worshipped the palm that was in the angel's hand. Therefore, when the Blessed Mary saw this, she was disturbed and said to the angel, "Lord, are you my God, because such

258 THE DORMITION AND ASSUMPTION OF MARY

power is accomplished by you, so that all the trees worship you?" And he said to her, "I am his angel, and I have been sent to you so that you will receive this palm."

Mary Returns Home, Prays, and Addresses her Friends and Family.

4. Mary then took the palm from the angel's hand and returned to her house, and immediately the house shook on account of its glory. And when she entered her room, she laid the palm in a fine linen cloth. And laying aside the garments that she was wearing, she took water and washed herself. With a blessing she took other garments and put them on, saying, "I bless you the sign that was manifest from heaven upon the earth, while you chose me and dwelt in me. Hear my prayer, for I cry out to you, and send your blessing upon me, so that no power will come upon me when I go forth from the body. But fulfill what was said by you when I was weeping before you, saying: 'What shall I do so that I will pass by the powers that will come upon my soul?' and you promised to me, saying: 'Do not weep, Mary my mother, for not only will angels and archangels come, but I myself will come upon your soul.'"

5. When Mary had said these things, she went forth and said to her maidservant, "Go and call those near to me." Then she went and called them all. And when they came, Mary said, "Fathers and mothers and sisters, let us help ourselves through good works and faith that is from God, since I am leaving. For tomorrow I will go forth from the body and depart for my eternal rest. Now then, do a great act of kindness with me: for I ask you neither for gold nor silver, because all of these things are vain and corruptible. I ask only this great act of kindness from you, that you will do what I say and remain with me for these two nights and that each of you will

THE LATIN BOOK OF MARY'S REPOSE 259

light your lamp and not let it go out for three days." And they all did as she said to them.

Mary Describes the Soul's Departure from the Body.

Then Mary turned to them and said, when the lamps were lit, "Let us be vigilant, because we do not know the hour when the thief will come.[1] For when one goes forth from the body, two angels will come upon a person, one of righteousness and the other of wickedness, and they approach with death. And when death begins to trouble the soul, the two angels come to examine the person's body. If it did works of righteousness, the angel of righteousness rejoices, and angels of righteousness come upon the soul, rejoicing before it, and they lead it to the place of the righteous. Then the angel of wickedness weeps because he has no part in it. Nevertheless, if someone is found to have done wicked deeds, the wicked angel rejoices and brings with him seven other spirits who are more wicked than him, and they take the soul and rip it from the body, and the angel of righteousness weeps greatly."

6. When Mary had said these things, the women said to her, "Our sister, who became the mother of the whole world, if we all weep, we are rightly afraid. You, however, what do you fear, you who are the mother of the Lord, the Savior? Therefore, we who are paltry and wretched, what shall we do or where shall we flee? If the shepherd fears the wolf, where will the sheep flee?" And Mary said to them, "Be silent, daughters, and do not cry, but glorify the one who is in our midst. Do not weep, O virgins of God, but sing a psalm instead of weeping, so that it will be renowned among all the generations of the earth."

1. Matt 24.43.

260   THE DORMITION AND ASSUMPTION OF MARY

When she had said these things, she called all those near to her and said to them, "Arise; let us pray." And when they had prayed, they sat down, discussing among themselves about the miracles of Christ and the signs that he did.

The Apostle John Arrives at Mary's House.

7. And while they were discussing these things, John came and knocked on Mary's door. He opened it and entered. Nevertheless, when Mary saw him, she was troubled in her spirit, and sighing, she could not endure. But on account of her great sorrow she could not remain silent, and she cried out with a great voice saying, "Father John, remember the words of your master, with which he advised you, which he said about me, on the day when he went forth from us, and I wept, saying: 'You are going away, and to whom do you send me, and with whom will I live?' Father John, do not forget what has been commanded to you regarding me."[2]

8. When she had said these things, Mary wept. John, however, did not know what to say, for she had not said that she was about to go forth from the body. Then John cried out with a loud voice, saying, "Mary, my sister, you who are the mother of the apostles of Christ, what do you want me to do for you? For I sent you my servant and provided you food. Now then, tell me what distresses your soul or what you need." And Mary said to him, "Father John, I have no need of this world, but tomorrow I will go forth from this world. I ask you, Father John, to do an act of kindness with me and watch over my body and simply place it in a tomb, and guard it with your brothers, the fellow apostles, on account of the priests of the Jews. For with my own ears, I have heard

2. Cf. John 19.26–7.

THE LATIN BOOK OF MARY'S REPOSE   261

them say: 'When we find her body, we will commit it to fire, because from her that deceiver came forth.'"

9. When John heard this, he fell on his knees and wept. Then John arose and wiped away his tears, and Mary said to him, "Come with me and bid the people to sing a psalm while I speak." And while they were singing a psalm, she led John into her room, saying, "Father John, you know all things, for I have nothing at all except my funeral garments and two tunics. There are two widows here: when I go forth from the body, give one to each of them." After this Mary went into where the palm was, and she said to him, "Father John, take this palm and carry it before my funeral bed, for thus it was given to me."

10. Then John said to her, "Sister Mary, I cannot accept it with my co-apostles and brothers absent. For there is one greater than I who has been appointed over us."

The Other Apostles Arrive at Mary's House.

11. Then after they went out of the room, there was a great thunder so that those who were in the house were disturbed. And after the sound of thunder, the apostles were sent forth on clouds before Mary's door. And they embraced one another, looking at each other and wondering how they came together in one place. And the apostles raised their voice, saying, "We pray that it will be made known to us why the Lord has gathered us together in one place."

12–13. Then Peter, raising his hands to heaven, said, "O Lord God Almighty, you who are seated upon the cherubim,[3] who dwell in the heights and look upon the lowly,[4] we raise

3. Cf. 4 Kgdms 19.15.
4. Ps 112.6 (LXX).

262 THE DORMITION AND ASSUMPTION OF MARY

our hands to you in the image of your cross, so that in recognition of this we will receive rest, for you are our rest and the glory of mercy, from now and unto the ages of ages."

14. When the apostles said Amen, they embraced one another. And John answered, saying, "All my brothers, bless me." Then they all embraced each other, according to the proper order. Then after they embraced, Peter and Andrew said to John, "Beloved of the Lord, how did you come here, and how many days have you been here?" And John said, "Listen to what happened to me. It happened while I was in the city of Sardis, among those whom I was teaching, who had believed in our Savior. Then it was the ninth hour of the day, and a cloud descended from heaven in the place where we were gathered and seized me up, with all those who were with me watching, and it brought me here. Then I knocked on the door, and she opened it, and I found many people standing around our sister Mary, who was saying to them, 'I will go forth from the body.' I did not remain in their midst, but my weeping weighed down upon me. Now then, my brothers, when she goes forth from the body, do not let her weep, lest the people will be disturbed, saying, 'They fear death themselves.'"

Mary Receives the Apostles
and Tells them of her Impending Death.

15. Then the apostles entered Mary's house, and embracing her, they said, "Mary, our sister, mother of all who are saved, grace be with you." And she said to them, "And with you brothers. **16.** How did you come here, or who told you that I am about to go forth from the body? For I see you gathered together." And they told, each one, the land from which he had been carried forth on a cloud.

THE LATIN BOOK OF MARY'S REPOSE   263

17. Then Mary rejoiced in her spirit and said, "I bless you, who are Lord of every blessing. I bless the dwelling places of your glory. I bless you who are seated on the great cherub, because you made your dwelling place in my womb, because you have done as you said. For you said, "I will send all of my apostles to you when you go forth from the body." And behold, I am in their midst, just like a fruit-bearing vine."

18. And saying this, Mary called Peter and the other apostles and led them into her room and showed them her funeral garments.

Peter Delivers an All-Night Discourse but is Rebuked for Revealing Secrets.

19. After this, she went forth and sat in the midst of all of them, with their lamps lit, and they did not go out for three days, just as the Blessed Mary had commanded them. Then Peter said to all the other apostles, "Brothers, let the one who has a learned discourse speak through the whole night until the sun rises, comforting the people." And the apostles said to Peter, "Who is more learned than you, and we would be delighted to hear your learning." Then Peter began to speak, "Brothers, do not think that death is the death of Mary. For it is not death but eternal life, because the death of the righteous will be blessed before God.[5] For this is glory, and the second death cannot afflict them."

20. While he was still saying this, a light shone in the house so that the light surpassed the lamps, and there was a voice, saying, "Peter, see that you do not reveal this, for it was given to you all alone to know and speak this knowledge." Then Peter turned and said, "Brothers, it is clear that we are not able

5. Ps 115.6 (LXX).

264   THE DORMITION AND ASSUMPTION OF MARY

to say what we want. But the one who directs our hearts, he himself directs us."

Peter Instead Compares the Kingdom of Heaven to Virgins.

21. Then three virgins fell at his feet, saying, "Make us worthy of the great wonders of Christ and show us what was revealed to you by him." Then Peter made them rise, saying, "Arise and listen to the things that are of our grace and honor. Do not think that the voice told me not to reveal on your account. For you are worthy of these things, and all who maintain purity and preserve the virtue of chastity in this world. Listen and learn what your master taught you, saying: 'The kingdom of heaven is like virgins.'[6] He did not say, 'The kingdom of heaven is like much time,' because time passes, but the name of virginity endures. And I believe that you are glorious, on account of which he compared the kingdom of heaven you."

"For when the end of each person comes, mighty death is sent. And when it comes upon the soul of one languishing in sin, who has gathered many iniquities to himself, and he will be afflicted by it, then he will beseech the Lord, saying: 'Be patient, Lord, while the sins that I have planted in my body are removed.' Death, however, will not indulge him. How can it indulge him when the allotted time is now completed? For if a soul has been with sins, having nothing of righteousness, it is led into the place of torments. But if he has done works [of righteousness], he rejoices and says: 'Nothing holds me back: I have nothing except the name and works of virginity. What shall I fear?' Then the soul goes forth from the body and is led to the bridegroom with praises unto

6. Cf. Matt 25.1.

THE LATIN BOOK OF MARY'S REPOSE 265

the place that he promised to all who keep his commandments, that is, in the seventh heaven. And seeing it, the Father rejoices and places it among the other saints." And while Peter was saying these things and the people remained steadfast until morning, the sun rose.

Christ Returns to Receive Mary's Soul.

22. And when Blessed Mary went out, she prayed. And after praying she lay down on the bed. **23.** Peter was sitting at her head, and the other disciples were around her bed. And around the third hour, there was a great thunder and a sweet-smelling fragrance, so that from the great sweetness sleep came upon everyone who was standing around Mary, except for the three virgins, whom he caused to remain awake so that they could testify concerning the glory with which Blessed Mary was received.

24. Then the Lord Jesus Christ arrived on clouds with an innumerable multitude of angels. And he entered into the house where Blessed Mary was lying, as the angels stood outside around the house singing hymns. The Savior entered, and he found the apostles around Blessed Mary and he embraced them all. After that he embraced Mary, saying, "Hail Mary, my mother."

25. And Mary opened her mouth and said, "I bless you, my Lord God, because you have done what you promised me, for you not only sent the apostles to me but also angels and even archangels, and not only archangels but you yourself have come upon my soul. Who am I that I have been found worthy of such glory!" And when she said these things, Blessed Mary completed her course, with her face smiling at the Lord.

26. Then the Lord received her soul and placed it in the hands of Michael the archangel. And it appeared white as

266   THE DORMITION AND ASSUMPTION OF MARY

snow. **27.** Then Peter rejoiced greatly and asked the Lord, saying, "Who among us has a soul as white as Mary's?" And the Savior said to him, "If someone keeps himself from many sins, his soul will be found white as Mary's."

The Apostles Bring Mary's Body to her Tomb.

28. And the Savior said to Peter, "Bury Mary's body, that is, my dwelling place, quickly, and go forth from the left side of the city, and you will find a new tomb. Place the body in it and guard it as I commanded you."

29. And when the Savior said this, Blessed Mary's body cried out before him, saying, "Remember me, Lord of glory, that I am your creation; remember me that I guarded the treasure that was entrusted that was sealed until it was sought." **30.** And when he had said these things, the Lord Jesus ascended into heaven.

31. Then Peter and the other apostles and the three virgins took care of Mary's body, and after they wrapped it in a clean linen cloth, they placed it on the bed. And after this, those who were sleeping awoke and began to be amazed, saying, "At what hour did Mary go forth from the body?"

32. Then Peter took the palm and said to John, "You are a virgin, and you must give praise before the bed, holding this palm." And John said to Peter, "You are our shepherd and bishop; you must go before the bed until we carry it to the place. And so that none of us will grieve, let us crown the bed with it."

33. The apostles got up and carried the bed. **34.** And Peter sang praise, saying, "Israel went out of the land of Egypt, alleluia." [7] And all the people were singing the psalm. **35.** Then

7. Ps 113.1 (LXX).

THE LATIN BOOK OF MARY'S REPOSE   267

the angels who were going above the clouds were singing a heavenly hymn and were not seen. Then only a noise was heard in all of Jerusalem.

The Jewish Attack on Mary's Body.

36. And when the high priests heard the tumult and the voice of those singing, they were disturbed, saying to one another, "What is this tumult?" **37.** And one of them said: Mary has gone forth from the body, and the apostles are around her singing praise." **38.** And Satan entered into them,[8] and they said, "Arise: let us go and kill the apostles and set fire to the body that bore that deceiver in its womb. And when they rose up, they went forth with swords and clubs[9] to kill them. Immediately the angels that were in the clouds struck them with blindness, and they smashed their heads against the wall, because they could not see where they were going, **39.** except for one of them who found the road to go out and see what was happening.

Then when he approached the apostles and saw the crowned bier and the apostles singing hymns, he was filled with great rage and said, "Behold the dwelling place of the one who despoiled us and our people: what glory she receives!" And he attacked it, wanting to overturn it. And he took hold where the [palm] was and wanted to throw it down to the ground. And immediately his hands withered.

40–41. Then the man cried in the presence of the apostles, begging them and saying, "Do not disdain me in such great need! Remember, Peter, my father's help when the doorkeeper

8. Cf. Jn 13.27.
9. Cf. Mt 26.47, 55 and par.

268 THE DORMITION AND ASSUMPTION OF MARY

questioned you, when she said to you that you are one of his disciples, how he set you free.[10] And now, help me!" Then Peter said to him, "It is not in my power to offer you help, nor anyone else of these. 42. But, if you believe that Jesus Christ the Son of God was born from the Holy Spirit and the Virgin Mary, touch Mary's body and you will be healed."

43. And with a loud voice he said, "I believe in Jesus Christ the Son of God, who was born from the Holy Spirit and the Virgin Mary." And Blessed Peter said to him, "Touch Mary's body." 44. And when he touched it, suddenly his hands were restored to health. 45–46. And Blessed Peter said to him, "Go into the city and tell all the people what happened to you. Whoever believes will see the light, but whoever does not believe will remain blind."

Christ Takes her Body to Paradise and Resurrects Her There.

47. Then they brought Blessed Mary's body before the tomb and spent three days there. The apostles were discussing the teaching of the Savior with one another. And as they were speaking, the Lord Jesus came on clouds with angels and archangels. 48–49. And he took up the apostles in the clouds with Mary's body, and they brought them to Paradise and laid down Mary's [body].

50. Then the Lord received her soul from the hands of the archangel Michael and restored it to Mary's body. Then, when Blessed Mary arose on her feet, she walked, and the angels sang hymns. The apostles, however, [were returned by the clouds] each to his own place, glorifying the Father and the Son and the Holy Spirit, to whom is honor and glory and power unto the ages of ages. Amen.

10. Cf. Mt 26.69 and par.

The Latin *Transitus Mariae*
Assumption of Holy Mary

An Angel Tells Mary of her Impending Death.

1. At that time, when Blessed Mary was keeping vigil and praying day and night after the Ascension of the Lord, the angel of the Lord came to her, saying, "Mary, rise up and take this palm which I have brought you, for in three days you will be taken up. And behold, I will send all of the apostles to you, so that they will see your glory, which you will receive."

2. And Mary said to him, "I ask, lord, that you tell me what your name is." And the angel said to her, "Why do you ask my name which is great and marvelous?"

3. When Blessed Mary heard this, she went up on the Mount of Olives. With the light of the angel shining forth for her, Mary held in her hand the palm that she received from the angel, and she rejoiced with great joy, one with all who were in that same place. Nevertheless, the angel who came to her ascended into heaven with great light.

Mary Returns Home and Addresses her Friends and Family.

4. Mary then returned to her house, and she laid down the palm that she had received from the hand of the angel with all care. And she laid aside the clothes that she was wearing and

270 THE DORMITION AND ASSUMPTION OF MARY

washed her body and put on her best garment. Rejoicing and exulting, she blessed God, saying, "I bless your holy and praiseworthy name unto the ages of ages, Amen. I ask, Lord, that you send your blessing upon me so that no power of the enemy or of the underworld will come upon me at the moment when you command me to go forth from this body, since indeed you promised me, saying: 'Do not be sorrowful, Mary.'"

5. And when she said this, she sent for and called to herself all those near to her and said to them, "Listen to me now you all and believe what I say, for tomorrow I will go forth from this body and will go to my Lord. Therefore, I ask you all to keep vigil together with me until the time when I will go forth from this body. And I make this known to you so that you will know that when a person is appointed to go forth from the body, two angels come upon him, one of righteousness and the other of wickedness. And if the angel of righteousness finds good and righteous deeds in this person, rejoicing and exulting it leads forth that soul to the place of the righteous. And then the angel of wickedness laments, because it was able to find nothing of its deeds in it. But if then the angel of wickedness finds its wicked deeds in that person, rejoicing and exulting it takes with it those whom it knows are wretched. And rejoicing thus they lead forth the soul of that one to the place of punishments. And the angel of righteousness withdraws with sorrow."

6. And all those who were around her said to her, "Why are you so sorrowful, when you are blessed among all and you are the mother of the Lord of the entire universe? What are we to say for ourselves, if you are sorrowful yourself?" And Mary said, "Do not weep but glorify the Lord with me."

THE LATIN TRANSITUS MARIAE   271

The Apostle John Arrives at Mary's House.

7. And as they were saying this, behold, suddenly Blessed John arrived and knocked on the door of the house and entered. And when Mary saw him, she was troubled in her spirit, and sighing, she was not able to hold back tears. And she cried out with a great voice, saying, "Father John, remember the word of my Lord, your master, with which he commanded me to you on the day when he departed from us, having suffered for the salvation of the world."

8. And John said to her, "What do you want me to do for you?" Mary answered, saying, "I ask nothing of you except that you care for my body and place it in a tomb, because tomorrow I will go forth from the body. For I myself have heard the Jews saying: 'Let us watch for when she dies, so that we will be able to seize her body and destroy it with fire.'" And when Blessed John heard this, that is, her saying that she would go forth from the body, he wept before God, saying, "O Lord, who are we to whom you have shown such great troubles?"

9. Then Mary asked Saint John into her room and showed him her garment that he should place on her for burial, and she showed him the palm of light that she received from the angel who had appeared to her and announced her assumption to her. And she said to him, "I ask you, father John, to take this palm and have it carried before my bier when I have been taken up."

10. And Saint John said to her, "Truly, I am not able to do this alone, unless my brothers and co-apostles arrive, for today we shall all be gathered as one in this place by the power of the Lord, to render honor to your body."

272 THE DORMITION AND ASSUMPTION OF MARY

The Other Apostles Arrive at Mary's House.

11. And when he said this, as they were going forth from the room, suddenly there was great thunder, so that the place was shaken and all who were in the same place in the house. And then suddenly all the apostles were seized up by clouds and were set down before the door of Blessed Mary's house. And seeing one another, they greeted one another with wonder, saying, "Thanks be to God, who today deemed it worthy to gather us together as one, for truly the saying of the prophet David is fulfilled: 'Behold how good and pleasant it is when brothers dwell in unity.'" [1] And the apostles said to one another, "Let us pray to the Lord, brothers, that he will make known to us what the reason is that he wanted to gather us together today as one."

12. And Peter said, "Brother Paul, rise and pray first, for my soul is very glad to see you." And Paul said, "How can I pray first, when you are a column of light? But indeed, all the brothers standing around me are better than me. You, then, who preceded us into the apostolate, pray for us all, that the grace of the Lord would be with us." Then all the apostles rejoiced at Paul's humility.

13. And then Peter got down on his knees, stretched forth his hands, and prayed, saying, "Lord God Almighty, you who sit upon the cherubim and gaze upon the depth of the abyss, we raise our hands to you in likeness to your cross, so that in understanding we might attain your rest, for you give rest to limbs that labor, you who humble all the proud, who have conquered death. For you, Lord, are our rest, the protector of all who call upon you, you who abide in the Father and the Father in you, one with the Holy Spirit unto the ages of ages." And all the apostles responded, "Amen."

1. Ps 132.1 (LXX).

THE LATIN TRANSITUS MARIAE 273

14. And Blessed John ran to meet them all, saying, "Bless me brothers." And Peter and Andrew said to John, "Beloved of the Lord, tell us how you came here today." And John said to them, "Bless God, brothers. Listen to what happened to me. It happened while I was teaching in the city of Agathen.[2] It was around the ninth hour of the day. Suddenly, a cloud descended in the same place where the people were gathered together listening to the word of God. Suddenly, the cloud surrounded me and seized me up from their midst, with all those who were in that place watching, and it brought me here. And immediately I knocked on the door, which opened without delay, and I found here many people standing around our sister and lady Mary, and she was speaking to the crowd, telling them that she is going to go forth from the body. And hearing this, I wept ardently. Now then, brothers, listen to me. If our lady goes forth from the body on the following day, do not weep for her, so as not to trouble the people, because this our Lord and master said to me before, on the night when I was reclining on his breast, while we were eating. Therefore, I remind you that the people should not see us weeping and begin to be doubtful and say in their hearts: why do they fear death, since they are apostles of God and preach the resurrection to others? But let us strengthen one another with the promises of the Lord, so that all the people will be able to be firm in faith and not doubt."

Mary Receives the Apostles.

15. When Blessed John had said this, all the apostles together entered Mary's house and greeted her with a great voice, saying, "Hail Mary, full of grace, the Lord is with you." And she responded, "And with you, brothers."

2. Athens?

274 THE DORMITION AND ASSUMPTION OF MARY

16. "I ask you, however, tell me how you came here suddenly today, or who told you that I will go forth from the body." And so all the apostles explained each of them had been seized up from the places where they were preaching with divine teaching and set down in the same place.

17. Then Mary rejoiced in her spirit and said, "I bless you who reigns over every blessing. I bless the dwelling place of your glory. I bless every promise that you promised to me, that you would appoint all of your apostles to my summons for my burial. I bless your holy name, which is and remains unto the ages of ages."

18. And after this Mary summoned all the apostles and led them into her bedroom and showed them every garment for her burial.

Peter Addresses the Crowd and Tells the Parable of the Virgins.

19. And when the third day arrived, when she was to go forth from the body, Blessed Peter said to all of the apostles and all the people, "Brothers who have come together in this place to keep vigil with us, let all of your lamps be lit, and let us be vigilant in soul and spirit, so that when the Lord comes, he will find us all keeping vigil together and will illuminate us with the grace of the Holy Spirit. Dearest brothers, do not suppose that the Blessed Virgin's summons is death. For it is not death for her, but life eternal, because the death of the righteous is praised with God, because this is great glory."

20. And when he said this, suddenly a great light shone in the house, so that scarcely anyone could look upon it or describe the greatness of the light. And there was a voice, saying, "Peter, behold I am with you all the days unto the end of the age." Then Peter raised his voice, saying, "We bless you, Governor

THE LATIN TRANSITUS MARIAE 275

of our souls, and we pray that you will not separate yourself from us. We bless you, illuminator of the world, who has mercy on all."

21. And when Peter said this, all the virgins who were there got up and fell at the Blessed Peter's feet, saying, "We ask you, master Peter, to pray for us, that we may be found worthy in the sight of Christ." And so Peter raised them all up from the ground, saying, "Arise and hear what your graces and glories are. For do not think that the voice spoke to me. Therefore, you heard this so that you would be able to know what you ought to observe. And so I tell you what you have given to the Lord, so that you will now serve him immaculately unto the end of the age, because if you guard your body completely and do not place a bridle on your tongue, you will [not] have eternal life, as it is written: 'If anyone thinks that he is religious, and does not bridle his tongue, but deceives his heart, his religion is vain.'[3] Indeed, our Lord and master thought it fitting to teach thus in the holy gospel: 'the kingdom of heaven,' he says, 'is like five virgins'[4] who, because they kept vigil and prayed, were worthy to receive the Lord. He did not say, however: the kingdom of heaven is like much time, because times passes away, but the name of virginity remains unto eternity, if it keeps itself from every evil, and what it does not wish to befall or be said about itself it does not similarly disparage in others, because the tongue is that which consumes our entire generation. For thus is virginity glorious before God, if it possesses innocence and purity and is troubled by nothing else except with vigils and prayer, so that, in keeping vigil and praying, it will be able to meet the coming Lord. For when the day of calling comes for each of

3. Jam 1.26.
4. Cf. Matt 25.1.

276 THE DORMITION AND ASSUMPTION OF MARY

us to go forth from this body, those who are worthy will be there, where the patriarchs Abraham, Isaac and Jacob are. For when he enters, death will be cast out. But the one who will be called from the body in his sins and sees the place of the righteous, he will say: 'Have patience, Lord, while I plead for my sins.' But death, having been dispatched, will not allow it, for his time has been fulfilled, and immediately he is led forth to the place of torment. If, however, he has done something good, he rejoices and exults. For when the soul goes forth from the body, first it is led forth before the Lord by angels. And after this each soul is addressed according to its action: if it did good, in Abraham's bosom; if, however, it was a sinner, it will be in the place of torments." When Blessed Peter said all these things, all the people were strengthened in the faith.

Christ Returns to Receive Mary's Soul.

22. And Mary stood up and went outside, and she prayed with the prayer that had been told to her by the angel, when he came to her. And after she finished the prayer, she went back into her house and laid down on her bed.

23. Blessed Peter, however, was sitting at her head, and the other disciples were around the bed. Then around the sixth hour of the day suddenly there was a great thunder and a fragrance of sweetness, so that all those who were in that place fell asleep on account of the excessive sweetness, except for the apostles and the three virgins, whom she had ordered to keep vigil without interruption and to bear witness regarding the glory of her Assumption in which Blessed Mary was taken up.

24. And while they were all sleeping, suddenly the Lord Jesus came on a cloud with a multitude of angels, and he entered the house in which Mary was lying. And Michael, the prince of the angels, was saying a hymn with all the angels. And when the Savior entered in, he found the apostles around Mary's bed and said to them, "Peace be with you."

25. And suddenly Blessed Mary's mouth opened, and she blessed the Lord, saying, "I bless you, for you have fulfilled what you promised me. For with such a great action of grace, I cannot repay your name as much as you have deemed worthy to bring me."

26. And thus the Lord received her soul and handed it over to the holy angel Michael: with the exception of all the bodily members, it had nothing in it except only the likeness of a human being and a whiteness seven times greater than snow.

27. Then Peter asked the Lord, saying, "Who among us has a soul as white as Mary?" And the Lord said to him, "Peter, the souls of all of my chosen, who have been chosen and sent to me, are thus when they came forth washed in the holy bath. But when they go forth from the body, they are not found so white, because they have been given differently and are found differently, because they have loved darkness more than light, on account of their many sins. For whoever has kept himself from all sin has such a white soul, just as you see Mary."

The Apostles Bring Mary's Body to her Tomb.

28. And again the Lord said to him, "Peter, take care of Mary's body, and go forth to the right part of the city, and you will find there a new tomb, and you will place her body in this tomb. And guard it as I have ordered you."

29. And when the Lord had said these things, suddenly Blessed Mary's body cried out before him, saying, "Remember me, King of Glory, because I am the work of your hands. Remember me, because I guarded the treasure that was entrusted to me." And the Lord said to Blessed Mary's body, "I will not abandon you, my pearl, because you were found faithful

278   THE DORMITION AND ASSUMPTION OF MARY

and you preserved the deposit that was entrusted to you. I will not abandon you, because you are the Temple of God."

30. And when he had said this, the Lord ascended into heaven.

31. Then Peter and the rest of the apostles held on, and the three virgins who had remained vigilant, and they washed Blessed Mary's body, and thus they placed her on the bier. And after this, all those who fell asleep arose.

32. Peter, however, took the palm that Blessed Mary had received from the hand of the angel, and he said to John, "You are a virgin. You should go before the bier and carry this palm and speak praises to God." And John said, "You precede us in the apostolate. You should go before and carry until we bear her to the place where the Lord commanded you. And let no one of us grieve, but rather let us crown the bed."

33. And when they got up, the apostles took up the bed, carrying it in their hands.

34. Then Peter raised his voice and began to say, "Israel went out of Egypt, alleluia."[5]

The Jewish Attack on Mary's Body.

35. Then the Lord protected the bed and the apostles with a cloud. And while walking and carrying the bed, they spoke praises, and they were seen by no one, except only their voices were heard like a great crowd.

36. And when the high priests of the Jews heard the great voices of those praising God, they were violently disturbed and began to say to one another, "What is this tumult and crowd of people?"

5. Ps 113.1.

THE LATIN TRANSITUS MARIAE   279

37. And someone of those standing by said, "Mary has gone forth from the body. Now the apostles are saying praises around her."

38. And immediately Satan entered into these high priests,[6] and they began to say to one another, "Let us go forth and kill the apostles and burn with fire Mary's body, which bore that seducer." And they got up and went forth with swords and clubs[7] to kill the apostles. Then at that same moment the angels that were in the clouds struck the Jews with blindness. And falling to the ground, they struck the walls with their heads. And feeling their way, they were feeling the ground with their hands: they did not know where they were walking.

39. But one of them who was a high priest, when he had drawn near to the apostles and saw the crowned bier, with the apostles saying hymns, filled with anger and rage, he said, "Behold, the tabernacle of the one who despoiled us and all our people: what glory she receives!" And suddenly he made an attack, crying out with a great voice, and he wanted to overturn the bier. Then, putting forth his hand, he wanted to seize the palm and cast it on ground. Then suddenly both his hands withered from the elbows and clung to the bier. And half of his body was holding on to the bier, but the other part was hanging toward ground.

The Jewish Attacker Repents and is Healed.

40. Then with tears he cried out with a great voice before the apostles. Pleading with them, he was saying, "I adjure you by the one God, do not disdain me in such great need. I beg you in particular, Saint Peter, to remember what my father

6. Cf. Jn 13.27
7. Cf. Mt 26.47, 55 and par.

280   THE DORMITION AND ASSUMPTION OF MARY

provided for you, when the doorkeeper questioned you and said, "Truly you were with him," how he made an excuse for you so that you were not arrested.[8] And now I beg you that you do not disdain me." Peter then said to him, "I do not have the power to provide help for you, nor does anyone of us, if you do not believe that Jesus Christ is the Son of the Living God, against whom you rose up."

41. And he answered, saying, "Do we not believe that he is the Son of God? But what will we do, since the enemy of the human race has blinded our hearts? But you do not wish to return evil for evil. For this, then, has happened to me because the Lord wants me to live."

42. Then Peter ordered them to set down the bed and said to him, "If you believe with your whole heart that you can be healed by God, approach the bed and embrace it and say: 'I believe in this body and in the one whom it bore.'"

43. Then the high priest blessed Mary in the Hebrew language for a period of three hours, and he did not allow anyone to raise up the bed, giving testimony from the books of Moses that it is written of her that she is the Temple of the Living God, so that the apostles themselves were amazed at the things that were said by him. And Peter said to him, "Take your hands and say: 'In the name of our Lord Jesus Christ, in whom I believe with my whole heart, let my hands be restored and be as they were before."

44. And it happened immediately, because he believed with his whole heart.

45. And again Peter said to him, "Now arise and take the palm that is before Blessed Mary, and enter the city, and you will find many people of the Jews who have been stricken with

---

8. Cf. Mt 26.69 and par.

THE LATIN TRANSITUS MARIAE 281

blindness. And speak to them, saying, "Whoever believes in the Lord Jesus Christ, that he is the Son of the Living God, his eyes will be opened.' And place this palm that you have received on their eyes, and immediately they will receive sight. Nevertheless, the one who does not believe will never see."

46. And the high priest went forth and did what Blessed Peter had directed him. And he found many people weeping and saying, "Woe to us! For as it happened to the Sodomites, so also it has come upon us, for first the Lord struck them with blindness, and then he sent fire from heaven.[9] Woe to us! Behold, we are full of iniquity." The high priest that Peter sent explained everything that happened, and how God had looked upon him. Whoever believed his words, who confessed Christ the Son of God, immediately received sight; the one who did not believe remained blind.

Christ Takes her Body to Paradise and Resurrects Her There.

47. Nevertheless, the apostles carried Mary and they reached the tomb where they buried Mary. Then they remained before the mouth of the tomb, as the Lord Jesus Christ had instructed them. And while they were sitting there, suddenly the Lord came with a multitude of angels and said to them, "Peace be with you, brothers."

48. And he ordered the archangel Michael to take up Mary's body into the clouds.

49. And as he was taking it up, the Lord told the apostles to draw near to him. And when the apostles approached the Lord Jesus, they were taken up into the clouds.

9. Cf. Gen 19.11, 24.

282   THE DORMITION AND ASSUMPTION OF MARY

50. And the Lord ordered the clouds to go to Paradise under the Tree of Life.[10] And thus the clouds set down Blessed Mary's body in Paradise, and there it is glorifying God with his elect. And the angels brought Holy Mary's soul and placed it in her body, as our Lord Jesus Christ rejoiced, and she will have glory there eternally, unto the ages of ages, Amen. Then the Lord ordered all the apostles to be restored whence they had been taken up.

Conclusion from Paris Bibliothèque nationale, fonds latin 3 550.[11]

... And they were sitting at the door of the tomb, as the Lord had said to them. And while they were sitting, the Lord came to them with a multitude of angels and said to them, "Peace be with you, brothers."

And the Lord ordered the archangel Michael to take up the body of Blessed Mary in the clouds, and he told the apostles to draw near to the Lord, and they were themselves taken up in the clouds, and the Lord ordered the clouds to go to Paradise. And thus they placed the body of Blessed Mary in Paradise, under the Tree of Life. And the angels of the Lord brought the soul of Blessed Mary and placed it in her body. And the Lord ordered the angels to go to their place.

10. The remainder of this paragraph is present only in certain manuscripts.

11. This manuscript largely concurs with the Latin version translated above, with some variants, until the ending, where it preserves a version of Mary's and the apostles' journey to hell as related in the earliest Dormition narratives. Text is from WENGER, *L'Assomption*, 258–9.

THE LATIN TRANSITUS MARIAE 283

Mary and the Apostles Visit the Places of the Damned.

1. And the Lord said to them, "It would be good for you if you did not see, but if you want and desire, now you will see it." And the Lord ordered the clouds, and they took up the apostles together with Mary. And the Lord said to Michael, "Open hell." And immediately it opened. And the Lord gave place to the apostles, so that they would see what hell was like.

2. And they[12] saw the angel Michael, and they wept with great tears, saying, "Michael, master, prince of the angels, whom you have always established,[13] intercede for us." Nevertheless, when the apostles heard this, they fell on their faces. The Lord, however, raised them up and said to them, "Remember what I said to you: 'I will lead you to the places where there is no light.'"

3. Then the archangel Michael said to those who were in hell, "The Lord lives, he who is and remains forever and will judge the living and the dead." For let them be inflamed for the human race; for he is beseeching the goodness of God.[14] But the Lord said, "Consider, Michael, that I love the human race even more than myself. I did not desist from shedding my blood, and nevertheless, they have not repented."

12. i.e. those in hell.

13. The text here seems to be corrupt, as the editor notes.

14. Again, the passage is corrupt. As Wenger suggests, this sentence seems to be a garbled summary of the prayer by the angel of the waters in the *Book of Mary's Repose*. "And the angel who is placed over the waters approached and beseeched God, saying, 'Let springs of water be abundant for the sake of the human race, because they are your image and likeness, Lord. Because of this, I beseech you to hear me, I who am your minister. Let your mercy be upon the waters and let them be abundant in all the earth.'"

284 THE DORMITION AND ASSUMPTION OF MARY

4. And again we saw the souls that had been consigned to the torments, and they cried out to Blessed Mary, saying, "Mary, mother of our Lord, Mary, Virgin and Immaculate, who is the true light, and Mary, Queen and Blessed forever, pray for us to our Lord that he gives us appeasement from the torments that we suffer." Likewise to Blessed Peter and John similarly.

5. And the Lord said to those who were consigned to the torments, "Why did you not remember when I suffered for your sake and when they whipped me and I did not respond, and when I received spit I endured patiently as you were sending me forth and pursuing eternal life.[15] But now on account of your weeping and that of Michael my archangel and Mary and the apostles you will have three hours of rest."

6. And when he said this, he ordered all the places of hell to close. And so the apostles were returned to the Tree of Life where Isaac and Jacob were with all of the saints who had gone forth from the body. They were resting there in the perpetual joy of the kingdom.

7. Truly the soul of Blessed Mary was assumed and placed in Paradise on the fifteenth day of the month of August, with the Lord Jesus Christ reigning, to whom is honor unto the ages of ages. Amen.

15. The final part of this sentence is quite peculiar and seems to be corrupt.

A Unique Early
Dormition Fragment in Georgian
A Reading from the Secret Apocrypha about the Departure of the Theotokos

17. ...in the mystical supper and reclining in spiritual marriage. **18.** Therefore they stood up and went to the ministers of the word and the eyewitnesses in order to serve his holy mother, as worthy of service and a revered treasure. But lest anyone is lacking in zeal for singing praise to God and honoring his mother, then Adam and Eve cried out and said, "O you daughter, you are worth of blessing, for you delivered us from the penalty for our disobedience. Behold, you truly are blessed, you, worthy of every blessing."

19. O Mother of the merciful God, I understand[1] many such words that the apostles spoke to the virgin in the company of the entire assembly. But when they saw her going forth from this world eagerly and willingly, they changed their words to praise the departure, and they spoke by receiving the gift of the Holy Spirit. And in order to fulfill the debt of the law, they plaited a crown of praise from many-colored flowers. **20.** Then they received a blessing given by God. And at that

---

1. It is not clear who is the first-person subject in this passage.

286 THE DORMITION AND ASSUMPTION OF MARY

time the King of his Glory came, and her pure soul was received in his divine hands.

Mary's Soul Goes Forth from her Body.

21. And holy Mary said, "Into your hands, O my son, I commend my spirit.[2] Receive my beloved soul unto yourself, which I have kept pure. Lead me with you, my son, so that where the fruit of my womb is, I will also be dwelling there. I beseech you, O my son and my God, who inseparably from the Father came down to me, to make my beloved children exalted. May their holiness please you to call them brothers. Add blessing upon blessing by placing your hands upon them."

22. At that time she raised her hands and blessed all those who were standing there after the plea and testament. And then a voice was heard, "Come, O my good mother, to your rest. Rise up and come, O my treasure, chosen of women, O my dwelling place, for your fragrance is more exalted than all perfumes." And when the Holy one heard this, she handed over her soul into the hands of her son. **23.** And at that moment the elements of heaven were stirred. And the angels mightily sang praises and went before her. And some were standing behind her, and some were standing around the pure soul of the holy Virgin. And they were going with her and sending her forth until they brought the holy Queen to the royal throne. Nevertheless, the souls were standing around her holy and pure body, and they were glorifying her as the Mother of God with angelic songs of praise, as this was a fitting glory.

24. And the holy ones were standing, and they handed over the pure body. Filled with blessings, they kissed her holy body

2. Cf. Luke 23.46.

with awe. In that moment, the infirmities of the sick were put to flight, and the firmaments were purified by the ascent of her soul, and the earth was blessed by her pure [body?]. After this they clothed her holy body with a holy shroud, and they anointed it with unguents and perfumes. And they placed it on a bier, and angels led the way with lamps [and] hymns of praise and magnified her with tongues of fire.

Mary's Funeral Procession.

25. Nevertheless, the joyful apostles struck up the trumpet and praised God as they had been instructed by the Holy Spirit. Then the apostles raised up the Ark of God on their shoulders and took it from Mount Zion, and placing it in the tomb, it ascended to the heavenly bridal chamber.

26. But before that, like a beautiful bride, adorned by the light of the Holy Spirit, they brought her outside the city and thus placed her in a holy tomb in Gethsemane. And angels went before them and with wings...

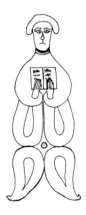

A Liturgical Apocryphon
from *Jeremiah* for
the *Dormition of the Virgin*

August 13. The assembly in Bethlehem, when the apostles took the Theotokos [from Bethlehem] to Zion. A reading: The things said by the prophet Jeremiah about typology of the ark of the old and new Law.[1]

1. "Rejoice and be glad, daughter of Edom, you who live in the land, for the cup of the Lord will go forth on you."[2] **2.** *This Jeremiah gave a sign to the priests of Egypt, that their idols will be shaken and knocked down and destroyed through a savior, a child born from a virgin* in Bethlehem in a cave *and laid in a manger,* **3.** *on account of which to this very day they* glorify the child as divine and *honor a virgin giving birth, and they place the child in the manger* every year *and worship him,* for in the second year the

---

1. The italicized passages in this translation are taken from the "Life of Jeremiah" in the apocryphal collection the *Lives of the Prophets,* while the passages in roman type have been added to the original. For the Greek text, see Theodor SCHERMANN, *Prophetarum vitae fabulosae, Indices apostolorum discipulorumque Domini, Dorotheo, Epiphanio, Hippolyto aliisque vindicata, inter quae nonnulla primum edidit* (Leipzig: In aedibus B. G. Teubneri, 1907), 45–6.

2. Lam 4.21.

290   THE DORMITION AND ASSUMPTION OF MARY

Magi came from Babylonia when the child was placed in the manger.

4. *And King Ptolemy asked about the cause of this,* "Why is it that at the completion of the year they place the child in the manger, which is in a cave? **5.** *And they told him, "This mystery is handed down from the fathers, which was given to our fathers by a holy prophet, and we will reach the completion of this mystery."* **6.** *This prophet Jeremiah, before the captivity* and destruction *of the Temple, seized the Ark of the Law and what was in it, and hid it in a rock.* **7.** *And the Lord has gone forth from Sinai and has ordered a giving of the Law on Zion* with the power of a new grace so that people will abandon the old and come to the new grace of the new child who was born from a virgin without a father and laid in a manger.

8. And the prophet said, *"It will be a sign to you of his coming* and of the consummation of the world of future children, *and this hidden ark no one will bring forth except Aaron* the priest, the brother of Mary, *and the tablets in it no one will remove and no one will be able to read them except Moses the lawgiver, the Lord's chosen one.* **9.** *And at the resurrection of the dead, the Ark will be the first to be resurrected from the rock and will be placed on Mount Sinai*, so that the saying of the prophet David would be fulfilled which says: 'Rise up, Lord, to your resting place, the Ark of your holiness,'[3] **10.** which is the Holy Virgin Mary, who goes forth from the world before God, whom today the holy apostles exclaim at Zion with laudation of anointing with myrrh. This day she is sent forth from Bethlehem to Zion, and today she passes away from the earth to heaven, *and all the saints will be gathered to her, and they await the Lord and flee from the enemy who wishes to destroy them.*

---

3. Ps 131.8.

11. *Nevertheless on the rock is the seal of our God*, sealed by all of the prophets, and no one is able to draw near to it or bring forth from it. **12.** For unto time it is kept there, *and it was made in the form as if written with iron. And a cloud of light covers* the house, where the Ark stands, *and no one knows the place, and no one is able to read it unto the ages.* **13.** *And* the place *is in a desert place*, and no one from humankind comes to this place. And *the Ark was at first between the two mountains where Moses* the law-giver of Israel *is buried. And all night a cloud of light stands over the place, just like the form of the earlier one, and the* grace *of God will not recede from the Law.*

14. *And therefore God granted to Jeremiah that he himself would enact the completion of his mystery, so that* the blessed Jeremiah *became a partner of Moses and Aaron, and they are together unto this day.* **15.** *For Jeremiah is also being from the line of the priests*, who fashioned the Ark as a type of the Virgin, which held the hidden mystery: the golden urn and the stone tablets inscribed by the finger of God, whose name is unchanging from age unto age.

The *Homily on the Dormition* Attributed to Basil of Caesarea

14 in the Month August.

The Departure of Our Lady the All-Holy and Pure, Most-Blessed and Ever-Virgin Mary, concerning her Assumption from Earth to Heaven

A Discourse of Our Holy Father Basil of Caesarea concerning the Ascension from Earth to Heaven and concerning the Mysterious and Tremendous Wonder Accomplished by God between Heaven and Earth on behalf of His Mother. Bless us O Lord!

1. The holy, living, magnificent Trinity, without beginning and the Creator of all creatures, which is the Father, Son, and Holy Spirit, One Lord and One God, the Merciful one, has made me worthy to search the tremendous mystery, on account of which it also brought me to find the mystery that I desire with clarity, from the discourse of John the Theologian and Evangelist, which is written with wisdom and written for spiritual devotion.

294   THE DORMITION AND ASSUMPTION OF MARY

Mary Learns of her Impending Death from the Holy Spirit.

2. When the Theotokos Mary learned the time of her departure from this world from the Holy Spirit, she understood that she would go forth and ascend with her son. Then she rejoiced in the wisdom of the Holy Spirit and was compassionately filled with love for eternal life, which is the fully endless glory of the exalted kingdom, in which she also dwells, for she is the Mother of God, the refuge of Christians, the sweet guardian, the pride and joy, the hope and confidence, the tranquil harbor, the protector and guardian of the entire world, the mediator between God and humanity, Queen of heaven and earth, who also unites the two as one.

3. She was always present at Zion, and three virgins with her, her servants and disciples, armed with her grace and happy in disposition. Nevertheless, Mary was their teacher, adorned with many virtues, more holy than the holy ones, always worn out from vigils, fasting, and prayer; nothing at all separated her from the tomb of the Lord.

Mary Prays at the Tomb of Christ.

4. Nevertheless, on the Sabbath she went, according to custom, to the tomb to burn incense. Then she placed the incense and lit the candles and bent her knees and seethed with ardent tears. She raised her hands and besought Christ our God who was born from her to look upon her, and so she said silently:

5. "My Creator God, Jesus Christ, Lover of humankind and All-merciful, you who are seated on the lofty, glorious, and exalted throne, Creator, with the consent of the Father and the Holy Spirit, of the heavens, the earth, and the boundaries, my kind son and God, you know how my life in this transient world has been, and you know well how my soul has longed

THE HOMILY ATTRIBUTED TO BASIL OF CAESAREA   295

for you. Mighty and Living God, you know as you will, thy will be done on earth as it is in heaven,[1] on account of which I am your servant and mother."

6. "Thus you know what your beginningless Father has mercifully fulfilled for his creatures, lest he delivers them to the enemy for destruction. Therefore, he chose me as his bride and sent to earth Gabriel, the angel who stands in his presence, who greeted me initially with 'Hail' and blessing."[2]

7. "Nevertheless, you sent yourself, his Word, from heaven at the direction of the Holy Spirit, and put on flesh from me and became incarnate from me for the salvation and life of humankind, you who sought the lost, showed mercy on the repentant, raised up the dead, comforted the poor, and finally were put to death on the cross by the Jews, placed in the tomb as dead, and arose on the third day as immortal. You despoiled hell and led forth the captives to the light and gave them paradise, ascended to heaven and sit at the right of the Father and the Holy Spirit and will come again to judge the living and the dead. Now on account of all this, glory and honor and worship to your mercy and magnanimity and charity with the Father and together with the Holy Spirit. Amen."

8. "Now do not forget or forsake me, but have mercy in your great mercy, and may you deem it fitting according to your will that you fulfill and grant my taking up, which you promised me at your ascension, so that the Jews, who are planning and intending to burn my body, will not accomplish their plot.[3] O

---

1. Matt 6.10.

2. Cf. Luke 1.19, 28.

3. Two of the oblique verbal forms here are unusual and seem to indicate a perfect tense (and so van Esbroeck renders them in his Latin translation), while one is in the present. Nevertheless, a translation in the present and future, as above, seems most appropriate, given the

296   THE DORMITION AND ASSUMPTION OF MARY

you who went forth from my flesh and have your spirit, hear me now and send to me the apostle John the Evangelist, for I desire to see him, so that he also will care for my distress at the time of my going forth. Behold, Savior and King, glory to you."

Gabriel Gives Mary an Olive Branch
and She Goes to Bethlehem.

9. When she finished this fervent prayer, behold, the heavens opened, and the archangel Gabriel came down and came to the Virgin and said to her, "Hail Mary, who gave birth to our God! Your prayers have gone up before God your son and have been received. Henceforth you will leave the world, Blessed one, and ascend with your son. Your existence has been prepared by the beginningless Father and the Holy Spirit, who is glorified together and remains unto the ages of ages. Nevertheless, your son has ordered that you go forth to Bethlehem."

10. And he placed in her hands his olive branch. Then Mary was filled with joy, and she turned toward Bethlehem, and with her were three virgins, her disciples. And when she went to Bethlehem, it was enlightened, and they rejoiced all together. The Queen, however, rested a little. And when night fell on that day, Tuesday, she bade the virgins to supper. And when they had dined and got up, she ordered them, "Bring me the censer and light three candles, so that we may pray."

11. Then she stood in prayer and said, "O my Lord Jesus Christ, who took on flesh from me, hear my voice and send to me John the Evangelist, so that I may see him and with him the holy apostles and all those who are holy before you and have been found worthy of your Kingdom. And when I

context. It would seem that the translator used this normally perfect form in an uncommon manner as a present oblique form.

THE HOMILY ATTRIBUTED TO BASIL OF CAESAREA   297

see them, I will bless and glorify and exalt greatly your utterly beautiful and lauded holy name."

Mary Prays Before an Image of her Son.

12. And according to custom, since the Ascension this pure Virgin had the visage portrayed on linen, given to her from divine hands, so that she would always see and behold the beautiful face of her son. And when she would pray, she placed the image to the east and thus prayed before it with raised hands. And also at the time of her departure, she made all her prayers before this image of the being. She lit three candles and placed incense on the fire, and with tears, prayers, and vigilance thus she spent the rest of the night.

13. When the sun rose it was Wednesday. She returned to Zion with her disciples. And again she placed incense and lit candles and stretched forth her hands and said, "You who receive the offering of the sun, receive my prayer and have mercy on your creatures and those you made with your hands, you who are a lover of humankind and because you have great mercy."

14. And she spoke this prayer, and the image of God said to her, "Do not fear, mother, I am with you." And again Mary said to Christ, "With John coming and the other apostles, you have made my soul glad." And again Christ said, "You are the guardian and faith of the apostles—how would you not see them? I myself will care for you, O caretaker of all who yearn for me. The time of your honor has drawn near, and you will be received as the mother of your son."

The Apostle John Arrives at Mary's Bethlehem House.

15. And when Mary ceased from prayer and sat on her bed, behold, John the Evangelist arrived and said in a great voice,

298   THE DORMITION AND ASSUMPTION OF MARY

"Peace be with you, mother of the Savior and deliverer of mercy and giver of blessing!" Then the Pure one cried out, "Behold, the Son of Thunder, behold the visage of Christ my God, behold the wise interpreter of the mysteries. Peace to you, virgin and theologian!"

16. When she saw, she was filled with joy, and thus she was thinking as if she had seen Christ. They greeted one another as the prophet David said, "Mercy and truth met, righteousness and peace kissed one another."[4] Mary said to John, "Today on account of my mystery, my master and yours has brought you here, a guardian over me. God is always blessed, but the one who brought you, is he not also capable that I may see all of the apostles?"

17. John said, "Not only will your son gather his disciples here, but also all of their disciples and the entire assembly of heaven and earth will be summoned to you, O bride unwed, throne of the Father, dwelling place of the Holy Spirit, behold beloved of the Trinity and always blessed and glorified."

The Other Apostles Arrive at Mary's House.

18. Behold, in an instant a cloud assembled the theologians from throughout the world together on Zion: John from Ephesus, Peter from Rome, Paul from Tiberias, Matthew who was traveling at sea, Mark from Alexandria, Bartholomew from the Thebaid. Andrew, James, Luke, Philip, Simon—these four[5] he raised from the dead. And when they assembled together in Zion, they greeted the Mother of God and venerated her.

19. Then Mary quickly sat down on the bed and cried out, "Behold, this is the day of my rejoicing. Has no one among

---

4. Ps 84.11.

5. Although these are five, the text says four.

women said such fitting words in her days? With regard to this day of my fulfillment, let it not be so at all, for the tongues of all humankind call me blessed since the Most High looked upon me in my humility."

20. Peter said, "Peace be with you, mother of the Savior, God before the ages!" Then Mary said, "Behold Peter, the rock of strength and foundation of the divine law, and Paul, teacher of the church and preacher of the true faith!"

Mary Greets the Apostles.

21. And the other apostles brought forth a shout and cried out together, "Peace be with you, mother of Christ, boon and pride of angels and humankind, joy of the living and the dead, and light of the world!" Mary said, "And peace be also with you, the spiritual elect, men of light, illuminators of the entire world, vanquishers of error, heirs of the Kingdom, disciples of the good Teacher, who do the will of the Word of God! Andrew the clear light, James the colorful, fragrant flower, Philip the font of grace and healer of the sick, Bartholomew the profound river of glorious wisdom, James the treasury of God's kindness and grace, Simon the beloved of the Trinity, eradicator of injustice and cultivator of justice, Jude the star not overtaken by the night that puts to flight the darkness of sin and abounding in praise, Matthias called from heaven and preacher of the resurrection raised up in place of the fallen one, Matthew the depths of divine Providence, the leader of the evangelists, Mark the doer of the will of the beginningless and endless God, Luke the precious pearl without price and the fortifier of the altar![6] Blessed is the one who sent you and blessed is your coming."

6. საკეთხეველისათ, which does not correspond to any form in the lexica, is presumably a typo for საკურთხეველისათ.

THE DORMITION AND ASSUMPTION OF MARY

22. And when they had completed this spiritual embrace and the disciples happened to be full of joy, they also cried out to her, "We confess you who gave birth to God; we glorify you who united heaven and earth; we venerate you who made angels and human beings one flock; glorified and praised one, may the grace of your right hand be our protector in soul and body: have mercy on us."

Mary Shows the Apostles
the Palm Branch Given by Gabriel.

23. Then Mary told all of the apostles of Gabriel's greeting and what he said, and she showed them the branch from a date palm that he brought her. James the Bishop said, "Behold the incomprehensible Providence of God that has been fulfilled in you, and this place on Zion, your cell, has been filled with the multitude of all the saints, comprehensible and incomprehensible. And what is the mystery of this vision? Who could explain it to us clearly? But it is clear that we should be patient for a little while, and everything will be explained to us without error."

The Apostles Explain their Miraculous Journeys.

24. And again Mary said to John, "I want you to explain for me whence you knew that I am being brought to completion, how you came to me, from which land, how much time you traveled here, so that you hurried for the sake of my departure."

25. John said, "O apostles and brothers, explain for the Mother of the Lord and our God, how it was made known to you by the Holy Spirit."

26. Peter said, "In Rome today, just at the time of dawn, I heard the voice of the Holy Spirit and it said to me: 'The

THE HOMILY ATTRIBUTED TO BASIL OF CAESAREA 301

time has drawn near for the departure of your Queen and the mother of Christ, and suddenly you will be at Zion in the presence of Mary.' And when I ascended to the altar, in a moment I was caught up by a cloud and was between heaven and earth. And also by clouds these brothers came with me, and behold we are found together here."

27. Paul said, "I was in Arimathea, in the region of Tiberius, and the Holy Spirit said to me: 'The mother of your Lord is about to go forth, and you will be at Zion in the presence of Mary.' And when I raised the cross, in a moment, behold, I was found here."

28. John said, "I was in Ephesus, and when I ascended to the altar for the holy liturgy, the Holy Spirit said to me: 'The mother of your Lord is about to go forth, and you will be at Zion in the presence of Mary." And when I was going down from the platform, in a moment I was caught up, and behold, I was found here."

29. Mark said, "I was in Alexandria, in the liturgy of the eucharist and in my prayer, and when I consecrated the body and blood of Christ the Savior, I put down the chalice and took off the cloth, the Holy Spirit said to me: 'Why do you delay? The mother your Lord is about to go forth; go forth to Zion before her.'"

30. James said, "I was in Jerusalem. I was reciting David [i.e. the Psalms], and I said this: 'Remember, Lord, David and all of his peacefulness.'[7] The Holy Spirit said to me: 'The mother of your Savior is about to go forth; suddenly you will be before her at Zion.' And in a moment, behold, thus I was found here."

31. Matthew said, "I was sitting on a ship at sea. The sea was stirred up, and we were troubled. Suddenly, it became

7. Ps 131.1.

302   THE DORMITION AND ASSUMPTION OF MARY

calm. The Holy Spirit said to me: 'The mother of your Lord is about to go forth. You will be at Zion before her.' And in a moment, behold, thus I was found here."

32. Bartholomew said, "I was in the Thebaid. At the time of sunrise, I was sitting among the congregation and was teaching. The Holy Spirit said to me: 'The mother of your Lord is about to go forth from the flesh and ascend to heaven. You will be at Zion before her.' And when I heeded the giving of the word, a cloud came down and caught me up, and in a moment I was found here."

33. Andrew, James, Philip, Luke, and Simon said, "We Were in Paradise with the souls of the saints, and the Holy Spirit said to us: 'The mother of the Builder of the Kingdom and Paradise and of the Destroyer[8] of Hell is about to go forth to heaven. You, these five, will be at Zion before her. And do not think this is the resurrection of the dead, but it is according to this grace that you will be counted in the number of twelve with your living brothers and will come together adorned with crowns.' And when it said this, behold we were caught up by clouds of light, and we went to where we were buried in our bodies. Invisibly we were revived and caught up by clouds, and once again we were joined together with our brothers and we came here. And all this happened in a moment, and behold we were found here."

34. And the other apostles also told everything, and together they glorified God. Then the apostles were awed by the lands that they had come from or from where some of them came together at Zion. But according to the grace of the Mother of God, they became satisfied and glorified God, for there were Dionysius the Areopagite and the great Hierotheus

8. შემმოსრჳელისაჲ is presumably an alternate spelling from შემმუსრჳელი.

THE HOMILY ATTRIBUTED TO BASIL OF CAESAREA 303

and Titus and Timothy. Nevertheless, they told the Holy Theotokos everything that happened.

35. Then she raised her hands and said, "Glory to the beginningless Father, glory to the beginningless Son, glory to the beginningless Holy Spirit, who has thus consoled my spirit, who illuminated you with his Gospel, O lights of the world. I bless his holy name who alone is compassionate and all-merciful."

36. Mary said to Andrew, James, and Philip, Simon and Luke, "I want you to tell me in which place you were." Andrew said, "I went to the shores of Bithynia and Pontus and Thrace and the land of the Thracians. And I went to the great city of Sebastopolis,[9] where the military camp of Afraeli (?) also was. In all these places, I preached your son. And when they crucified me in Patra, one of the locals buried me."

37. Philip said, "I was in Phrygia and I preached your son, and when I died, I was buried in Hierapolis." James said, "I preached your son in Judea, and I was put to death by Herod by the sword and was buried." Simon said, "I preached your son in Eleutheropolis and its environs and up to Egypt, and when the Egyptians crucified me, they buried me in the village of Lystra."

38. Mary said, "O who is like you among all, Jesus Christ our God, or who is more merciful than you who magnified your apostles, the twelve columns of the firmament, the foun-

9. სიბასტგინელთა. Presumably, this refers to Sebastopolis in Cholchis on the eastern shore of the Black Sea—the modern city Sukhumi, capital of the Russian-occupied Georgian territory of Abkhazia. Although there are other cities, named Sebastopolis in the region, according to early medieval tradition, Andrew was believed to have visited Sebastopolis in Cholchis. The military camp of Afraeli remains mysterious, however.

304   THE DORMITION AND ASSUMPTION OF MARY

dations of the world, friends of your Father and as offspring of the parent."

The Jews Plot to Kill the Apostles and Burn Mary's Body.

39. And the Jews heard the activity of the apostles. So they conspired to go to Zion to kill the apostles, but they were planning to burn the Mother of God. And an innumerable assembly went forth with swords and clubs, and while they were going, their feet were bound and their eyes blinded and their tongues were stuck in their mouths, and they no longer were speaking to one another.

40. Then there was a certain one among them named Abraham. Because of this, this one of them remained determined to teach his friends the way of life. And he was filled with lamentation and said, "You wretched ones, from the beginning I told you that Mary is truly the mother of Christ, and the disciples of Christ are healers of soul and body. Are you not now able to understand against whom you are intending evil? He will repay your retribution with vengeance, for I believe that Mary is the Theotokos and the apostles are disciples of Christ. Will you not now confess, you who have been burned by divine fire? For I have previously confessed the truth, and by it God has protected me in peace."

41. Then they all let forth a cry of misery and said, "We believe that Christ is God and Mary is the Theotokos and the apostles are revivers of the dead. Lord, have mercy on us; Lord, pardon us for this error." Then they were freed from their torment, and they thanked Abraham and quickly went to Zion and venerated the Theotokos. And they confessed all of their plot and told everything that had happened to them. Then they were baptized and converted, and they went to their homes illuminated by the Lord's cross and glorified God.

THE HOMILY ATTRIBUTED TO BASIL OF CAESAREA   305

Mary Addresses the Apostles before her Death.

42. And night fell on Wednesday. And the holy Theotokos and the twelve apostles and all of their disciples began supper in the name of the Father, the Son, and the Holy Spirit, who was dwelling among them in his wisdom. Then James the bishop said, "I want all of the disciples to go outside, and only the twelve apostles themselves to remain with us."

43. And when this happened, the holy bride Mary said, "O you chosen of God from above, for this reason I besought God regarding your coming here with me, for the day of my fulfillment has drawn near, so that the departure of my soul from my body will be observed. Even if I know this, nevertheless I know nothing of what will transpire after my going forth. Now I ask you, shepherds of the articulate sheep, columns of the foundation and hopes of God, to be guardians of my frailty and humility."

44. "Remember the love of my son and God and your master, and the time of his Passion for the sake of all creatures, how he left me among you, and at the time of his Ascension to heaven he entrusted me to you. And you know his joy [10] over me. Thus you will also be benevolent and compassionate to me. What will I say to you or my son who is equal to him who himself chose you in a moment for my sake? He established your posterity and his likeness and truly my glory for your sake from age to age." [11]

45. "He is your master and my son, and you are his beloved disciples and doers of his will. You are my sons. I beseech you with tears and ask of you that you will beseech

10. "Gospel" would be a more standard translation of this word, but that does not seem right for the context.

11. These last two sentences seem to be garbled, and their meaning is not entirely clear.

306   THE DORMITION AND ASSUMPTION OF MARY

your master for my sake that he will have mercy on me in his great mercy and deem it fitting that I will go forth in peace. He is holy, and you are also holy. As he is my protector, so you also are my protectors and your blessing is my rampart. Now receive and accept my soul and body. As my son, so you also have peace and great mercy."

The Apostle Weep and Lament Mary's Death.

46. And with these words of the Most-Blessed one, the apostles were seething[12] vehemently with bitter tears, and Mary also wept. Then John the Evangelist cried out fervently and deeply, "Behold this terrible and wretched day for us sinners, like that great day when the Lord, the slayer of death, was willingly handed over to death, and the terror of our sadness, for with your going forth to the Kingdom, we will be left as orphans, unless you protect us there from temptation, you who are blessed in soul and body!"

47. Peter and Paul said, "Why do you come thus with humility among us paupers, you who contained the Most-High whom heaven cannot contain? Behold, delight of angels and human beings, why do you entreat us, you who bore the Creator, who are, like your son, ruler of heaven and sovereign of the earth? To you are entrusted the souls of the living and the dead. We dispatch you before your son as an intercessor[13]

---

12. აღდღუნეს is presumably a misprint for აღდუნეს.

13. მობუაიმნედ is a rather uncommon word, and its use is somewhat peculiar here. According to the lexica, it means something equivalent to "informer" or "malcontent," neither of which seems appropriate here, and clearly the word also has some other meaning, presumably something along the lines of intercessor or advocate, as translated above.

THE HOMILY ATTRIBUTED TO BASIL OF CAESAREA   307

for our sins, and from you all human beings expect forgiveness of faults. For you are the eternal Queen and endless Providence, and you have peace and immeasurably [14] great mercy."

48. And the other apostles said, "Torments have seized us and troubles have besieged us. O day like the day when we were dispersed and Annas and Caiaphas were the high priests and Pilate and Herod were ruling over your son! Go then, go to the eternal mansion with your son, for you have peace and great mercy."

Mary and the Apostles Pray through the Night.

49. Then Mary ordered everyone to spend the night in fasting, ardent tears,[15] and prayer, and to glorify the crucifixion, burial, and resurrection of the Savior and his ascension into heaven with the Father and the Holy Spirit. And especially he has the second coming to judge the living and the dead. And all the apostles gathered together and began to sing hymns with great enthusiasm. And in the middle of the night, an unattainable light shone before the image of the Savior.

50. Then all the apostles let forth a shout, and Mary cried out, "O Light of light, do not take your Holy Spirit from us, for there is no other light except you." And a command shone from the light, "Apostles hear and disciples understand: glorify the departure of my mother fittingly." Then Mary said, "O

14. ურაცხელი seems to be a hapax legomenon, although its meaning is fairly clear.

15. მჭლარებითა does not find any equivalent in the lexica. Van Esbroeck translates "vigilia," but how he arrived at this interpretation is not clear to me. I have assumed instead that this is either a misprint or variant spelling for მღუდარებითა.

308   THE DORMITION AND ASSUMPTION OF MARY

servants of the Word, now I want you to adorn the image of my beloved son with glory."

51. Then the twelve apostles and the disciples and all began saying litanies, Kyrie eleison and Alleluia, with genuflections and tears and mixing in the songs of David. Nevertheless, Peter and Paul, with hands raised, uttered a hymn as follows: "Creator of all creatures, Ruler of the ages, Foundation of Heaven and Earth, Savior of angels and human beings, praised and magnified by all, the Most High, alone Mighty, the living Lord, and visible in condescension, Creator of brilliance, Gladsome Light, himself the Light not overtaken by night, eternally True and the unshadowed Illuminator of all, the Infinite, the Incomprehensible, the Ineffable, the Inscrutable, the Unattainable, the Sovereign most beautiful of all, we magnify with a hymn."

52. James and John said, "Glory to the Son and Word of the Father, who came into the world with wisdom, became incarnate from the Virgin Mary, became human for the sake of our salvation, pardoned the repentant, offered repentance, forgave sins, had patience, was ungrudging, showed mercy and took the enemy captive, sought the lost, was crucified by sinners, willingly tortured and tormented for our sake, laid in the tomb for our sake, rose from the dead on the third day, worked miracles, raised the dead, was beneficent and destroyed Hell and freed the captive Christians, the giver of every good thing and joy, source of light and blessing, giver of his own flesh and blood, clothed in his own grace, exalted power and grace, who puts down the haughty and proud and raises up those who have fallen and abundantly crowns the faithful, Jesus Christ who ascended into heaven, is seated at the right of the Father, and will come again a second time to judge the living and the dead, for there is no God other than him. Come, faithful, let us worship him as God."

THE HOMILY ATTRIBUTED TO BASIL OF CAESAREA 309

53. And this they said and sang with a voice of laudation. Nevertheless, the holy Theotokos drenched the earth with tears and spent the night with such prayers. And when dawn broke, it was Thursday. And the apostles remained at Zion. Then Mary secretly stood in prayer in her bedroom before the image of the Savior and was praying silently and said as follows:

Mary Prays to her Son in Anticipation of Death.

54. "O beginningless Father and only begotten Son and life-giving Holy Spirit, we glorify you because you are merciful, we bless you because you are a lover of humankind, we hymn you because you are kind. Glory to you who is patient and ungrudging. O my beautiful son, who revealed the light of your divinity among the apostles, make them glad and fill me with fragrance."

55. "Receive now my soul in the presence of the apostles and have mercy. Deliver me in peace from the guardians of the air with the assistance of your inaccessible servants Michael and Gabriel, and with the prayers of all those born of women, of the senior and exalted prophets, of the bishops, preachers, and lights of the desert, and the martyrs who were battered for your sake, victors in the struggle, having toiled here and honored there, and your friend and my beloved John the Baptist your Forerunner, and all of your saints who have pleased you through the ages. Protect me in soul and body from the robbers partaking of souls, from corruption and evil, for I am greatly terrified and afraid, and I do not know where I will go or where I will flee except to you my comforter. Glory and worship to you with the Father and the Holy Spirit, you who have great mercy."

310   THE DORMITION AND ASSUMPTION OF MARY

The Image of Christ Again Addresses Mary.

56. And again a brilliant light shone before the image of the Savior. A fragrant smell went forth ineffably,[16] and from it a command went forth and said to Mary, "Do not fear, mother, for I am with you, and do not be terrified, Blessed one: all my creatures venerate your holiness, for I am with all who glorify you." Seething with tears, she fell to the ground.

57. Again the voice said, "Arise, pray, and receive what you want from me." Then she raised her hands and said, "Have mercy on your exalted ones and the works of your hands, O terror of Hell, forgive sins in error, and do not deliver them to Hell, but make them worthy of your light: behold, for their sake you came from heaven to earth."

58. And again the voice said, "Mother, those who glorify you, I will glorify them unto eternity. And what you asked, it has been granted beyond what you asked. I will grant it to you on account of your glory, and now you have boldness, and above all your wish will be granted as the beloved mother."

59. Mary said, "Lord God, might I somehow see John the Baptist now, here in the flesh?" Christ said, "I am pleased to do anything. Nevertheless, you will not only see him in the flesh, but my entire Kingdom, for I will lead forth your soul myself and peace to you." Mary said, "As is fitting for your divinity, so may your will be done, and without you nothing at all is done. Glorious Lord, glory to you."

Mary and the Apostles Prepare for her Departure.

60. And again the apostles gathered around the Queen, mourning and in anguish and grieving exceedingly on account

---

16. მიუთხრომელად is a typo for მიუთხრობელად.

THE HOMILY ATTRIBUTED TO BASIL OF CAESAREA   311

of her departure. And the All-Pure one told the twelve the entire vision. Then John the Evangelist said, "We also understand this, for as your son's willing Passion and going forth were dreadful, so also your going forth from the world is dreadful, for you are the Mother of the King."

61. Philip said, "If your son thought it fitting to be placed in a tomb as one dead, the Creator of the heavens, so now also, you, his mother, receive the cup of death."

62. And when evening fell, it was Friday. They prepared supper, and when they had finished the prayer of evening and sat at the table in the church of Holy Zion, they brought the image of the Savior there from the bedroom and sat down for supper.

Mary Washes the Apostles' Feet.

63. Then Mary said, "Disciples of the Lord, the command that your master gave you as a law and an order, he said to you also there at the washing of the feet: do this. It is fitting to fulfill this, and now you also need to have your feet washed." [17] And when they arose from supper, they prepared the wash basin and poured water. The mother of the Lord put on her shroud and began to wash the feet of the disciples. Peter and John cried out, "We bless the Father, we bless the Son, we bless the Holy Spirit, now unto the ages." And all were saying this while standing around. And she not only washed the feet of the chief disciples, but also of their disciples. Nothing, however, compelled the Pure one to fulfill the washing of feet, but so that the entire plan of Christ Passion would be fulfilled in her departure.

17. Cf. John 13.14–15.

312   THE DORMITION AND ASSUMPTION OF MARY

Archangels and Patriarchs Arrive for Mary's Death.

64. Then the Mother of God ordered them to spend the night in prayer and praise. And when they began to pray, behold, the earth moved with its foundations, and heaven and earth together groaned with fear, and Michael and Gabriel suddenly came and cried out, "The King of Glory comes!" Gabriel said, "Hail blessed one, the Lord is with you!" Michael said, "Glory to God in the highest, peace on earth and good will among men!" Mary said, "O great, splendid luminaries, until I see my son, my soul will not go forth from my body."

65. And again Abraham, Isaac, and Jacob came and said to Mary, "Behold then, the one you are expecting comes, O daughter of Adam!" The elder Simeon came and cried out, "O more exalted than the cherubim, the boast of virgins!" John the Baptist came and cried out, "Peace to all!" And they all said. "Amen." Peter cried out, "Behold, the morning star of the sun, the sprout in the desert!" And Mary said, "Come to me, desire of my soul!"

66. Behold, the earth moved with its foundations, and heaven and earth groaned with fear, and behold, around midnight a light more brilliant than the sun shone forth. And the precious cross was put up, and before it the multitude of myriads of myriads of the heavenly host, who were saying, "Holy, holy, holy is the Lord Sabaoth. Heaven and earth are full of his glory," and "every soul and every creature, praise the Lord!"

Christ Appears and Receives Mary's Soul.

67. Then Christ cried out, "Peace be with you! I am. Do not fear!" The apostles cried out, "Lord God!" and "he has appeared to us!"

68. "Peace be with you, mother, Queen of all creatures above and below, ask what you want from me, and receive

THE HOMILY ATTRIBUTED TO BASIL OF CAESAREA   313

generously, All-Blessed." Mary said, "You know everything, and nothing that I ask from you is concealed from you, my God and King."

69. Christ took her right hand and said, "O blessed mother, I have come to you, your son, with power for your sake so that you will come with me. Behold then, here are myriads of myriads of the incorporeal heavenly host, visible and invisible. Behold, all my saints and the patriarchs and the high priests, mothers and fathers, for you are the pride of all, the hope and bulwark of all. O my throne and my rest, come to me so that I may give you rest and crown you before me, go forth to the Kingdom and immortal glory, for previously it seemed fitting to me that you were on earth, and now I want you to be in heaven. For because you are my mother, it is fitting that your glory should also be like mine. Behold, my joy, my and your immortal destiny, go forth to the eternal Kingdom, for all the creatures that have turned to you in a moment in heaven and on earth, they behold you, mother greater than all things!"

70. And when they began to ascend, the King himself took the Mother's soul in his arms, and all the assemblies began to ascend to heaven with uninterrupted songs and laudations. And when the All-Pure one ascended to heaven with acclamations of victory, she settled into an invisible dwelling place. Immortally she shines in body and soul and stands before the face of God, and she pleads for peace and mercy for our souls.

The Apostles Prepare Mary's Body for Burial.

71. Then the apostles began to take care of the body that received the Lord. They wrapped it in a holy shroud and covered it with fabric and anointed it with perfume and sang

314 THE DORMITION AND ASSUMPTION OF MARY

praises to the mother of the King of all. Tongues of fire were giving praise, and all the disciples were giving glory.

72. Nevertheless, the virgin disciples said, "Do not forget us, Theotokos, and do not make us unable to sing praises, but take care of our souls before your son and the God of us all."

73. Thus they spent the night in prayers and vigils, and when dawn broke on Friday, the virgins were preparing her bier, and they were preparing to go forth to Gethsemane, for so it had been commanded by God. And when they went forth from Zion and began to go, then the Jews assembled to prevent the deposition of her body. With swords and spears[18] they surrounded the apostles, and they insolently attacked the body that received God, for they wanted to throw it down and burn it.

The Jewish Attack on Mary's Body.

74. Then one of them named Jephonias brazenly grabbed the bier with his hands, and they all saw that his hands suddenly were severed, and they fell to the ground. Then they were all stricken with fear at the horrible sight. The apostles said, "Brotherly men, we told you from the start not to touch the life-giving and miracle-working body. Did you not know that it is fitting that we bring it to Gethsemane?" The Jews said to them, "Now we will know that it is miracle working, if the severed hands are restored to his body."

75. Then the all the apostles began to beseech the Theotokos with tears, and Peter said pleadingly, "You who are immortal in soul and body like your son and God, O Merciful one, for every need and care we plead to you our ready helper.

18. Cf. Mt 26.47, 55 and par.

THE HOMILY ATTRIBUTED TO BASIL OF CAESAREA 315

If your son came for the sake of sinners,[19] now, you, his mother, who knows the frailty of our earthly nature, how will you not pardon this wretched and injured man?"

76. John said, "Now you understand that Mary is the Mother of God" And they pleaded with tears, "Behold your wonder, Lord who has glorified your mother beyond all creatures!" And behold, in a moment the severed hands were restored to Jephonias as before.

77. Then they all cried out, "You are great Queen, and great is God who was born from you, Mary. We believe that you, the Theotokos, are exalted above all creatures." And they were converted and baptized and sealed with the seal of Christ. Nevertheless, Jephonias was praising the Theotokos without interruption and beseeching her with tears. And filled with joy they joined the apostles along their way, and they all gave glory to God.

The Apostles Bury Mary's Body.

78. They led before them the image of the Savior and went to Gethsemane. Along the way they were crying out, "Go forth, then, go forth, glory of all things, for he calls you to endless glory. Rejoice now, living Mother of the Merciful one! You are in the presence of your son; secure great mercy for the faithful."

79. And when they reached Gethsemane, as was fitting they laid the body that received God in a tomb and placed the image of the Savior on the grave. And they spent the night with prayers and singing praises, and dawn broke on Saturday.

---

19. წოდვილთა, which does not seem to have a corresponding form in the lexica, is undoubtedly a typo for ცოდვილთა, which is consistent with van Esbroek's Latin translation "peccatores."

316 THE DORMITION AND ASSUMPTION OF MARY

And at the third hour, they completed the offering and again began to spend the night with great diligence and prayer until midnight.

80. And at midnight, they were slumbering in a deep sleep, and while they were sleeping, the body of the All-Holy Theotokos was invisibly snatched up to heaven. And at dawn, Paul and John were fearfully awakened with force by an earthquake, and they cried out as if enraged, "Wake up brothers! Behold, why are you wretches sleeping?[20] Could we not last the night of Sunday, wretches, to remain awake?"

The Late Arrival of Thomas.

81. And when they all stood up, I realized[21] regarding Mary's body that one of the twelve was not with the apostles for the departure of the Mother of God. He was not able to come, for the holy apostles were expecting him all the time, and even more on this night of Sunday, so that he too could meet with her holy body and receive a blessing from our blessed Queen.

82. Nevertheless, he arrived with the earthquake and found the other apostles assembled with their disciples. And those who were followers of Paul were the great Dionysius the Areopagite and Timothy, Titus, and Hierotheus, who were praised in many various ways. And the angels of heaven were helping them. And Thomas heard the sweet and pleasing praises of the heavenly powers.

83. He was sad on account of his arriving last and beset with sorrows. Then, by divine providence he thought of the

20. Cf. Luke 22.46.
21. The first person form, although very strange here, is in the manuscript.

THE HOMILY ATTRIBUTED TO BASIL OF CAESAREA   317

time of the resurrection of Christ from the tomb, when he entered the closed doors with the apostles and no one opened the gates of the house, for also he had arrived there last, and the resurrection of Christ was confirmed even more when he saw the evidence of the nails and the wounds of his hands and feet and placed his hand in the side dyed with blood.[22]

84. Then Thomas said, "This mystery is like that occasion, and it was desirable that something would be revealed." And the apostles greeted him and told him what had happened, and they asked Thomas, "Where were you? To which land were you sent far away?"

85. Thomas said, "I was in India in a great city. I baptized the son of the king and his niece, they were sealed by me. And the Holy Spirit said to me: 'Thomas, do not delay any longer, for the mother of your Savior is going forth from the world to heaven. Go forth immediately to Gethsemane in the presence of Mary.' And as I was looking around, a cloud of light came down upon me and caught me up, and behold, I am found here. You are blessed who came more quickly and are filled with blessings."

Thomas Pleads to Enter Mary's Tomb and the Body is Gone.

86. And he pleaded with the apostles to let him go to her life-giving tomb so that they would open the closed tomb. Then, at the command of the Holy Spirit, they granted his request and invited Paul to open the tomb. Filled with tears, Paul said to John the Evangelist, "O son of thunder, do I grasp the ark of the old and new covenants with my hands? Shall I

---

22. Cf. John 20.24–9.

318 THE DORMITION AND ASSUMPTION OF MARY

embrace it, frail with sin?" They said to John, "You are like Christ, Son of Thunder. It is fitting for you to touch it." John said, "O chosen vessel, Peter, dwelling place of the grace of the Trinity, rock of strength, you are the chief of the apostles. It is fitting for you to touch it. I will hold the censer."

87. Then Peter, compelled by them, with fear and trembling put forth his hands, and also James the brother of the Lord, and they opened the tomb. And when they looked inside, they did not find the body of the All-Holy Theotokos, and they saw the empty girdle and shroud lying together to one side. When the apostles saw this, they were amazed, and they understood that it was for the sake of this that Thomas came late: so that he would be the cause for opening the tomb and revealing the transfer of the body of the holy Queen in soul and in the flesh to heaven.

The Apostles Establish Commemoration of Mary's Dormition.

88. Then all of the apostles gave glory to the wonder-working God. And they placed incense, lit candles, and with tears began to pray with the canon and litany, "We worship, we praise you without cease, we honor you continuously, and we magnify the feast day, we sing praise of the Dormition, and we beseech your mercy." And on Sunday they completed the holy liturgy, and they glorified God and the holy Theotokos, and received the body and blood of Christ.

89. And the holy virgins were consoled. And they appointed the Memory of the Holy Theotokos on the fourteenth, as a precursory feast day, the 15th the departure itself, on the sixteenth the Dormition and the laying in the tomb, the 17th the Assumption into heaven for the sake of this, for she is living in body and soul. The four days the apostles established.

THE HOMILY ATTRIBUTED TO BASIL OF CAESAREA 319

90. Nevertheless, Peter stood among the apostles and said, "Let anyone who does not fulfill this be cursed, and whomever the Lord does not enable is not condemned. Nevertheless, regarding the fast, there are, then, three fasts ordained by us, and there is no other communal fast beyond these. Nevertheless, whoever fasts for the departure of the holy Theotokos becomes worthy of great blessing and will receive great mercy from it. The day of the departure of the holy Theotokos is a day of rest while she was in the tomb. Work is not allowed except for vigils, prayers, and litanies."

Concluding Exhortation.

91. O beloved believers in Christ, what would be sweeter than remembering the holy Theotokos with praise? For she is a mediator between God and humankind, and so also the tomb of the holy Theotokos works cures and miracles, as if her body were alive in Gethsemane. And I, Basil, say: Let anyone who does not fulfill this [command] of Peter, who is sufficiently able, be cursed, but those who magnify the holy Theotokos are blessed with the blessing of Abraham.

92. Nevertheless, the apostles prepared what they saw fitting with regard to the tomb, and they placed the miracle-working image of the Savior there permanently, and, in order to establish all of this, they gathered at the tomb. And they went forth to the ends of the earth to preach the holy gospel, to praise and magnify the All-Holy, Blessed, and Beloved Theotokos.

93. Now it is fitting for us, of faithful, to praise and magnify, to give thanks, to worship and bless, to adorn with song, to exalt in the highest our hope and pride, the Queen, the Theotokos and Ever-Virgin Mary, who stands in the presence of her son and constantly pleads with tears for mercy on us and forgiveness of sins, and deliverance from all affliction and trials for hymns in praise of her departure.

94. Come, faithful, let us complete her memorial with praise, and to show respect for her departure, we offer intercession and praise, grace and mercy, to Christ our God, who is worthy of glory and honor and worship with the Father and the Holy Spirit now, always, and unto the ages of ages.

Bibliography

General Bibliography
on the Early Dormition Traditions.

B. BAGATTI, "La verginità di Maria negli apocrifi del II-III secolo," *Marianum* 33 (1971), 281–92.

—, "Ricerche sulle tradizioni della morte della Vergine," *Sacra Doctrina* 69–70 (1973), 185–214.

—, "La morte della Vergine nel Testo di Leucio," *Terra Sancta* 50 (1974), 44–48.

D. BALDI and A. MOSCONI, "L'Assunzione di Maria SS. negli apocrifi," *Atti del congresso nazionale mariano dei Fratei Minori d'Italia (Roma 29 aprile–3 maggio 1947)* (Rome, 1948), 75–125.

R. BAUCKHAM, "The Four Apocalypses of the Virgin Mary," *The Fate of the Dead*, 332–62, 332–8

M. BONNET, "Die ältesten Schriften von der Himmelfahrt Mariä," *Zeitschrift für Wissenschaftliche Theologie* 23 (1880), 227–47.

L. CIGNELLI, "Il prototipo giudeo-cristiano degli apocrifi assunzionisti," in B. BAGATTI, *et al.* (eds), *Studia Hierosolymitana in onore di P. Bellarmino Bagatti*, 3 vols. (Jerusalem, 1976), 2:259–77.

M. CLAYTON, "The *Transitus Mariae*: The Tradition and Its Origins," *Apocrypha* 10 (1999), 74–98.

É. Cothenet, "Marie dans les apocryphes," in H. Du Manoir de Juaye (ed.), *Maria : Études sur la Sainte Vierge*, 7 vols (Paris, 1952), 6:117–56.

—, "Traditions bibliques et apocalyptiques dans les récits anciens de la Dormition," in J. Longère (ed.), *Marie dans les récits apocryphes chrétiens* (Paris, 2004), 155–75.

B. E. Daley, *On the Dormition of Mary: Early Patristic Homilies* (Crestwood, NY, 1998), 1–45.

—, "'At the Hour of Our Death': Mary's Dormition and Christian Dying in Late Patristic and Early Byzantine Literature," *Dumbarton Oaks Papers* 55 (2001), 71–89.

F. de La Chaise, "À l'origine des récits apocryphes du '*Transitus Mariae*,'" *Ephemerides Mariologicae* 29 (1979), 77–90.

M. van Esbroeck, "Les textes littéraires sur l'Assomption avant le xe siècle," in F. Bovon (ed.), *Les Actes apocryphes des apôtres* (Geneva, 1981), 265–85.

—, "Bild und Begriff in der Transitus-Literatur, der Palmbaum und der Tempel," in M. Schmidt (ed.), *Typus, Symbol, Allegorie bei den östlichen Vätern und ihren Parallelen im Mittelalter* (Regensburg, 1982), 333–51.

—, *Aux origines de la Dormition de la Vierge : Études historiques sur les traditions orientales* (Brookfield, VT, 1995).

H. Förster, *Transitus Mariae: Beiträge zur koptischen Überlieferung mit einer Edition von P. Vindob. K 7589, Cambridge Add 1876 8 und Paris BN Copte 129¹⁷ ff. 28 und 29* (Berlin and New York, 2006).

P. González Casado, "Los relatos árabes apócrifos de la dormición de la Virgen: narrativa popular religiosa cristiana," *Ilu* 3 (1998), 91–108.

—, "Textos árabes cristianos sobre la dormición de la Virgen," *Ilu: Revista de Ciencias de las Religiones* 4 (2001), 75–95.

—, *La dormición de la Virgen: Cinco relatos árabes* (Madrid, 2002), 15–78.

M. Jugie, *La Mort et l'Assomption de la Sainte Vierge, Étude historico-doctrinale* (Vatican City, 1944).

A. van Lantschoot, "L'Assomption de la Sainte Vierge chez les coptes, " *Gregorianum* 27 (1946), 493–526.

S. C. Mimouni, "La lecture liturgique et les apocryphes du Nouveau Testament: le cas de la *Dormitio grecque* du Pseudo-Jean," *Orientalia Christiana Periodica* 59 (1993), 403–25.

—, *Dormition et Assomption de Marie: Histoire des traditions anciennes* (Paris, 1995).

—, *Les Traditions anciennes sur la Dormition et l'Assomption de Marie: Études littéraires, historiques et doctrinales* (Leiden: Brill, 2011).

—, "Traditions sur le sort final de Marie. Remarques et réflexions fragmentaires sur une question en débat," in F. P. Barone, *et al.* (eds), *Philologie, herméneutique et histoire des textes entre Orient et Occident: Mélanges en hommage à Sever J. Voicu* (Turnhout, 2017), 641–70.

E. Norelli, *Marie des apocryphes: Enquête sur la mère de Jésus dans le christianisme antique* (Geneva, 2009), 103–47.

—, "La letteratura apocrifa sul Transito di Maria e il problema delle sue origini," in E. M. Toniolo (ed.), *Il dogma dell'assunzione de Maria: problemi attuali e tentativi di ricomprensione. Atti del XVII Simposio Internazionale Mariologico (Roma, 6–9 ottobre 2009)* (Rome, 2010), 121–65.

—, "Les premières traditions sur la Dormition de Marie comme catalyseurs de formes très anciennes de réflexion théologique et sotériologique. Le cas du Paradis terrestre," in J. Schröter (ed.), *The Apocryphal Gospels within the Context of Early Christian Theology* (Leuven, 2013), 403–446.

—, "La littérature ancienne sur la Dormition de Marie: La transformation de ses formes et de ses fonctions," in Géraldine Veysseyre, Barbara Fleith, Réjanne Gay-Canton, Audrey Pérard and Aude Mairey (eds.), *De l'(id)entité* *textuelle au cours du Moyen Âge tardif. XIIIe-XVe siècle*, (Paris, 2017), 63–84.

J. Rivière, "Rôle du démon au jugement particulier : Contribution à l'histoire des *'Transitus Mariae*,'" *Bulletin de littérature ecclésiastique* 48 (1947), 49–56, 98–126.

S. J. Shoemaker, "'Let Us Go and Burn Her Body': The Image of the Jews in the Early Dormition Traditions," *Church History* 68.4 (1999), 775–823.

—, "Gender at the Virgin's Funeral: Men and Women as Witnesses to the Dormition," *Studia Patristica* 34 (2001), 552–58.

—, *Ancient Traditions of the Virgin Mary's Dormition and Assumption* (Oxford, 2002).

—, "Death and the Maiden: The Early History of the Dormition and Assumption Apocrypha," *Saint Vladimir's Theological Quarterly* 50 (2006), 59–97.

—, "Marian Liturgies and Devotion in Early Christianity," in S. J. Boss (ed.), *Mary: The Complete Resource* (London, 2007), 130–45.

—, "The Virgin Mary's Hidden Past: From Ancient Marian Apocrypha to the Medieval *vitae Virginis*," *Marian Studies* 60 (2009), 1–30.

—, "From Mother of Mysteries to Mother of the Church: The Institutionalization of the Dormition Apocrypha," *Apocrypha* 22 (2011), 11–47.

—, "A New Dormition Fragment in Coptic: P. Vindob. K 7589 and the Marian Apocryphal Tradition," in D. Bumazhnov, *et al.* (eds), *Bibel, Byzanz und Christlicher Orient. Festschrift für Stephen Gerö zum 65. Geburtstag* (Louvain, 2011), 203–29.

—, "Mary in Early Christian Apocrypha: Virgin Territory," in P. Piovanelli, *et al.* (eds), *Rediscovering the Apocryphal Continent: New Perspectives on Early Christian and Late Antique Apocryphal Texts and Traditions* (Tübingen, 2015), 175–90.

—, "The Ancient Dormition Apocrypha and the Origins of Marian Piety: Early Evidence of Marian Intercession from Late Ancient Palestine," in L. M. Peltomaa, *et al.* (eds), *Presbeia Theotokou, The Intercessory Role of Mary across Times and Places in Byzantium (4th–9th century)* (Vienna, 2015), 23–39.

—, *Mary in Early Christian Faith and Devotion* (New Haven, 2016).

—, *The Dormition and Assumption Apocrypha* (Leuven, 2018).

E. Testa, "Lo sviluppo della 'Dormitio Mariae' nella letteratura, nella teologìa e nella archeologìa," *Marianum* 44 (1982), 316–89.

—, "L'origine e lo sviluppo della Dormitio Mariae," *Augustinianum* 23 (1983), 249–62.

A. Wenger, *L'Assomption de la T. S. Vierge dans la tradition byzantine du VIe au Xe siècle : Études et Documents* (Paris, 1955).

The *Book of Mary's Repose / Obsequies of the Virgin.*

Texts.

V. Arras, *De transitu Mariae apocrypha aethiopice*, 2 vols (Louvain, 1973), vol. 1.

M. van Esbroeck, "Apocryphes géorgiens de la Dormition," *Analecta Bollandiana* 92 (1973), 55–75, 64–5, 69–73.

L. S. B. MacCoull, "More Coptic Papyri from the Beinecke Collection," *Archiv für Papyrusforschung* 35 (1989), 25–35.

T. Mgaloblishvili, კლარჯული მრავალთავი *(Klarjuli mravalt'avi [The Homilary of Klarjeti])* (Tbilisi, 1991), 420–21, 423–25.

C. Müller-Kessler, "Three Early Witnesses of the "Dormition of Mary" in Christian Palestinian Aramaic from the Cairo Genizah (Taylor-Schechter Collection) and the New

Finds in St. Catherine's Monastery," *Apocrypha* 29 (2018), 69–95.

—, "An Overlooked Christian Palestinian Aramaic Witness of the "Dormition of Mary" in Codex Climaci Rescriptus (CCR IV)," *Collectanea Christiana Orientalia* 16 (2019), 81–98.

—, "Obsequies of My Lady Mary (I): Unpublished Early Syriac Palimpsest Fragments from the British Library (BL, Add 17.137, no. 2)," *Hugoye* 23 (2020), 31–59.

—, "Obsequies of My Lady Mary (II): A Fragmentary Syriac Palimpsest Manuscript from Deir al-Suryan (BL, Add 14.665, no. 2)," *Collectanea Christiana Orientalia* 19 (2022), 45–70.

P. SELLEW, "An Early Coptic Witness to the *Dormitio Mariae* at Yale: P. CtYBR inv. 1788 Revisited," *Bulletin of the American Society of Papyrologists* 37 (2000), 37–69.

S. J. SHOEMAKER, "New Syriac Dormition Fragments from Palimpsests in the Schøyen Collection and the British Library: Presentation, Edition and Translation," *Le Muséon* (2011), 259–78.

W. WRIGHT, *Contributions to the Apocryphal Literature of the New Testament* (London, 1865), 11–16 and ܣܟܘ-ܟܡ.

Modern Translations.

M. ERBETTA, *Gli Apocrifi del Nuovo Testamento*, 3 vols., vol. 1/2, *Vangeli: Infanzia e passione di Cristo, Assunzione di Maria* (Torino, 1966), 421–64.

L. MORALDI, *Apocrifi del Nuovo Testamento*, 2 vols (Torino, 1971), 1:896–900.

S. J. SHOEMAKER, *Ancient Traditions of the Virgin Mary's Dormition* (Oxford, 2002), 290–350.

W. WRIGHT, *Contributions to the Apocryphal Literature of the New Testament* (London, 1865), 42–51.

Selected Studies.

T. ABRAHÀ, "La *Dormitio Mariae* in Etiopia," in E. M. TONIOLO (ed.), *Il dogma dell'assunzione de Maria: problemi attuali e tentativi de ricomprensione. Atti del XVII Simposio Internazionale Mariologico (Roma, 6–9 ottobre 2009)* (Rome, 2010), 167–200.

—, "Some Philological Notes on the *Mäṣəḥafä 'Ǝräfətä läMaryam* «Liber Requiei» (*LR*)," *Apocrypha* 23 (2012), 223–245.

V. ARRAS, *De transitu Mariae apocrypha aethiopice*, 2 vols (Louvain, 1973), 1:75–105 (Latin).

R. VAN DEN BROEK, "Manichaean Elements in an Early Version of the Virgin Mary's Assumption," in A. HOUTMAN, *et al.* (eds), *Empsychoi Logoi—Religious Innovations in Antiquity* (Leiden, 2008), 293–316.

J. GRIBOMONT, "Le plus ancien *Transitus* marial et l'encratisme," *Aug* 23 (1983), 237–47.

S. J. SHOEMAKER, "Rethinking the 'Gnostic Mary': Mary of Nazareth and Mary of Magdala in Early Christian Tradition," *Journal of Early Christian Studies* 9 (2001), 555–595.

—, "A Case of Mistaken Identity? : Naming the 'Gnostic Mary,'" in F. S. JONES (ed.), *Which Mary? Marys in Early Christian Tradition* (Atlanta, 2002), 5–30.

—, "Jesus' Gnostic Mom: Mary of Nazareth and the Gnostic Mary Traditions," in D. GOOD (ed.), *Mariam, the Magdalen, and the Mother* (Bloomington, 2005), 153–83.

—, "Asceticism in the Early Dormition Narratives," *Studia Patristica* 44 (2010), 509–13.

328 THE DORMITION AND ASSUMPTION OF MARY

The *Six Book* Apocryphon.

Texts.

S. P. Brock and G. Kessel, "The 'Departure of Mary' in Two Palimpsests at the Monastery of St. Catherine (Sinai Syr. 30 & Sinai Arabic 514)," *Khristianskiĭ Vostok* 8 (2017), 115–52.

M. Chaîne, *Apocrypha de Beata Maria Virgine*, 2 vols (Rome, 1909) 1:21–49.

M. Enger, اخبار يوحنّا السليح في نقلة امّ المسيح (*Akhbâr Yûhannâ as-salîh fi naqlat umm al-masîh) id est Joannis apostoli de transitu Beatae Mariae Virginis liber* (Elberfeld, 1854).

S. J. Shoemaker, "New Syriac Dormition Fragments from Palimpsests in the Schøyen Collection and the British Library: Presentation, Edition and Translation," *Le Muséon* (2011), 259–78.

—, *The Six Books Dormition Apocryphon in Syriac: Critical Edition, Translation, and Commentary* (in preparation; delayed due to manuscript access).

A. Smith Lewis, *Apocrypha Syriaca* (London, 1902), ܣܡܒ-ܟ. ܡܠܪ-ܡ.

W. Wright, "The Departure of My Lady Mary from This World," *The Journal of Sacred Literature and Biblical Record* 6–7 (1865), 417–48 and 108–28.

—, *Contributions to the Apocryphal Literature of the New Testament* (London, 1865), ܟܒ-ܐܟ.

Modern Translations.

M. Erbetta, *Gli Apocrifi del Nuovo Testamento*, 3 vols., vol. 1/2, *Vangeli: Infanzia e passione di Cristo, Assunzione di Maria* (Torino, 1966), 534–73.

P. González Casado, *La dormición de la Virgen: Cinco relatos árabes* (Madrid, 2002), 169–210.

J. P. Migne, *Dictionnaire des apocryphes*, 2 vols (Paris, 1856–8), 2:509–32.

S. J. Shoemaker, *Ancient Traditions of the Virgin Mary's Dormition and Assumption* (Oxford, 2002), 370–96.

—, "New Syriac Dormition Fragments from Palimpsests in the Schøyen Collection and the British Library: Presentation, Edition and Translation," *Le Muséon* (2011), 259–78.

A. Smith Lewis, *Apocrypha Syriaca* (London, 1902), 12–69.

W. Wright, "The Departure of My Lady Mary from This World," *The Journal of Sacred Literature and Biblical Record* 6–7 (1865), 129–60.

—, *Contributions to the Apocryphal Literature of the New Testament* (London, 1865), 18–41.

Selected Studies.

S. Ashbrook Harvey, "Incense Offerings in the Syriac *Transitus Mariae*: Ritual and Knowledge in Ancient Christianity," in A. Malherbe, *et al.* (eds), *The Early Church in Its Context* (Leiden, 1998), 175–91.

E. Grypeou and J. P. Monferrer-Sala "'A Tour of the Other World': A Contribution to the Textual and Literary Criticism of the '*Six Books Apocalypse of the Virgin*,'" *Collectanea Christiana Orientalia* 6 (2009), 115–66.

A. Kateusz, "Collyridian Déjà Vu: The Trajectory of Redaction of the Markers of Mary's Liturgical Leadership," *Journal of Feminist Studies in Religion* 29 (2013), 75–92.

S. J. Shoemaker, "A Peculiar Version of the *Inventio crucis* in the Early Syriac Dormition Traditions," *Studia Patristica* 41 (2006), 75–81.

—, "Epiphanius of Salamis, the Kollyridians, and the Early Dormition Narratives: The Cult of the Virgin in the Later Fourth Century," *JECS* 16 (2008), 369–99.

330 THE DORMITION AND ASSUMPTION OF MARY

—, "The Cult of the Virgin in the Fourth Century: A Fresh Look at Some Old and New Sources," in C. MAUNDER (ed.), *The Origins of the Cult of the Virgin Mary* (London, 2008), 71–87.

—, "Apocrypha and Liturgy in the Fourth Century: The Case of the "*Six Books*" Dormition Apocryphon," in J. H. CHARLESWORTH and L. M. McDONALD (eds), *Jewish and Christian Scriptures: The Function of 'Canonical' and 'Non-Canonical' Religious Texts* (London, 2010), 153–63.

The Greek Revision of the *Book of Mary's Repose*.

Texts.

F. MANNS, *Le Récit de la Dormition de Marie (Vatican grec 1982)* (Jerusalem, 1989), "Synopse des textes."

A. WENGER, *L'Assomption de la T. S. Vierge dans la tradition byzantine du VIe au Xe siècle: Études et Documents* (Paris, 1955), 201–41.

Modern Translations.

M. ERBETTA, *Gli Apocrifi del Nuovo Testamento*, 3 vols., vol. 1/2, *Vangeli: Infanzia e passione di Cristo, Assunzione di Maria* (Torino, 1966), 465–74.

P. GEOLTRAIN and J.-D. KAESTLI (eds), *Écrits apocryphes chrétiens II* (Paris, 2005), 207–39.

F. MANNS, *Le Récit de la Dormition de Marie (Vatican grec 1982)* (Jerusalem, 1989), 240–9.

S. C. MIMOUNI and S. J. Voicu. *La Tradition grecque de la Dormition et de l'Assomption de Marie: Textes introduits, traduits et annotés* (Paris, 2003), 63–98.

L. MORALDI, *Apocrifi del Nuovo Testamento*, 2 vols (Torino, 1971), 1:825–40.

BIBLIOGRAPHY

331

S. J. SHOEMAKER, *Ancient Traditions of the Virgin Mary's Dormition* (Oxford, 2002), 351–69.

M. STAROWIEYSKI, *Apokryfy Nowego Testamentu*, vol. 1.2, *Ewangelie apokryficzne* (Lublin, 1986), 552–64.

M. VALLECILLO, "El 'Transitus Mariae' según el manuscrito Vaticano G. R. 1982," *Verdad y vida* 30 (1972), 240–52.

A. WENGER, *L'Assomption de la T. S. Vierge dans la tradition byzantine du VIᵉ au Xᵉ siècle : Études et Documents* (Paris, 1955), 201–41.

Selected Studies.

F. MANNS, *Le Récit de la Dormition de Marie (Vatican grec 1982)* (Jerusalem, 1989).

M. VALLECILLO, "El 'Transitus Mariae' según el manuscrito Vaticano G. R. 1982," *Verdad y vida* 30 (1972), 187–260.

A. WENGER, *L'Assomption de la T. S. Vierge dans la tradition byzantine du VIᵉ au Xᵉ siècle : Études et Documents* (Paris, 1955), 201–41.

The Latin Revision of the *Book of Mary's Repose* and Latin *Transitus Mariae*.

Texts.

B. CAPELLE, "Vestiges grecs et latins d'un antique "*Transitus*" de la Vierge," *Analecta Bollandiana* 67 (1949), 21–48.

G. MAROCCO, "Nuovi documenti sull'Assunzione del Medio Evo latino: due transitus dai codici latini 59 e 105 di Ivrea," *Marianum* 12 (1950), 449–52.

A. WENGER, *L'Assomption de la T. S. Vierge dans la tradition byzantine du VIᵉ au Xᵉ siècle : Études et Documents* (Paris, 1955), 258–9 ("Type N"), 245–56 (The Latin Revision of the Book of Mary's Repose).

332 THE DORMITION AND ASSUMPTION OF MARY

A. Wilmart, *Analecta Reginensia : Extraits des manuscrits latins de la reine Christine conservés au Vatican* (Vatican, 1933), 323–62.

F. Manns, *Le Récit de la Dormition de Marie (Vatican grec 1982)* (Jerusalem, 1989), "Synopse des textes."

Modern Translations.

M. Erbetta, *Gli Apocrifi del Nuovo Testamento*, 3 vols., vol. 1/2, *Vangeli: Infanzia e passione di Cristo, Assunzione di Maria* (Torino, 1966), 475–82.

L. Moraldi, *Apocrifi del Nuovo Testamento*, 2 vols (Torino, 1971), 1:879–84.

Selected Studies.

B. Capelle, "Les plus anciens récits de l'Assomption et Jean de Thessalonique," *Recherches de théologie ancienne et médiévale* 12 (1940), 209–35.

J. Rivière, "Le plus vieux '*Transitus*' latin et son dérivé grec," *Recherches de théologie ancienne et médiévale* 8 (1936), 5–23.

A. Wenger, *L'Assomption de la T. S. Vierge dans la tradition byzantine du VIe au Xe siècle : Études et Documents* (Paris, 1955), 68–95.

An Early *Dormition Fragment* in Georgian.

Texts.

M. van Esbroeck, "Apocryphes géorgiens de la Dormition," *Analecta Bollandiana* 92 (1973), 55–75, 62–64.

T. Mgaloblishvili, კლარჯული მრავალთავი *(Klarjuli mravalt'avi [The Homilary of Klarjeti])* (Tbilisi, 1991), 421–23.

A Liturgical Apocryphon from *Jeremiah* for the *Dormition of the Virgin*

Texts.

M. van Esbroeck, "Nouveaux apocryphes de la Dormition conservés en géorgien," *Analecta Bollandiana* 90 (1972), 363–69.

Studies.

G. Dye, "Lieux saints communs, partagés ou confisqués : aux sources de quelques péricopes coraniques (Q 19 : 16–33)," in Isabelle Dépret and Guillaume Dye (eds.), *Partage du sacré : Transferts, dévotions mixtes, rivalités interconfessionnelles* (Brussels, 2012), 55–121.

S. J. Shoemaker, "Mary between Bible and Qur'an: Apocrypha, Archaeology, and the Memory of Mary in Late Ancient Palestine," in Harald Buchinger, Andreas Merkt and Tobias Nicklas (eds.), *Extracanonical Traditions and the Holy Land* (Tübingen, 2023), forthcoming.

The *Homily on the Dormition* Attributed to Basil of Caesarea.

Texts.

M. van Esbroeck, "L'Assomption de la Vierge dans un *Transitus* Pseudo-Basilien," *Analecta Bollandiana* 92 (1974), 125–63.

Index

General Index

Aaron: 290–91.
Abgar: 51, 182.
Abkhazia: 303.
Abraham: 76–77, 80, 106, 123, 144–45, 201–2, 212, 228, 276, 304.
abyss: 102, 164, 272.
acheiropoieta: 51, 297, 310.
Adam: 61–62, 64, 69, 201, 212, 285.
Addai: 182.
Adonai'el: 82.
Aeons: 83.
Afraeli: 303.
Agathen: 97, 273.
Alexandria: 179, 193, 298, 301.
altar: 185–87, 202, 218, 221–22, 299, 301.
Andon: 164.
Andrew: 97, 128–29, 131, 141, 187, 190–91, 247, 262, 273, 298–99, 302–3.

Angel, Jesus as manifestation of a Great (Angel Christology): 23–24, 27, 36, 55–56, 60, 65–66, 74, 82–83, 92–93, 235–39, 244, 249.
angels: 25, 41, 64, 69, 74, 81, 85, 87–88, 100, 106–8, 111–13, 119–20, 122, 131–36, 144, 171, 174, 191–92, 196–98, 202, 209–14, 216–17, 228, 240, 248, 250, 252, 255–59, 265, 267–71, 276–79, 281–83, 286–87, 295, 299–300, 306, 308.
anger: 57, 62, 79, 103, 105–6, 115, 122, 160, 163, 168, 180, 204, 253, 279.
Annas: 307.
anointing: 222, 287, 290.
apocalyptic: 29–30, 36, 38, 47, 133, 137, 145.

338   THE DORMITION AND ASSUMPTION OF MARY

apocalyptic, tour of the
   other world, Mary's:
   132–46, 172–74, 225–33.
apparitions, of Mary: 34,
   206–8.
Aramaic: 3, 8, 17–20, 26,
   93–95, 98–99, 118–22,
   139, 141, 150–52, 160–62,
   164, 312–13.
archangels: 69, 84, 134, 175,
   228, 240, 258, 265, 268,
   281–84, 296.
Archelaus: 184–85.
Archon: 68–69.
Arimathea: 301.
Ark of the Covenant: 46,
   145, 287, 289–91.
ascension: 23, 36, 66–68,
   257, 269, 293, 295, 297,
   305, 307.
asceticism: 25, 28, 314.
asceticism, apostolic debate
   over: 126–31.
Athens: 193, 273.
August commemoration of
   Mary: 10, 13, 41–46,
   48–49, 218, 220, 284,
   289, 293.
Axumite: 23.
Babylonia: 290.
Bartholomew: 187, 191,
   298–99, 302.
Beirut: 193.

Bethlehem: 11–12, 30,
   32–33, 42–44, 47–48, 111,
   183–97, 201, 211, 289–90,
   296–97.
Beyatar: 97.
bilocation: 34.
birds: 149–50, 152–54.
Bithynia: 303.
blindness: 113, 115, 117–18,
   149, 152–55, 157, 192,
   197, 207, 252, 255,
   267–68, 279–81, 304.
book, secret/of mysteries:
   23–24, 36, 55–57, 83,
   92–93, 111, 114, 243–44.
Brakke, David: 15.
branches: 12, 47, 61, 71, 111,
   116–18, 145–46, 227, 243,
   254–55, 296, 300.
bread: 33–34, 73, 149,
   153–54, 207, 221–22.
bridal imagery: 100–1, 106,
   184, 229, 236, 239, 249,
   264, 266, 287, 295, 298,
   305.
burial: 7, 24, 41, 55, 80,
   109–11, 180, 206, 210,
   216, 218, 252, 271, 274,
   281, 291, 302–3, 307.
burning: 113, 117, 137, 177,
   230–31, 294, 304.
burning, Jewish attempts to
   burn Mary: 25, 113, 191,

198, 209–10, 252, 279, 295, 304.
Caesar: 185.
Caesarea: 1, 47, 293, 320.
Caiaphas: 307.
Caleb: 199–200.
Calletha: 184–85.
candles: 294, 296–97.
caves: 42, 201, 208–11, 223, 289–90.
censers: 185–86, 188, 191–92, 205, 207, 212–13, 218, 221–22, 296.
Cephas: 186–87.
chariot: 96, 171–72, 175, 185, 188–89, 191, 212–13, 217, 225, 227, 231, 246.
Cherub of Light, Jesus as: 23–24, 39, 98–99, 248, 261.
cherubim: 69, 85, 96, 137, 227–28, 231, 241, 246, 261, 272.
chiliarch: 195, 209, 228.
Cholchis: 303.
clouds: 24–25, 30, 94, 97, 99, 107, 113, 122, 132–33, 136, 147–48, 162, 164, 171, 186, 188–92, 221–23, 242, 245, 247, 250, 252, 256, 261–62, 265, 267–68, 272–73, 276, 278–79, 281–83, 291, 298, 301–2.

commemorations of Mary: 13, 33–34, 41, 43, 45, 176–77, 180, 214–16, 220–21, 224–25, 232.
Constantinople: 50.
Coptic: 13–14, 19, 83, 92–94, 100, 109, 239, 311–13.
cross: 96, 165, 170, 176, 182, 193, 212, 222, 246, 262, 272, 295, 301, 305.
cross, hiding and discovery of: 181, 203–4.
Cyriacus: 178.
Cyrus: 178–79.
damned, visit to the places of the: 132–44, 230–31, 283–84.
David: 144–45, 177, 212, 218, 228, 272, 290, 298, 301, 308.
deacon: 138, 177.
deceiver (as Jewish name for Jesus): 92, 113, 195, 197, 200, 208, 243, 252, 261, 267.
demiurge: 23–24, 68, 239.
demons: 120–22, 126, 149, 156, 193–94, 203.
devil: 19–21, 26, 62, 109, 146–47, 158, 169–71.
Dionysius the Areopagite: 48–50, 302.

340 THE DORMITION AND ASSUMPTION OF MARY

drunkenness, Joseph's:
    29, 59.
Eden: 145, 214, 217, 219,
    225–27, 232.
Edessa: 51, 182.
Egypt: 13, 18, 51, 56, 59, 61,
    74–80, 112, 179, 193–94,
    200, 203, 208, 237, 252,
    266, 278, 289, 303.
Egypt, Christ–Angel as
    destroyer of firstborn in:
    74.
Egypt, Flight into: 56–63.
Egypt, Israel's servitude in:
    74–82.
Eleazar: 75–76.
elect: 65, 108, 238, 282, 299.
Eleutheropolis: 303.
Elijah: 202, 226, 228.
Elisha: 202.
Elizabeth: 144, 212.
emperor: 162, 182–83, 195,
    199, 204, 206.
encratite: 28.
Enda/Endan/Endon: 156,
    161.
Enoch: 26, 145–46, 213, 226,
    229.
Ephesus: 32, 179–80,
    185–86, 189, 298, 301.
Epiphanius: 34.
Esbroeck, Michel van: 17,
    40–43, 46–49.

esotericism: 22–24, 27, 36,
    239–40.
Ethiopia: 156, 169.
Ethiopian: 169.
eunuchs: 148.
Euphrates: 182, 226.
Eve: 64, 68, 176, 212, 285.
Exodus: 78.
famine: 215, 218, 232.
farmers: 217, 220, 222.
fasting: 127, 129–30, 145,
    294, 307.
feet, Mary' washes the
    apostles': 311.
flood: 145–46, 226.
flour: 221.
fragrance: 202, 219–20, 222,
    227, 240, 250, 265, 276,
    286, 299.
funeral, Mary's (see also
    garments, Mary's
    funeral): 7, 107, 109–12,
    208–9, 250–52, 266–67,
    277–78, 287, 313–14.
Gabriel: 211, 229, 250, 255,
    295–96, 300.
Gamaliel: 184.
garments, Mary's funeral: 93,
    100, 244, 248, 261, 263.
Gehenna: 73, 133, 166,
    230–31.
Gethsemane: 41, 45, 287.
Gihon: 226.

GENERAL INDEX

Gilead: 202.

gnostic: 23–24, 27, 36, 68, 239–40.

gold: 86, 104–5, 124–25, 140, 167, 201, 210, 241, 258.

Golgotha: 51, 181, 183–84.

governor: 33, 181, 183, 191, 195–201, 203–6, 210, 216, 274.

Great Angel: see Angel.

grief: 61, 77, 82, 85, 91, 98, 111, 123, 126, 213, 242, 247, 250, 252, 266, 278.

hail: 215, 218, 221, 265, 273, 295–96.

hallucinations: 113, 117.

Hebrew: 180, 221, 224, 254, 280.

hell: 283–84, 295, 302, 308.

Herod: 57, 303, 307.

Hierapolis: 303.

Hierotheus: 302.

horses: 158–61, 170–171.

ice: 222, 227.

idols: 289.

image of Christ, miraculous: see *acheiropoieta*.

incantations: 197.

incense: 175–76, 179, 181, 185–86, 188, 191–92, 205, 207, 213, 218–19, 221–23, 294, 297, 316.

incubation: 32.

India: 156, 187, 189–90.

intercession: 25–26, 33–34, 134–35, 137, 140–41, 214, 231, 283, 306–7, 312.

Irenaeus of Lyon: 15.

Isaac: 76–77, 80, 106, 144–45, 202, 212, 228, 276, 284.

Isaiah: 177, 213.

Israel: 70, 112, 149, 173–74, 199–200, 203, 208, 219, 252, 266, 278, 291.

Israelites: 75–76, 78, 80–82.

Jacob: 76–77, 80, 106, 144–45, 202, 212, 228, 276, 284.

James: 49, 178–79, 187, 190, 298–303, 305, 308.

Jephonias: 208, 253–55.

Jeremiah: 1, 11, 13, 42, 46, 289–91, 320.

Jerusalem: 11, 24, 30, 32–33, 35, 40–46, 48–49, 56, 75, 89, 112, 120–21, 136, 147, 178–85, 187, 190, 192, 194–200, 204–6, 208–11, 227–29, 236, 252, 257, 267, 301, 317–19.

Jews: 24–25, 30, 33, 178, 181–84, 187, 189, 191, 195–98, 200, 208–11, 260, 271, 278–80, 295, 304, 311.

342 THE DORMITION AND ASSUMPTION OF MARY

Jews, attack on Mary's funeral: 112–18, 208–9, 252–55, 267–68, 278–81, 314–15.

Jews, attempt to burn Mary: 25, 113, 191, 198, 209–10, 252, 279, 295, 304.

Joachim: 58.

John: 15, 32, 90–93, 97, 106, 111, 127–29, 131, 141, 178–80, 185–86, 188–89, 196, 217, 224, 232, 242–44, 247, 250–52, 260–62, 266, 271, 273, 278, 284, 296–98, 300–301, 306, 308.

John, presbyter of Mount Sinai: 177.

John the Baptist: 58, 144, 212.

(Ps-)John the Theologian: 9, 47, 235, 293.

John of Thessalonica: 35.

Joseph, father of Jesus: 29, 42, 57–61, 89–90, 183.

Joseph, patriarch: 78–82.

Judea: 201, 303.

Justin Martyr: 43.

Kathisma Church: 11, 42–46.

Kerseson: 81.

Kidron: 120.

Kishon: 81.

kissing: 186, 188, 212–13, 239, 254, 286, 298.

Klarjeti: 18, 40–42, 45–47, 49, 312, 319.

knowledge, secret: see secret knowledge/mysteries.

Kollyridians: 34.

Kush: 161.

ladder, Jacob's: 202.

lamentation: 76, 80, 90, 242, 270, 304, 306.

lampstand, Mary as golden: 140.

late apostle motif: 316–18.

law: 28, 60, 115, 168, 200, 285, 289–91, 299.

Legion (demons): 158, 194.

leprosy: 149, 155, 193.

Levi: 123.

Lewis, Agnes Smith: 31–32.

lightning: 191, 207, 222, 225, 229, 231.

lion, beast with body of and tail of a snake: 68.

locusts: 215, 217, 220.

Lot: 78.

Ludan: 187, 189.

Luke: 187, 190, 298–99, 302–3.

Magi: 145, 201, 290.

magicians: 77–79, 156–58, 160, 162–63, 169.

Malchu: 193.

Mandylion: 51.
Manns, Frédéric: 35, 319.
mansions: 188, 217, 307.
Maranatha: 97, 246.
Mark: 188, 190, 298–99, 301.
Maruyal: 97.
Mastinpanes: 62.
Matthew: 187, 190, 298–99, 301.
Matthias: 299.
(Ps-)Melito of Sardis: 37.
Memphis: 51.
Michael: 24, 78, 82, 107–8, 131–37, 140, 144, 174, 229, 250–51, 255–56, 265, 268, 276–77, 281–84.
miracles, performed by Mary: 192–95, 205–8.
Moses: 80–82, 116, 178, 183, 203, 213, 254, 280, 290–91.
Mount of Olives: 24, 56–57, 119, 174, 219, 223, 236–37, 255, 257, 269.
Müller–Kessler, Christa: 17, 20.
myrrh: 201, 290.
mysteries, secret: 19, 22–26, 28, 36, 39, 58, 65, 74, 84, 92–93, 96, 102, 118–19, 126, 131, 146, 152, 242–44, 246, 255–56, 293, 298, 303.

Nablus: 43.
Nador: 97.
Nativity: 42–44, 46, 217, 220.
Neapolis: 43.
Nerdo: 97.
Nero: 185.
Neshra: 184–85.
Nicodemus: 184.
Noah: 145–46, 212, 220.
Norelli, Enrico: 3, 15–16, 26.
offerings: 33–34, 193, 214–18, 220–21, 223, 232.
olive branch/tree: 47, 145–46, 296.
orphans: 115, 125, 253, 306.
pagans: 139.
Palestine/Palestinian: 3, 17–20, 26, 40, 44, 93–95, 98–99, 118–22, 139, 141, 150–52, 160–62, 164, 312–13.
palimpsest: 31–32.
palm tree/branch: 11–12, 14, 27, 30, 35, 37–38, 47–49, 58–63, 93, 111, 116–17, 137, 235–37, 239, 244, 251, 253–54, 257–58, 261, 266–67, 269, 271, 278–81, 300.
papyrus: 19.
parable, of virgins: 103–6, 264–65, 274–76.

344 THE DORMITION AND ASSUMPTION OF MARY

parable, of the wormy trees:
70–73.
Paraclete: 175, 229.
paradise: 7, 15, 25–26, 30,
33, 41, 55, 61–64, 66, 107,
131–32, 148, 164, 174, 214,
217, 219, 225–27, 231–32,
236–38, 256, 268,
281–82, 284, 295, 302.
paradise, Mary and apostles
visit: 144–46, 172, 219,
256, 268, 281–82.
Paragmos: 152, 154, 156–58,
160, 162–66, 167, 169–70.
Patra: 303.
Paul: 28–29, 44, 94–95, 99,
118–21, 146–49, 151–52,
155–60, 162–63, 169–71,
178–79, 187, 189, 196, 206,
217, 224, 245, 248, 272,
298–99, 301, 306, 308.
Paul, contendings against the
devil with Peter: 19–21,
26, 147–72.
Paul, debate with other
apostles about asceticism:
25, 126–31.
Paul, questionable status as
an apostle: 28.
Paul, seeks knowledge of
heavenly mysteries: 19,
25–26, 118–20, 126, 131,
146–47, 255–56.

perfume: 222, 227, 230,
286–87.
Persia: 201.
pestilence: 215, 221.
Peter: 24, 39, 49, 94–97,
99–103, 105–6, 108–11,
114, 116–17, 119–20,
126–29, 131, 141, 148–60,
162–71, 173, 178–79,
188–89, 196, 203, 206,
209, 212, 217, 224, 226,
245–55, 261–68, 272–81,
284, 298–300, 306, 308.
Peter, all–night discourse by:
100–6, 249–50, 263–65,
274–76.
Peter, contendings against
the devil with Paul:
19–21, 26, 147–72.
Pharaoh: 59, 75–82, 203.
Philip: 177, 187, 190,
298–99, 302–3.
Philippi: 19, 155–56, 161,
168–69, 171.
Phrygia: 303.
Piacenza Pilgrim: 51.
Pilate: 199, 307.
Pishon: 226.
plague: 221, 323.
Pleroma: 240.
Pontus: 303.
powers, heavenly: 25, 69, 84,
174, 197, 239–40, 258.

praetorium: 195, 198, 205.
Prayer, secret, of ascent: 23–24, 36, 66–68, 92, 106, 238, 243–44, 249, 276.
Priest(s), Jewish High: 92, 112, 116–17, 181, 183, 192, 195–99, 209–10, 243, 252, 254, 260, 267, 278–81, 307.
priests: 138, 141, 175, 179, 216, 218, 221, 289, 290–91.
procurator: 182, 193.
Protevangelium of James: 30, 42–43.
Providence: 299–300, 307.
psalms: 96, 106, 135, 217–18, 244, 259, 261, 266, 301.
Ptolemy: 290.
punishments: 25, 30, 34, 137–38, 270.
queen, Mary as: 92, 140–41, 284, 286, 294, 296, 301, 307.
Rabbuli: 213–14, 217, 226, 230–31, 233.
Rachel: 75–77.
rain: 222, 227, 229.
relics: 48–51.
resurrect: 66.
resurrection: 7, 33, 64, 66, 144, 176, 188, 190, 201, 214, 229–30, 237, 256,

268, 273, 281, 290, 299, 302, 307.
Rome/Romans: 19, 33, 148, 152–54, 156–58, 162–63, 165, 179, 183–84, 186–87, 189, 193, 205–10, 289, 298, 300.
Ruler (Archon): 68–69, 308.
Sabbath: 212, 294.
Sabinus: 182, 193.
sacristan: 180.
Sadducees: 198–99.
sailing: 206–7.
Sardis: 247, 262.
Satan: 68, 77, 88, 112, 147, 155, 177, 193, 215, 252, 267, 279.
scribes: 69, 208.
sea: 194, 203, 206, 215, 298, 301, 303.
Sebastopolis: 303.
secret knowledge/mysteries: 19, 22–26, 28, 36, 39, 55, 65–67, 92, 102, 118, 229, 237–39, 243, 255, 263, 285.
Sellew, Philip: 19.
seraphim: 85, 172–74, 185, 190–91, 212–13, 219, 228, 241.
Seth: 201, 212.
sheep: 70, 89, 115, 211, 222, 259, 305.

346 THE DORMITION AND ASSUMPTION OF MARY

Shem: 212.

Sheol: 166, 188.

shepherds: 70, 89, 259, 266, 305.

ships: 190, 206–7, 301.

shroud, burial: 287.

silver: 86, 124–25, 167, 241, 258.

Simon: 185–87, 203, 217, 298–99, 302–3.

Simon the Canaanite: 187, 190.

sin, Mary's: 29, 89–90.

Sinai: 20, 32, 52, 177–80, 290, 315.

sinlessness, Mary's: 29.

snake: 68, 208.

snow: 222, 227, 266, 277.

Sodom/Sodomites: 78, 117, 255, 281.

soldiers: 33, 156–61, 163–65, 168, 175–76.

Solomon: 120–26.

Sophron: 194.

soul: 90–91, 95, 101, 109, 115, 122–24, 129, 136, 139, 144, 163, 194, 256, 260, 272, 274, 294, 297, 300, 304.

soul, ascent past the cosmic powers: 24, 69, 240.

soul, departure from the body: 64–66, 84–89,
106–7, 238, 240, 258–59, 264, 270, 276.

soul, Mary's: 7, 13, 25, 30, 33, 41, 84–85, 107–8, 132, 213, 217, 240–41, 250–51,256, 258, 265–66, 268, 277, 282, 284, 286–87, 305–6.

staff: 82, 111, 114, 116–17, 203, 209, 235–37, 239, 244, 251, 253–54.

storms: 190, 206, 215.

strangury: 193, 205.

sun: 67–68, 100, 106, 133, 174, 192, 202, 207, 227, 238, 248–49, 263, 265, 297, 302.

synagogue: 183–84.

Tabetha: 184–85.

Tarsus: 149, 187.

Tartarouchos: 171.

tears: see weeping.

temple: 115, 138, 253–54, 278, 280, 290.

Thebaid: 187, 191, 298, 302.

Theotokos: 44, 52, 175, 186, 194, 197–98, 205, 207–9, 221, 223, 225, 235, 254, 285, 289, 294, 303–5.

Thessalonica: 35, 193.

Thomas: 30, 187, 189, 196, 217.

Thrace: 303.
throne: 167, 174, 176, 185, 205, 216, 231, 286, 294, 298.
thunder: 94, 191, 216, 225, 229–30, 245, 250, 261, 265, 272, 276, 298.
Tiberias: 187, 189, 298.
Tiberius: 182–83, 195, 199, 301.
Tigris: 226.
Timothy: 303.
Titus: 303.
Tobia: 184.
tomb: 190.
tomb, Christ's: 181, 183–84, 294–95, 308.
tomb, Mary's: 24–25, 33, 41, 45, 92, 109–10, 118, 120, 131, 243, 251, 255, 260, 266, 268, 271, 277, 281–82, 287.
treasure: 74, 82, 96, 110, 201, 246, 251, 266, 277, 285–86.
trees: 12, 27, 56–58, 61–63, 70–73, 128, 132, 136, 144–46, 164, 218–19, 221, 227, 237, 256–58, 282, 284.
Trinity: 293, 298–99.
trumpets: 175, 190, 219, 228, 230, 287.

tunics, Mary's: 93, 244, 261.
urn, Mary as golden: 291.
Veronica, veil of: 51.
vespers: 221.
virginity: 28, 58, 103, 106, 153, 264, 275.
virgins: 28, 102, 107, 110, 174, 184–86, 250–51, 259, 264–66, 274–76, 278, 294, 296.
watchers: 175, 212.
weeping: 84, 88–90, 92, 98, 109, 117, 134–37, 144, 156, 181, 207, 209, 220, 230, 240, 242–44, 247, 254, 258–59, 261–62, 270–71, 273, 279, 281, 283–84, 294, 297, 306–8.
Wenger: 35, 37–38, 319.
whirlwinds: 202, 227, 232.
whiteness of Mary's soul: 251, 266, 277.
widows: 115, 207, 244, 261.
winds: 136, 149, 188, 232.
worms: 70, 72.
Yabus: 187.
Yuphanya: 208–9.
Zechariah: 58.
Zion: 41, 190, 287, 289–90, 294, 297–98, 300–302, 304.

Ancient Writings Index

Biblical References

Genesis,
— 2.10–14: 226;
— 3.24: 227;
— 5.22–9: 146;
— 7.19: 226;
— 15: 201;
— 16: 201;
— 19.11: 93, 255, 281;
— 19.24: 93, 255, 281;
— 22: 202;
— 28.10–17: 202;
— 32.29: 55, 236.
Exodus,
— 3.13: 55, 236;
— 12: 74;
— 14: 203.
Leviticus, 5.11: 221.
Deuteronomy, 28.12: 227.
2 Kingdoms (2 Samuel), 2.1–12: 202.
4 Kingdoms (2 Kings), 19.15: 96, 246, 261.
1 Chronicles, 18.40–5: 81.

Psalms (LXX),
— 27.2: 85, 241;
— 84.11: 298;
— 112.5–6: 96;
— 112.6: 246, 261;
— 113.1: 112, 252, 266, 278;
— 115.6: 101, 263;
— 131.1: 301;
— 131.8: 290;
— 132.1: 95, 245.
Isaiah,
— 6.2: 172;
— 6.3: 228;
— 7.14: 177;
— 45.3: 96, 246;
— 53.2: 177;
— 64.4: 229.
Lamentations, 4.21: 289.
2 Maccabees, 6.16: 246.
Matthew,
— 6.10: 295;
— 8.28–32: 203;
— 9.32–3: 203;

— 11.28: 96, 246;
— 14.28–33: 203;
— 19.28: 219;
— 24.30–1: 107, 250;
— 24.43: 87, 259;
— 25.1: 103, 264, 275;
— 25.1–13: 249;
— 26.47: 267, 279, 314;
— 26.55: 267, 279, 314;
— 26.64: 107, 250;
— 26.69: 268, 280;
— 27.60: 110;
— 27.66: 181;
— 28.19: 91, 243.
Mark,
— 12.26: 80;
— 14.41: 113;
— 14.43: 252;
— 14.66–7: 114, 253;
— 16.16: 236.
Luke,
— 1.19: 295;
— 1.26–38: 211;
— 1.28: 98, 247, 295;
— 1.38: 108, 251;
— 1.42: 177;
— 1.47: 99, 248;

— 1.48: 108, 251;
— 5.3: 194;
— 8.5–6: 154;
— 14.26: 128;
— 22.46: 316;
— 23.46: 286;
— 24.50–3: 203.
John,
— 2.16: 115, 253;
— 8.24: 66;
— 8.52: 201;
— 8.54–8: 201;
— 13.14–15: 311;
— 13.23: 91, 179, 242;
— 13.27: 112, 252, 267, 279;
— 14.2: 66;
— 15.12: 96;
— 19.26–7: 91, 242, 260;
— 20.24–9: 317.
Romans, 1.26–7: 139.
1 Corinthians,
— 2.9: 229;
— 3.2: 130.
2 Corinthians, 11.23–5: 163.
1 Timothy, 6.16: 96, 246.
James, 1.26: 275.
Apocalypse, 21.12: 228.

Christian Apocryphal Literature

Acts of Thomas: 187.
Apocalypse of Paul: 29, 87, 134, 137.
Apocalypse of Peter: 26.
1 Enoch: 26.
Gospel of Ps.–Matthew: 57.
Infancy Gospel of Thomas: 30.
Ps.-JOHN THE THEOLOGIAN, *Transitus Mariae*: 9, 47, 293.
The Letters of Pilate: 199.
The Lives of the Prophets: 11, 46, 289.
Protevangelium of James: 30, 211.
Ps.-MELITO: *Transitus Mariae*, 37.
The Story of Peter and Paul: 19–21.
Testament of Adam: 201.
Testament of Solomon: 121.

Other Early Christian Texts

Doctrina Addai, 182.
EPHREM, *Hymns on Paradise*, 15.
JOHN OF THESSALONICA, *Homily on the Dormition*, 35, 103, 115, 249, 253, 254.
Jerusalem Armenian Lectionary, 44.
Jerusalem Georgian Chantbook, 45.
Jerusalem Georgian Lectionary, 45.
JUSTIN MARTYR, *Dialogue with Trypho*, 43.
The Klarjeti Mravaltavi, 18, 40–42, 45–47, 49.
Ps.-DIONYSIUS THE AREOPAGITE, *On the Divine Names*, 49.

APOCRYPHES

COLLECTION DE POCHE DE L'AELAC

1. *L'Évangile de Barthélemy*, par Jean-Daniel KAESTLI,
   avec la collaboration de Pierre CHERIX, 1993, 281 p.
2. *Ascension d'Isaïe*, par Enrico NORELLI, 1993, 186 p.
3. *Histoire du roi Abgar et de Jésus*, par Alain DESREUMAUX,
   1993, 184 p.
4. *Les Odes de Salomon*, par Marie-Joseph PIERRE, avec
   la collaboration de Jean-Marie MARTIN, 1994, 225 p.
5. *L'Épître des Apôtres et le Testament de Notre Seigneur*,
   par Jacques-Noël PÉRÈS, 1994, 152 p.
6. *Salomon et Saturne,* par Robert FAERBER, 1995, 209 p.
7. *Actes de l'apôtre André*, par Jean-Marc PRIEUR, 1995, 209 p.
8. *Les Actes de l'apôtre Philippe*, par François BOVON,
   Bertrand BOUVIER & Frédéric AMSLER, 1996, 318 p.
9. *L'Évangile de Nicodème*, par Rémi GOUNELLE
   & Zbigniew IZYDORCZYK, 1997, 273 p.
10. *Les Reconnaissances du Pseudo-Clément*,
    par Luigi CIRILLO & André SCHNEIDER, 1997, 652 p.
11. *Les Actes de Mar Mari*, par Christelle JULLIEN
    & Florence JULLIEN, 2001, 175 p.
12. *La Gloire des Rois*, par Robert BEYLOT, 2008, 490 p.
13. *Les Apôtres Thaddée et Barthélemy*, par Valentina CALZOLARI,
    2011, 260 p.
14. *The Syriac Pseudo-Clementines*, par F. Stanley JONES, 2014,
    354 p.
15. *The Ever-New Tongue*, par John CAREY, 2018, 208 p.
16. *The Gospel According to Thomas*, par André GAGNÉ, 2019,
    288 p.
17. *The Dormition and Assumption of the Virgin Mary*,
    par Stephen J. SHOEMAKER, 2023, 368 p.
18. *Xanthippe et Polyxène, Un roman chrétien*, par Éric JUNOD,
    2023, 200 p.